Praise for *"The World's Richest Busboy"*

"In the true spirit of "Talk Story" and like story tellers before him, J.J. tells tales of travel adventures that'll make you want to pack a bag with your board under your arm and hit the road."

—Peter "PT" Townend, 1976 World Surfing Champion

"The World's Richest Busboy" is a wonderful, functionally spare narrative honoring the best traditions of the adventurer-surfer. Brito has taken the time to tell his adventures and tell them well, recounting his early and pointedly dedicated creation of a Tom Blake-like low-overhead personal economy, which allowed him to remain financially independent, unencumbered and free to travel and surf. Brito's narrative offers an insight into how a young surfer can, with limited – very limited – means, see and surf the waves millions of surfers only dream of but never experience. Two shakas, up. Brito's brio deserves a "bravo."

—Craig Lockwood, author of *"The Surfing Heritage Foundation Guide to Oral History"*; and *"Peanuts: An Oral Biography Exploring Legend, Myth and Archetype in California's Surfing Subculture."*

"….inspiring and spine tingling…..the path he chose for himself was an unpretentious and self-sufficiently modest journey that landed him in situations and introduced him to people that would impact his life profoundly."

—Jon Perino, Solspot

"The World's Richest Busboy" beautifully reflects who J.J. is –a winsome man with a robust spirit of adventure…. his unquenchable optimism carries him through the most perilous moments. As you read his story, you realize this is a man you'd love to have as a friend

—Maralys Wills, author of *"Higher Than Eagles"*

"Cool book….exciting from the first page."

—Bud Llamas, pro surfer, owner of 17th St. Boardshop, H.B. CA.

"….an extreme adventure with amazing stories that will keep you stoked!"
—Gary Sahagen, Director, International Surfing Museum

"It's a hard book to put down because of his natural way with words, describing diverse encounters in descriptive, easy-to-read detail. You get to tag along with him and experience a rollercoaster ride of emotion, excitement and envy."
—Chris MacDonald, Surf City News

"The story of "*The World's Richest Busboy*" is a throwback to the days of core surf travel rooted in the truth of "it's not about the destination but the journey."
—John Hinkle, team captain, Malibu Surfing Association

"…..an awe-inspiring adventure described with crisp prose and vivid detail. It's the sort of story that anyone with a dream and aspirations to break out of binding societal norms must read. The reward will be a fresh outlook on what's out there to explore and accomplish if you put your mind to it and desire enough. "Richest Busboy" is a testament to the strength of the human spirit and dogged determination of one man to surf that "perfect wave."
—Dan Koven

"Excellent... I couldn't put it down; from cover to cover I was inspired and entertained. You captured the feel of traveling and the sense of adventure only a true citizen of the world could do. Thank you so much for having the courage to travel at such a young age and the humility to write it all down truthfully."
—Michelle Faires

"This was one of those books that I didn't want to end! It was captivating, humorous, romantic and dramatic all at the same time. This was truly the best adventure book I've read to date."
—Kai Brant, singer/songwriter

The World's Richest Busboy

A True Story of One Guy's Unpredictable Life on the Road

To Matthew
Good luck on
your adventures!

July 2011

J.J. Brito

i

The World's Richest Busboy
First Edition
Published in California by Sundaze Publishing
P.O. Box 2951
Anaheim, CA 92814

Visit our Website at:
www.sundazepublishing.com

ISBN: 978-0-9826967-1-2

Cover photo by Christy Lynn Burleson
Christy Burleson Photography.com

Printed in U.S.A.

For my daughter, Melita

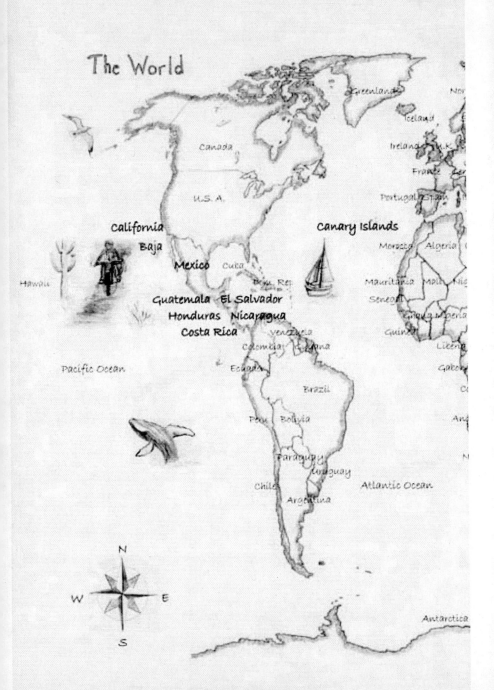

The World

Greenland

Nor

Iceland

Ireland U.K.

France

Canada

Portugal Spain

U.S.A.

California

Canary Islands

Baja

Morocco   Algeria

Mexico   Cuba

Mauritania   Mali   Nig

Dom. Rep.

Guatemala   El Salvador

Senegal

Honduras   Nicaragua

Ginea   Liberia

Hawaii

Costa Rica

Guinea

Venzela

Liberia

Colombia   Guiana

Gabon

Pacific Ocean

Ecuador

C

Brazil

Ang

Peru   Bolivia

N

Paraguay

Uruguay

Atlantic Ocean

Chile

Argentina

N

W   E

S

Antarctica

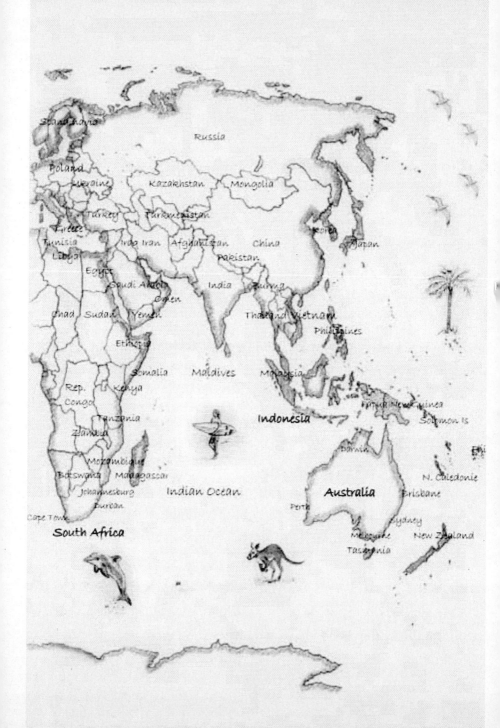

Author's Note

Although the characters in the story are real, some of their names and identities have been changed to protect their privacy. Events and conversations are written as accurately as I remember them and are not intended to be exact quotations.

Acknowledgments

I would like to thank my mom and dad for all they've done for me through the years, I couldn't ask for better parents. I'd like to thank my sis, and all my family and friends for their endless support through both good times and messed up times. My thanks to author Maralys Wills and her creative writing class for their invaluable critiquing and constructive criticism. I'm grateful to Chiwah Carol Slater for her excellent editing and unlimited straightforward advice. I thank Jon J. Noeth of New Wave Web Designs for delivering top quality graphic design. Special thanks go to artist Susan Hull for whipping up a splendid world map and also for her love, which has taken me to places I never thought I'd reach. And finally, my absolute appreciation goes to the many amazing people of this world whose paths I've crossed, for it is truly they who have made my experiences abroad so rewarding.

Contents

1

CANARY ISLANDS

Punished... Off the Coast of Morocco

Long after midnight I sat at the bar in the smoky, neon-lit nightclub feeding cheesy lines to Elina, a blonde Norwegian beauty. I was making fine progress. She laughed at my jokes, bought me a beer, and playfully brushed her fingers across my forearm. Her touch gave me tingles.

A few stools to my left, my Portuguese roommate, Miguel, was having trouble getting to know Elina's friend. But her friend wasn't his problem; he'd been dealing with the angry Moroccan who also fancied her. I'd been concentrating on Elina, and I had no clue that a tiff was going down behind me. That is, until Miguel tapped my shoulder and whispered in his thick Portuguese accent, "Hey J.J., we'd better get outta here. I think we're in danger."

This wasn't how I'd intended to use the buzz I had flowing. I didn't even know how the whole stupid mess started. In a flash, I heard a shout and a shatter, and Miguel yelling, "Run, J.J., run!" We jammed for the front doors with eight maddened Moroccans dead on our heels. The second we escaped the club, Miguel and I branched out in different directions—not on purpose; we were just running for our lives.

At full speed I approached a wide set of cement stairs that descended about ten feet and separated the club floor from the main street. The Moroccans were clawing at my tail, so I couldn't slow to take the stairs. With one huge leap I soared through the air. I cleared the bottom step, landed feet together on the sidewalk, and tucked into a roll. Without the slightest hesitation I bounced up to my feet, sprinted to the street, and turned to face the enemy.

Four Moroccans crept up to surround me. Two of them picked up empty booze bottles from the littered street and created crude weaponry by smashing the bottoms off against the hard ground (they must have seen that done in the movies). The other two pulled the belts from their waists and swung the heavy buckles from the bitter ends (I'd never seen that done in a movie). I took it they had experience.

By sheer luck, I stumbled upon a busted crate in the street and quickly scavenged up a three-foot nail-infested plank. I cocked the thing back and got ready to strike. Miguel was caught up in his own confrontation with the other four guys, and I heard him callout from down the road.

"J.J.!"

"Miguel!" I yelled back. Then we got back to our respective battles.

The Moroccans' shiny metal belt buckles reflected off the street lamps. I felt the pressure of them closing in, and wanted to run. But if I ran, they'd chase me. I didn't want to risk being taken down from behind.

A violent strain of adrenalin flared up, fueling my core and igniting my temper. The hairs on the back of my neck stiffened. Without thinking, I erupted, "Rrraaaaaaaaw!" and charged them. My hand clenched the plank as I darted toward the closest guy, attempting to bash him. But the dude lurched away from my attack. I turned my aggression on the others, moving forcefully, ready as hell to club someone, but they backed up as well.

Expecting them to come at me, I planned a scenario in my head. *If they all rush at once, I'll hit the big guy as hard as I freaking can. Maybe I can take down the one next to him, too.* But the Moroccans remained at a safe distance. Thank goodness. A quiet moment passed in the face-off.

I stepped back several feet and chucked the piece of wood onto the ground, careful not to toss it too far away. "Alright, enough," I said. "Enough!" I held up my empty hands to flag a truce. To my relief, it worked. The Moroccans lowered their weapons. I backed off cautiously, and so did they.

Concerned about how Miguel was holding up, I jogged in his direction. My friend the Portuguese man at war had already repelled his adversaries. In a raging fit, he stood in the street yelling obscenities, ordering them *back*.

"C'monnnnnn! Get back here, you *pussies!*"

I couldn't believe my ears. "Hey, Miguel, are you out of your mind? Shut the hell up! There's eight of them!" A lot more than I wanted to deal with.

"I'm gonna kill those bastards!"

"Look, man, cool it. They're over it . . . *I'm* over it."

Miguel finally calmed down. We hoofed it over to his friend's house, opting to catch up with the Norwegian girls at another time. For some reason, I no longer felt like a Casanova.

Ten minutes later, my adrenalin had faded entirely but my right heel had begun to suffer a nagging pain. The jump over the stairs had taken its toll. Soon I was moving around the house with an awkward gait.

"Hey you look pretty bad," said Miguel.

"Thanks."

"C'mon, let's get you home."

"Sounds good. I feel like crap." We drove across the island to our place.

The next morning I awoke in my small, bare, white-walled room. My heel still felt achy. *It couldn't be too bad,* I thought. *I'll just ignore it.* I got up to hit the head. In one agonizing step, a sharp pain shot up from my foot and stabbed my brain. My leg faltered and I crumbled to the floor. At that moment I realized I'd been truly injured. I crawled back into bed, still needing to pee.

Lying there wounded gave me time to reflect. In the month since I'd arrived to ride the waves of the Canary Islands, I had taken more physical abuse than Wiley Coyote.

Take the burly Spanish bouncer for example. I hadn't even seen that untamed control freak coming. Three days after landing in the Canaries, I'd been hanging out in a crowded nightclub (there happened to be a lot of night life) minding my own business when four drunk young English girls shuffled past. The last gal, the most intoxicated, face-planted in front of me. She had been using her friend as a crutch when her mini-skirted legs finally gave out. She sort of slid slow motion down her friend's back and collapsed on the ground.

Her friends noticed she had gone down and struggled to drag her out of the crowd. It only took me a second to realize they could use a hand. Like any Good Samaritan would, I lifted the girl's drunken body off the floor and threw her over my shoulder. The limp lush only weighed about a hundred pounds. She looked like a cutie, but that was beside the point.

With a decent grip on the gal, I said to her friends, "Let's go, girls."

"Oh, thank you, thank you!" they said.

Together we searched for an exit and some fresh air. We forced our way through bodies rock-concert thick and found a closed door under a green "Exit" sign, not far from the main entrance, where the previously mentioned bouncer sat trying to look all tough. I didn't pay him much mind during my quest to leave the club. But it seems he was watching me, and closely.

With one arm I kept the girl secure on my shoulder, and with my free arm I pushed the unguarded door ajar. The door pried halfway when, out of nowhere, the bouncer grabbed its long handle and stopped me cold. He muttered something in Spanish, but I couldn't understand him. I didn't care what he had to say, anyway. I wanted to get the heck out of the claustrophobic club before someone puked on me.

He yanked on the door, trying to close it. And I pushed at it, wanting to get outside.

The dude was pretty adamant about me not exiting that particular door. But I figured he was just being hard-headed, so I kept my back to him and continued pushing on the handle. Surely he could see I was trying to help the girls? I hoped he would find it in his heart to let me out. Yeah, right.

The bouncer released the door handle, alright, although with my back to him I didn't see why. To my joy, the door started to open. I leaned toward my escape. Suddenly a crushing blow struck the side of my skull and I dropped to the ground, girl and all. The bouncer had blind-sided me. He followed that up with a series of powerful wallops. *Bam! Bam! Bam! Bam!* There I was, getting beaten, while half-stuck under the drunk chick.

I heard her friends screaming, *"Stop! Please, stop!"*

Two other bouncers rushed to the scene and stabilized the situation, taking their aggressive friend away before I had time to realize what had happened.

"Hey, *que pasó?"* I said, trying to set the girl down softly so I could get up off the floor. "Was all that really necessary?"

"Well," said one of the bouncers, "I don't know what happened with you guys, but our friend's been known to punch first and talk later."

One of the girls vouched for me. "This guy was just helping us and that jack-hole was being a bully."

"Maybe," said the other bouncer. "But he's good to have when there's a real problem."

So that was that. The lumps on my head and face eventually healed, and the manager made it up to me by letting me slide on all future cover charges. Whenever I encountered the original unsmiling face of Mr. Quickpunch at the door, I had the satisfaction of passing him without paying. To me, that meant he knew his own people understood that he had been in the wrong.

Not that he cared.

* * *

Out on the town wasn't the only place those islands roughed me up. I faced trouble in the water, too. The place to party was located on one side of the island, and I lived on the other side, where the surf was. From the balcony of my rented room at Miguel's place I could check the waves directly out front, which happened to be an out-of the-way surf spot. I liked its lack of surfers, and the island's volcanic reefs provided waves with some grunt. At times the surf would get downright mean.

One day the swell was up. The waves were good but a bit lumpy and broke at shorter intervals—the effect of a wind swell. Some of the bigger sets were chunky. Anyway, there were two guys in the water: me and Miguel.

Two minutes after we paddled out, I scored a great ride. I'd dropped cleanly into an overhead beauty and leaned hard into a bottom turn. In front of me, the wave's face stood tall and steep. With all my speed, I rocketed up the wave, careened off the top, and flew straight down the vertical wall of water. At the bottom, I jammed a turn under the pitching lip and stalled into a nice bowling section. After shooting out of that, I saw another sweet section forming up. I pumped my board on the open face and met the new wall with a solid carve, slicing my rail through the water and pushing with everything I had. What a rush. After one last good whack off the lip at end of the ride, I kicked out and began paddling toward the lineup for another.

The waves had slowed to a brief moment of peace, giving me a chance to cover some ground. Miguel was still way outside when the ocean sprang to life again. A nice inside wave approached, and I paddled for it. I stroked hard, but missed it. When I turned around, the ocean gave me the unpleasant surprise of a large set ready to unload on my head.

It may not have been the biggest set that had ever caught me inside, but when the first wave broke, the mass of whitewater was definitely too furious to duck-dive. I bailed my board, took a breath, and plunged feet-first toward the bottom.

The wave rag-dolled me hard. It flung my body in a circular whoosh, and the fierce energy drove me deeper. Spun upside down, I covered my head with my arms to protect it from a possible smash against the reef. Luckily, I didn't hit.

Seconds passed, and I began to wonder when things were going to mellow out. The damn thing didn't want to let go. During the thrashing I felt myself get pushed deeper still, which surprised me, as I hadn't thought the water *was* that deep.

Not wanting to think about it anymore, I turned the channel in my mind and let my thoughts float as if in a dream. I was traveling south through the Baja desert on a motorcycle. In every direction I saw big boulders and tall, spiny pitchfork cacti. The road was quiet and lonely. Fresh air flowed all around me, and I felt the vibration of the bike's engine massaging my arms. I had no place to be, and felt no sense of responsibility. A free-spirited happiness pumped through my heart.

My brain switched back to my current underwater situation, ripping me from the dream. But it hadn't been a dream at all—I had just recalled a vision of myself from six months earlier, after I'd left home to begin another trans-world wander. I'd come a long way since then.

After a while my lungs began to crave air. But the wave had me, and there was nothing to do but stay relaxed. As the wave started to let go, I developed a new worry.

Due to the nature of the swell, the waves were breaking in close succession. It seemed this wave had kept me an underwater prisoner longer than it should have, and I now feared I'd surface without a chance to snag a breath before the next wave of the set would hit. But I didn't have time to worry about that. Just as I began to swim for the top, my undersea world shook once more. *Another wave.* At the mercy of the ocean, I tumbled.

The urgency for air grew. *I can't take my last breath today,* I thought. Dwelling on it would be the worst thing to do. Knowing that surviving meant staying mellow and not wasting precious oxygen from my already depleted brain, I searched for a relaxing song to sing in my mind.

Soon my desire for air faded. My lungs no longer burned, and my brain no longer cared. I began to feel . . . *good.* A peaceful feeling engulfed me. *Oh, look, I'm standing in line to see Santa. Oh, and there's my sister, trying to roller skate away from me. She couldn't stand me when we were little. There's my Uncle John, in the middle of one of his hearty laughing spells. I love that guy!*

Random memories from long ago flashed through my mind, preparing me for the surrender to dreamland.

When the second wave finally released me, instinct raised my arms above my head and I took a lethargic stroke in the direction I thought to be the surface. My second feeble stroke started at my chest. I was so weak I relied more on floating up than on swimming. Anyway, floating probably took less energy and therefore used up less oxygen. Bottom line: I simply hadn't the gusto to swim.

Floating to the surface, mouth first, head tilted back, I began to hear the foam of the wave's aftermath crackling on the surface. The sound grew louder. Then, just as a quieting blackness promised to take over, I felt my fuzzy head come out of the water. My eyes opened, and I sucked air into my lungs.

Light, dark, light, dark. My sight wobbled on both sides of consciousness until the oxygen kicked in. I was that close to fading out.

Now back on earth, I glanced out to sea to check whether there were more waves in the set. Luckily the ocean surface was now dormant. I reeled my board in and paddled toward Miguel. My muscles were drained, but the air sure tasted good. I breathed, and paddled slowly.

I finally reached Miguel, who was sitting on his long board, smiling.

"What a set, huh," he said.

My wits still hadn't been completely collected. "Man, that had to have been my longest hold-down ever," I said. "Two waves."

"I know," said Miguel. "I barely made it over both waves. When I looked down behind me, I saw your board tombstoning in the impact zone as the second whitewash rolled over it."

Let me explain: When a surfboard is tombstoning, it's half submerged and half out of the water with its nose aiming straight up at the sky, mimicking a tombstone. A board does this when the surfer is deep under, anchoring it, pulling its leash taut.

* * *

I'd taken some punishment in the Canaries, but had a great time. Although one side of the isle buzzed with a party scene, most everywhere else was exceptionally peaceful. I liked that.

The raw volcanic landscape, not too different in appearance from a red moon, had a quiet spiritual quality. Along the reef crusted shoreline the Atlantic crashed rhythmically, as it had for eons. Perhaps because the place was so wildly different from home, everything felt magical, as if I'd reached this world by traveling through time.

On top of that, I enjoyed the companionship of friendly people from the far reaches of the globe. One new person after another would pop into my life. Some of them seemed like long-lost friends from the moment we said hello.

And, of course, there were the waves. I practically had my own surf spot, and some fantastic moments in the water. Many blue wave sessions I surfed with only a few friends, and many I surfed alone. I enjoyed both the company and the solitude.

For all of its elements, I loved life on the road.

2

CALIFORNIA

Grommethood

I was born into a working class family in Southern California. Of Mexican descent, my father was the eighth of ten siblings raised in a barrio a gunshot away from L.A. Although my grandparents spoke perfect English, they mixed it up and often talked to their kids in Spanish. With so many brothers and sisters, most of them supported by his father's foundry worker wages, my dad learned early in life that if he wanted something he had to earn it. As a youngster, he sold newspapers and forked over fistfuls of his earnings to his mother. My old man claimed his family was so poor he had to wear his older sister's hand-me-down blouses to school—a great visual, but I didn't buy it.

He told colorful tales of blood-shedding brawls breaking out on the streets of his rowdy neighborhood, and of how as a teenager he had held the spoon while his doper friends' sautéed their fix. Growing up surrounded by drugs, thieves, and an increasing number of peers stuck in either a crackhouse or a jailhouse, Dad couldn't wait to get out. So one day, at the beginning of his junior year in high school, he didn't bother going to class. Instead, with his father's written consent, at seventeen, he joined the few, the proud, and the brave.

Back from Vietnam, my father met my mother through a friend. Mom was a Cali transplant from Chicago. Her mother was a full-blooded Greek whose folks had come to America fresh off the boat from Kythdia, a small island in the Mediterranean. My mom's dad was a mostly white boy, in and out of orphanages, 1930s depression-impressioned, WWII-hardened Marine Corps vet. Apparently, my granddad, James Frazier Bonham, was a direct descendant of semi-famous U.S. Lt. James Butler Bonham, who fought and died at the Alamo during the Mexican-American War. My ornery grandfather was strongly opposed to his daughter marrying a Mexican, even though my dad happened to be a U.S. Marine Corps vet himself, and as American as Taco Bell.

My dad however, didn't give a rat whether or not he had his future father-in-law's approval. Only months after Mom graduated high school, my folks married in spite of my crusty old granddad. They eventually produced two mutts. My sister, Christy, came first. Over two and a half years later, I entered the world.

Dad borrowed money from none other than old Granddad for a down payment on a neglected tract house in Anaheim, just two blocks from Disneyland. Our clan moved in. Unfortunately, other than a few words I shouldn't mention here, Spanish was not spoken in our home. And I'm still *pinche* pissed about that!

My dad job-hopped for a few years before settling into a serviceman position at a large restaurant supply outfit. There he began to shine. They soon acknowledged him with a "Serviceman of the Year" award, and subsequently "Man of the Year." They promoted him from serviceman to consultant, and his green utility service van and workingman's attire gave way to a boxy late model sedan and a closet full of outrageous 1970s suits.

On the surface, it appeared things were going smoothly— the house, the decent job, and two healthy kids. However, as we all know, life is obstaclistic. I've never attempted it myself, but I've heard that working your way up in a large corporation can sometimes require brown-nosing asinine know-it-alls who think they're God's gift to enterprise. My dad bit his tongue for a while, but he eventually got sick of corporate politics and jumped into business for himself, taking many of his former company's clients with him. He didn't care that his collar reverted from white to whatever was on sale.

With a wife and two kids to support, it was a ballsy move. But my old man tackled his tasks and maintained a good rapport with his customers. He kept his business rolling, and he kept his promise to himself that his children would have more than he had while he was growing up. I never had to wear my sister's blouses to school.

Meanwhile, my loving mother, who was always there for us, was also quick on the keyboard. As she became liberated from the duties of caring for her two growing children, she enrolled in adult education courses. In a few years she landed a sweet position working for the state, complete with a company car and more paid vacation days than an elementary school teacher.

With our parents busy living their lives, my sister and I got on with our own.

When she was younger, Christy and trouble were pretty

good friends. Getting caught smoking in the girls' room and sneaking out late at night with her friends turned her relationship with our father into an ugly war, one she almost won.

Once out of high school, she focused on cosmetology and became a dynamite hairstylist. I'll dig for a little credit here: Early on, I helped boost her career by guinea pigging her latest fashions . . . that is, until she really blew it, right during my first week of eighth grade.

"Oh, I've got this really hot haircut to give you. All the girls will dig it!" she promised. She plopped me down on a chair in the middle of our kitchen, grabbed a pair of dull scissors, and hacked away. *Snip, snip, snip.* Clumps of brown hair slid down the black plastic trash bag she'd wrapped around my neck.

When she claimed her cut a success, the only thing *hot* was my temper. The instant I glimpsed myself in the mirror, I cried out, "What girl will dig . . . *this?*" Then I literally cried. I looked like Bert from Sesame Street.

Long story short, I eventually forgave my sis, but it was at least a year before she could approach me holding a pair of scissors. I got a good deal in the long run, and haven't paid for a haircut since, financially or emotionally.

My sister is an amazing photographer. A few clicks of the shutter through her creative eye, and you'll see the beauty in things you've never noticed before.

She's a genuine cowgirl. While I headed west to the beach, she hightailed it in the opposite direction, into horse country. She'd been stepping barefoot in horse manure since she could first walk. My mom has pictures of Christy as a toddler, poised on our Aunt Punkin's mare in Yorba Linda, at that time (early 1970s) a swelling semi-rural town. She's never stopped horsing around. And I'm *still* trying to ride a surfboard with as much bravado as my sister rides a horse. She has more energy than the sun, and somehow juggles two young kids, a camera, hairstyling, rodeos, and whatever may be cooking in the oven.

While not as artistic as my sis, I'd like to think I'm as driven. Mom's waning hope of university-bound doctor or lawyer career-minded kids wasn't due to our lack of motivation, but to the direction in which we channeled it.

From the time I was five until my freshman year in high school, I played baseball. According to the roster, I wasn't a bad player, and during those years I really enjoyed the game. A regular on the All Star team, first base was my spot, circus catches my specialty. As a young boy I'd pile up pillows on the living room floor across from where my dad kicked back on the couch and watched games on the tube. I'd charge out of the hallway as he tossed the ball toward the soft stack, where I'd dive for it. I did this over and over, unaware that this exercise would later help me out in the field. During game time, I pulled off some of these diving catches in front of a small but cheering crowd. My old man, who's crazy about the sport, envisioned me becoming the lead-off hitter for the L.A. Dodgers.

All men are different, and my father's fantasies and my own didn't equate. High school baseball lacked the pizzazz of the Little League days, and things were getting dull. As any loving son would do, I loafed through a year of freshman ball, burned out, called it quits, and shattered Dad's hopes and dreams forever. Organized team sports became a thing of the past.

Ironically, almost two years earlier, a Hawaiian kid on my Little League team had led me to my first surfboard. He and I had been doing a lot of boogie boarding. He kept talking about an upgrade, and about how in the water, surfing was superior. He said it was time to stand up and be noticed, and I went along with it.

One day I received a call.

"Hey, J.J., there's an outlet sale goin' on right now and they're sellin brand-new surfboards for a hundred and fifty bucks. I got one. There's still one left, bra. Ya'd betta hurry!"

He had me all fired-up. I had enough cash buried in my savings, and I got the board. I was thirteen years old.

I leaned the surfboard up against the wall in my room and admired its glossy finish. My mind swept back to earlier beach days with my family. I had caught my first wave at age four. On a hot summer day in Huntington Beach, I'd sat perched high on my Uncle Bill's shoulders. He'd shuffled innocently through waist high water and inched gradually toward the sea. You see, my uncle was far too bold. As for me, I was just having fun.

Nowadays I know that it's unwise to turn your back on Mother Ocean, for you never know what surprises she may throw at you. My uncle, who hailed from Illinois, was about to learn this golden rule. When he turned to face the beach, and my concerned parents, he waited just a little too long.

I didn't even know what hit me.

Ripped from my Uncle's grip by the force of the wave, my light frame tumbled helplessly in a series of underwater somersaults. The sound of roaring water rumbled ruthlessly in my ears. Out of fear and curiosity, I opened my eyes for a split second. I was lost in a sea of rushing white bubbles, and all I could do was hold my breath.

After what felt like an eternity, I hit the sand feet first in belly-deep water.

Shoulders slumped low and head held down, I staggered toward shore while watching a thick stream of water drain off my head.

I wasn't sure what had just happened. But my parents must have watched the whole scene, because by that time they'd hurried to my side. My mother, trying to console me, kept repeating enthusiastically, "Wow, J.J., you were body surfing! You were body surfing!"

* * *

In the wake of a fading baseball career, I nurtured my new pastime. In no way did I make an intentional switch from the diamond to the beach. Wielding a ball and glove, I knew what I was doing. Playing around on a surfboard was a novelty.

* * *

Entering into my teenage years I had the same interests as other kids my age, and ditching authority ranked high on the list. Luckily, I wasn't a dedicated delinquent, although I had my moments.

Our group of friends would always hang out at the guys' houses where there were no curfews, rules, or parental guidance. One of these getaways belonged to Dan. Our eyes bulged the first time we entered his bedroom and saw the walls plastered with magazine clips of bare-breasted women striking tasteless poses. We walked in slowly, and carefully examined each saucy pinup as Dan strolled across the room and reclined on his bed. He reached into the nightstand drawer for a pack of cigarettes, sparked up a smoke, and puffed three perfect rings into the air, all casual, like it was no big deal.

We freaked. "Dude! Your mom's in the next room, man! What are you doing?" I guess nothing should've shocked us at that point.

"Oh, she'll stay in there," he said. "Don't worry about it." And heck, since he didn't care, we *really* didn't care. His place instantly became our preferred hangout.

Dan was ahead of our time. He practically raised himself. Clean cut and clever, he could play a parent like a hand of poker. When my mom first met him, he talked so slick and respectful she never suspected that spending the night at his house was a teenager's wet dream.

"Mom, I'm sleeping over Dan's tonight, okay?"

"Okay, honey. Have fun." And I'd be free.

Little did Mom know that her eighth grader pounded wine coolers and popcorn while porn flicks pumped on his friend's television screen. And that was just dinner. We'd skateboard around town till three in the morning. I loved skating through the empty late-night streets to the a.m./p.m. mini-mart and dispensing myself a ninety-nine-cent cup of soft ice cream. To make sure I got my money's worth, I'd pile it ridiculously high and overflow the thing with crushed Oreos and M&Ms. From there, we'd skate home and sleep until ten or eleven the next day.

All that stuff would *not* have flown at my house. The moral of the story is that sometimes strict parenting is overrated. I say that because Dan ended up being more responsible than I.

* * *

Huntington Beach was a good half-hour car ride from my parents' house in land-locked Anaheim. Before I started surfing, beach trips had been with family or friends and had always included the watchful eye of an adult. But now things were different. Itching to be self-reliant and to reach the beach on my own, I discovered an alternate mode of transport that didn't require the help of anyone else: the bus.

A ten-minute walk from my front door was a stop for OCTD bus #37. For seventy-five cents, this bus would carry me and my surfboard through thirteen miles of traffic lights and deposit us on the south side of the Huntington Beach pier, in the same area where my uncle had accidentally sent me hurtling from his shoulders into the sea years before. But these days, I knew what to expect.

* * *

The year we finished junior high, my friend Scott Silvey and I hung out nearly every day. Scotty and I were born a week apart. For our fourteenth birthdays we bought season passes to Disneyland, where *Videopolis* was a teenage hot spot on warm, summer nights. At that age, our main goal was to make out with the girls (what's changed?) on the slow rides. We lived within walking distance of Disney, and declared our independence.

The ritual went like this: Scotty and I would wake early, bag sandwiches, grab our boards, and stroll out of the neighborhood to the bus stop. We had summer wired, relying on our parents only for bus fare. Neither Scott nor I surfed well. In fact, we were complete kooks. We spent more energy dodging sets and getting drilled than riding our boards. But that didn't matter to us. Summertime at the beach ruled, and we loved every minute. The smell of the ocean's salty air was intoxicating, and we'd be on it before the crowds covered the sands. By late morning the same bus would deposit more boys and girls from our school, and there'd be a bunch of us kids basking in the sun like socializing seals.

Summer faded, high school started, and the frequency of our surf sessions dwindled. My time with Scott had come to a halt now that we attended different schools. Though I'd find other friends to paddle out with from time to time, surfing had yet to develop into a true passion.

Then, shortly after I turned fifteen, something changed. Or maybe I should say . . . snapped. I'm not sure how it happened, but I suddenly felt a fiery enthusiasm for the water. Whether this new hunger was triggered by a particular wave or session or by a blurry confluence of the many glorious beach days combined, I don't know. What I do know is, that was the year wave riding transformed from a fun recreational activity into a fullblown addiction. I no longer felt lackadaisical about getting to the beach; I most definitely *had* to get there. The mere thought of it pumped my blood.

Finding a surf buddy around Anaheim in the dead of winter was sometimes impossible. But that didn't matter. I'd wake early on weekends, throw on my sweat pants and jacket, grab my board, and stride alone to the bus stop while watching my frosty breath dissipate into the nippy air.

The bus would drop me off at an empty beach, its cold morning sand void of sunbathers. I'd wrap my towel around my waist and change out of my warm sweats into a leaky wetsuit. Wetsuits in the mid-'80s weren't as warm as the ones made today, and I lacked decent gear even for those days. Without a proper surf mentor to guide me, I had to learn the hard way. I nearly froze my *cojones* off.

I'd stay in the water until I was a shivering mess, hands so stiff and dysfunctional I had to wrestle my wetsuit off my body, fingers so numb that tying the drawstring to my sweatpants was easier to do with my teeth. Why do this to yourself? Where's the fun in it? Good question. During those chilly moments I wondered the same thing. But once I thawed out, frozen nerve endings gave way to a satisfying tingling sensation I could find nowhere else. After the session, feeling mellow and surfed out, I'd sit in the sand and watch the waves tumble to shore.

Winter's effects were only temporary. Spring held the promise of longer, warmer days. Friends with cars came out of their hovels and offered after-school and weekend rides to the beach. This equaled more water time and a slow but inevitable progression. As my ability improved, surfing seeped deeper into my core. I looked forward to my sixteenth birthday.

This is a good place to pause and explain something that played a key factor in shaping the years that followed: I grew up in a land of plenty, for which I'm grateful. However, from the moment we're born, consumerism is practically fed to us like baby formula from a plastic bottle. Roadside billboards and TV commercials tempt us with a never-ending array of dazzling products sure to enhance our lives. Credit card apps are crammed into our mailboxes, persuading us to over-spend and enslave ourselves to the anxieties of financial debt. We dig deep into our shallow pockets to buy luxuries we can't really afford. None of this is news to anyone, but for many of us, living within our means seems like mission impossible.

This is where I got lucky. For some unknown reason, I'm a saver—a trait I was born with. From as far back as I can remember I never squandered dough. At five years old, I proudly opened a savings account and deposited eleven dollars. That amount grew over the years. It was like a game. If Grandma slipped me a ten-spot in a birthday card, three dollars went into my pocket and seven into the account. By the time I hit fifteen, I'd banked over two grand from birthdays, allowances, and the occasional odd job. My free-spending sister loved making condescending cracks about my thriftiness. She couldn't understand that I simply didn't need much. But now, almost old enough to drive, I had a legitimate reason for the savings. I planned on getting my license, buying some wheels, and taking full advantage of that important privilege.

* * *

As I mentioned earlier, my father and sister battled constantly through her early teens. No matter how much grief she gave him, he refused to let his only daughter follow the dark path to no-good-ville. In the end he prevailed, and saved her from herself.

Having witnessed their conflict, I realized I was no match against his parental ordinance, and a transgression there would equal zero fun. But I also lucked out. Christy was stubborn and had the defending champ against the ropes more than once. By the time I stepped into the ring, I sensed some authority burnout. And I was a male, which probably helped. Nevertheless, I wasn't about to test my boundaries the way my sister had. The secret to maximum surf-time was to stay out of trouble. Except for a trickle of saltwater, I kept my nose pretty clean, and my grades, well . . . average.

During the second half of my sophomore year, I paid close attention in Drivers Ed and easily aced all the written exams. At the time, I wasn't concerned about whether Benedict Arnold was a traitor or ran a trading post, or how many atoms fit into a jar. I wanted to drive. Before I knew it, my learner's permit sparkled in my hand.

I scheduled my D.M.V. driving test for the afternoon of my sixteenth birthday, June 12, 1989, the day school let out for the summer. Little did I know that it would be one of the better summers for swell California had seen in years. I was about to have my cake and swallow it whole.

But wait. It got better.

Not only did I pass my driving test without trouble; my dad offered me the use of his old backup work van. He didn't know how stoked I was. Well, maybe he did, when he saw me pimp out the inside with spray paint, carpet, and a bed. I threw in my surfboard, grabbed some buddies, and virtually disappeared for the next three months . . . POOF!

We drove up and down the coast. Vacant lots and beachside suburb streets became our camping grounds. One of my favorite places to go was Lower Trestles, one of So Cal's supreme surf spots. Lowers could get absurdly crowded, but with ample swell pumping in, picking-off waves wasn't a problem. I favored the long rights that peeled down the point; they brought out the best in my novice abilities.

Once, I took my Uncle Jim and a few cousins from back East to Trestles because they asked for a true "Californian" surfing experience. I doubt my intentions were pure; I knew the swell was up and the waves were firing. I was so amped to get in the water that I left my innocent family to fend for themselves.

Pummeled by the pounding shorebreak, Uncle Jim ended up on the rocks. I'd had a feeling that might happen. The real beginners' spot lay just across the bay in the mellow rolling waves of San Onofre. I could've taken them there, but I had a one-track mind.

* * *

It was during this swell roaring time that I started hanging with Chris Malavar. I knew Malavar through my sister, so he had a few years on me. We were both surf-crazy and went on wave hunting missions. From Santa Barbara to San Diego, we took advantage of Mother Nature's hospitality.

Summer died before its time. I returned my dad's van to him, as I wanted something zippy and fuel-efficient. My school sat a half-hour inland, and I anticipated lots of commuting to the beach. I used fifteen hundred of the two thousand dollars in my savings to buy a trusty dark blue 1983 Nissan Sentra, still branded with the old Datsun emblem on the trunk.

In the first month of my junior year, Malavar rented a crumbly old apartment on Seventh Street in downtown Huntington Beach, right across from the pier. We could see the waves from his front doorstep. My surfboard and wetsuit moved in. Although he rarely locked the door, Mal gave me a set of keys to his pad.

Before school, after school, and often during school, my winter water time not only expanded, it exploded. As long as I didn't flunk classes, my folks let me do my own thing. I have to admit I walked into first period English class late a few times, with damp, salty hair and wearing flip-flops on my sandy feet.

"Um, I'm terribly sorry Mr. Douglas, my darn car wouldn't start this morning."

"That's funny, son. You said that yesterday."

"Man . . . was it yesterday? Well then, um, sir, my dog died. The poor little guy choked to death on my homework."

I was lucky Teach liked me, because there's no way he ever bought those tardy stories. He'd usually smirk and make me take a seat. However, that sort of thing only happened during primo swells. I acted like a diligent student when I wanted to. But the satisfaction I got from going to school couldn't compare to the feeling of waking up on Malavar's couch and surfing good waves through a Monday or Tuesday morning when I *should've* been in class.

For the record, these days I understand the importance of a solid education. So, kids, I'm telling you to pay attention in school. This book would've taken half the time to write had I actually *listened* in English Class. Either way, like so many kids at sixteen, I felt high school was nothing more than a nagging nuisance. It soaked up what was usually the best time of the day to surf, before the wind hit and messed up the waves. But after school, regardless of the conditions, I paddled out in just about every mood ol' H.B. could produce.

* * *

Summer rolled around again, and I nearly lost my beach hangout. Malavar had abandoned his ocean apartment and moved to the other side of town. My saving grace was one Mr. Chris Weaver, whom I met through Malavar. We all three often paddled out together.

Weaver was a straightforward kind of guy. Both ambitious and wild, he had a schoolboy face, an athlete's build, and a punk rock attitude. He had just moved in a few blocks from Malavar's old place, and he said if I wanted to I could stash my gear at his place. I did.

The scene at Weaver's pad was busier than at Malavar's. He had four other roommates, all girls in their early twenties. The doors were rarely shut, let alone locked. With a good-sized duplex, the onset of summer, and a bunch of wild young adults (where's an adult?) living near the beach, it brewed the perfect recipe for one thing: PAR-TAY.

Most nights, there was hardly a dull moment. I witnessed the staggering power of the beer bong and the mental cloudiness of the water bong. Loud music echoed endlessly through open windows. One time, a drunken brawl broke out and the loser came into the house hunched over, clutching the nape of his neck.

"Someone just whacked my head with a pipe, hard," he complained.

That kind of stuff went down all time. It didn't matter whether it was Friday, Saturday, or Tuesday. The faces passed never-ending through the nights, yet I always managed to find an obscure corner of the house to curl up and sleep, occasionally discovered and half-seduced by an intoxicated female.

Another stellar summer ended. I counted on one hand how many times I'd driven inland to Anaheim, but couldn't add up the number of hours I'd spent in the water. I paddled out three times a day. As my surfing improved, I became as zealous as ever.

Thus began my senior year at Loara High School. Weaver bailed on his place near the beach, and without the luxury of a coastal crash pad I became a legitimate inlander again. But I still had wheels.

Through the years, I'd learned a lot watching my sister— mostly what not to do. But back when I was a freshman I noticed that as a senior, she left school every day at noon while we lower classmen were stuck in confinement long past lunch. I never asked her how she did it, but I wanted to follow her example.

When I got to be a senior, I made the mistake of speaking with a school counselor about how I too could have a four-period day. "No, sorry, that's impossible. Seniors are not allowed to leave campus till fifth period is over," she said matter-of-factly. I wasn't buying it. What did she know, anyway? I felt sure this broad only wanted me on campus because I wanted off. It was going to take a little research.

A senior who had never failed a class in their entire life would graduate with five extra credits, I learned, assuming he or she continued to pass until graduation day. That was how leaving after five classes became possible. But it still meant suffering through lunch while the ocean danced without me.

Then I found my escape: the school's work experience program. Working enough hours at a part-time job after school and attending a "zero" period one morning per week would soak up a class.

I needed a job, anyway. Gone were the days of bumming milk money off Mom and scraping the dregs of my exhausted savings account. A friend of mine who worked at a local Pizza Hut told me they needed delivery drivers. The only catch was that you had to be eighteen. I had just turned seventeen. He said all they required with an application was a photocopy of your driver's license and insurance. I Xeroxed a copy of my license and with a black ink pen I made the 3 in 73 look as much like a 2 as possible. Then I crinkled up the paper into a little ball and let the wrinkles set in. I flattened out the paper and made a Xerox of that, doing my best to hide any discrepancies. Not bad, I thought, looking at the distorted copy. I was instantly a year older.

I marched into Pizza Hut, filled out an application, and turned it in along with my fraudulent paperwork. The manager gave a quick glance at my app, never looked at my actual license, and put me to work.

"Can you start tonight?" she asked.

Mission accomplished. I wasn't going to mention a word to any authority figure at my school, and I was beach-bound come lunchtime whether I had to sneak away from government property or not.

As it turned out, no one made a fuss about my mid-day departures, nor did they notice that I often left with someone in my passenger seat. Eight times out of ten, that someone was Chris Valentin. I'd known of Valentin since junior high, and that he surfed. But it wasn't until my senior year that we began paddling out together.

Valentin and I were roughly the same age, but he was a grade under me, and I never gave him much thought until my sophomore year, when we happened to be seeing the same girl. I'd heard through the grapevine that he had some beef with me. Since his main surf territory was several miles down the coast from mine, I considered Valentin a sort of silent adversary.

Generally being one to stand my ground, but never looking to rumble, I passed him one day on campus. I saw him coming and mad-dogged him. He didn't acknowledge my scowl or even seem to know I was there, or maybe he didn't recognize me. That was it. I didn't see him for another two years.

I don't recall how we kicked off our first surf session together, and until then hadn't realized what a cool guy Valentin was, always polite, respectful, and mellow. What I really liked about him was that he was just as keen as I about getting into the water, and staying in the water.

One sunny day after school we headed to Golden West Street in Huntington, expecting average waist-high surf. Instead, we arrived to find clean, glassy six-foot peaks up and down the beach. We suited up and paddled out with urgency, watching the blue waves peel in both directions. My heart thumped with anticipation. I couldn't calm down until I had a wave under my belt.

A head-high right rolled in and I snatched it, charging down the line as the wave's face jacked up. Now, with the vertical wall of water in front of me, I became really excited! When the thick, pitching section approached, I had loads of speed. Using all my momentum, I hopped up over the lip and floated weightlessly across the wave's smooth, round roof, then sprang out and free-fell from the top of the wave all the way down to the flats. My weight and balance stayed over the board's center for a perfect landing. A rush from the ride vibrated through me.

As I paddled back out, I saw Valentin racing down the line on a beauty. "Whoooo!" I cheered.

Valentin and I spent hours paddling against energy-draining currents in swells of all shapes and sizes. Noodle-armed, rashed, cramped, dehydrated, and burnt, we caught some fantastic waves that year.

Some afternoons I'd coax Weaver into heading out for a surf, leaning on the fact that the previous day had been going off and promising him that the swell still had plenty of juice.

One day I called him, saying, "Man, the Cliffs were *good* yesterday. C'mon, let's get on it!"

We arrived at the beach to the sight of small, sloppy, wind-blown crap. He looked at me in disappointment.

"Hey, J.J., what's up? It's shitty out there."

"No, no, check out that section forming up . . . look, you can hit it right *there!*" I said, pointing toward the disorganized sea.

I wasn't kidding. It always looked fun to me. Weaver thought I was nuts, but paddled out anyway.

I probably both motivated and annoyed him, but I'll bet he didn't regret one windswept wave.

* * *

Although I couldn't wait until it was over, I actually enjoyed my senior year. Someone formed a surf club, which I joined, of course. Our group went on excursions down the coast and into Mexico. We competed against other schools with surfers of similar caliber, and I felt what it was like to win surf contests. My status in the club was cool, kind of like the king of the kooks. The kids at my school considered me pretty good.

While many may not have noticed the evident disparity, I certainly did not fall in the same league as some of the top kids from schools like Huntington Beach High. They had a legitimate surfing "team" and some boys on the verge of becoming professional surfers. Most of those guys had far more experience than I did and would've snuffed me in a comp. But competitions didn't concern me. I rode waves for pure joy.

* * *

A normal weekday after school went like this: I'd drive the half-hour to the beach and surf from one until four, and then jet back to Anaheim to deliver pizzas during the dinner hours. I'd earn minimum wage and fifteen or so bucks in tips. Good money to me. My savings account began to swell.

Like a typical urban surf-stoked grommet, I read the magazines and watched the videos. I saw colorful photos of perfect empty lineups in exotic lands and images of clean wet cylinders draining endlessly down a lonely tropical reef. Watching that stuff lulled me into a trance. So much was happening outside Southern California, and I was graduating high school soon. I was about to be free from the last detail separating me from the real world.

Those last few months choked me like a rabid dog on a short leash.

There was this thing called a senior trip—a grand finale, a celebration of mental and physical liberation and progression from young to young adult. At least that's how I looked at it. For those who went on this journey, it usually averaged a week or two in some party town in Mexico, where a person of eighteen could legally drink alcohol like the grownups they were supposed to be.

I had other ideas.

I was so eager to bust out of high school that I wanted to go somewhere far, far away. Like Neptune. And a two-week trip wouldn't do, either. I had to feel it, soak in it, and absorb it. I needed at least two months.

I'd taken an interest in Indonesia. Yeah, I could hardly pronounce it, but I'd seen it in the mags and vids. So mystical was its allure, so distant it seemed, almost unobtainable. I knew nothing about the place except that it helped frame the Indian Ocean and had warm, magnificent waves.

I wanted so desperately to go that nothing else mattered.

Reluctant to jump on a plane and travel alone to the other side of the planet, I planted a seed in my buddy Weaver's head. We had always talked about taking a real surf trip, and as potential travel companions went, he was a prime candidate. He and I got along hassle-free, and he had a job, hence money.

I baited a hook, and Weaver bit. The hard part would be reeling him in.

* * *

Planning the trip took work. First I asked the Pizza Hut manager to load my schedule with shifts. Then I went to the library to check out some books. The place to fly into was Bali, well visited and tourist friendly, like landing on a pillow. From there we could hop around to different islands.

Reading about those islands heightened my desire to get there. The reference books claimed rooms or bungalows rented for as little as two dollars a night, and the average meal cost fifty cents or less, depending on your taste. I read about all the tropical fruit, the monkeys that frolicked near sacred temples, the boat taxis, the festivals, and the magic mushrooms.

The travel section in the Los Angeles Times was loaded with flights to that side of the world—Kuala Lumpur, Singapore, Jakarta, ah and yes . . . Bali. I shopped for a deal, searching the specials and calling travel agents. After the first two agents quoted two very different prices, I thought, *I'm gonna have to call every travel agent in the paper.* And that's exactly what I did.

Along with the least expensive ticket, one agency quoted a complimentary three-night stay at a *losmen* (budget home-stay type accommodation) near Kuta, Bali's craziest tourist town. Not having to worry about a bed right off the plane would give us breathing room to figure the place out. I liked these tickets so much I called Weaver to pester him about going. "Hey, Weave, what's up? Any new developments in your position about taking this kick-ass surf trip that's guaranteed to be the absolute best time of your life?"

Weaver was motivated by his own forces, but I cheered him on from the sidelines, assuring him that he needed this trip as badly as I did.

Then he was in. His job granted him his requested "leave of absence."

I booked the flight, and we drove to L.A. and applied for our passports. Soon I received the little blue book to the world.

The rest of the year rolled along smoothly. I continued surfing as usual and mentally prepping for the end of the school year. Two weeks before graduation, I began packing a large duffle bag with everything under the moon—several pairs of shorts and tee-shirts, hats and sun-block, toothbrush and toothpaste, water purifying tablets, insect repellent . . . an inflatable pillow? I had no idea what to take with me.

A month earlier, I'd purchased a double board bag with the intention of stuffing it with three boards.

* * *

The last day of high school, class of 1991, was one of the most liberating days of my life. My stomach twisted and churned with an enormous sense of freedom. Girls cried nostalgically with their friends. I felt like shedding tears of joy. From now on, all my weekday mornings would be free for catching waves.

As if at the end of a lengthy prison sentence, I bid farewell to many I knew I'd never see again. To others, I promised to show my photos when I returned.

3

Indonesia
Getting Drilled

After more than two days of airtime and layovers, we arrived in Bali at dusk. Weaver and I walked out of the airport and the thick warm air soaked into our lungs. A soft breeze smelled of fresh flowers. We dragged our gear to the edge of the airport curb.

"Transport?" The voice came from the darkness.

"Yes . . . transport." We had arrived.

Weaver and I stuffed our large board bags inside a *bemo* (mini-van style taxi) and squeezed in around them. Our round-faced driver was just pulling away from the curb when a long-haired Australian stuck his head through the window.

"How ya goin? Ya blokes headin to Kuta? Mind if I scab a lift?"

"Sure, we don't care. Hop in," we said.

The driver *did* care, but couldn't do much about it because the Aussie had already molded himself into the packed vehicle. We began our short commute.

"How much is he charging ya, mate?" the Aussie asked.

"Ten thousand *rupiah*," I said.

"What? That's too much!" he scolded us, and then turned his

disapproval on the driver. "That's too much, and you know it! Five thousand, and that's it!" He turned to us and spoke loud so the driver could overhear. "He's taking advantage of you. It's a five thousand rupe ride, and he knows it!" He turned back to the driver. "Five thousand. That's it!"

The driver said no, a deal's a deal. The Aussie said five and that's it. They snapped back and forth at each other while Weaver and I stayed clammed and watched, silently cheering for the Aussie.

The bold Australian had the last word and the driver drove on, disgusted.

Once in town, the Aussie jumped out near a busy corner and disappeared forever. The *bemo* turned off the main road and sped through dark, twisting alleys with but a beep before shooting around blind corners.

We arrived in front of our *losmen* a little nerve-wracked.

Unfortunately for us, neither Weaver nor I had changed any U.S. dollars into Indonesian *rupiah* at the airport. Unsure of the exchange rate, we handed the driver a green five-dollar bill, which amounted to our original agreement before the hard-bartering Aussie stepped into the scene. Holding the note in hand, the driver put on a performance, looking at the foreign bill like, "What the hell is this?" I bought into his act and handed him another five. He still played stupefied, but he knew he'd scored, and he had to be stoked that the Australian hadn't prevailed in saving us naïve American tourists from a harmless price hike. We were lucky our first lesson of the trip had only cost us a few bucks each. Not a terrible deal.

* * *

The morning light woke my time-twisted, jet-lapsed brain. While Weaver slept, I strolled alone to the beach to meet the Indian Ocean, passing under several tall coconut trees to a sandy beach. My eyes feasted on a large, smooth lagoon outlined by big blue lefts firing off in the distance. I wasn't looking at a surf spot; these were random waves breaking onto a barrier reef. My stomach gripped with excitement.

* * *

The island looked like a holiday brochure, more foreign and fantastic than I could've fathomed. Beaches were bordered in tropical lushness, and rice terraces shaped the hillsides. A volcanic mountain pierced through the clouds over the heads of women who walked around balancing large woven baskets on their heads.

The people were warm and welcoming. Weaver and I met Made, a man who lived in a house near Uluwatu, on the Bukit peninsula. He had hopped onto the back of Weaver's rented motorcycle to "show us the way" to the beach. I followed without getting lost; the trail was all too obvious.

"You come, stay at my house," he said.

At first I was skeptical. But after visiting his small but clean two-bedroom home and meeting his wife, son, and two daughters, Weaver and I trusted Made enough to stay. To make matters better, he didn't automatically try to rip us off, asking each of us for only fifteen thousand *rupiah* ($7.50 U.S.) per night for a room and meals. We couldn't argue about price.

Made's whole family shacked up in one room to make the

other available to us. Even though they didn't have much, he and his family were better off than most of his friends. That was the conclusion I came to when a big boxing match was televised and he broke out an old thirteen-inch color TV for the special event. The thing somehow powered up off a car battery. Its rabbit ears were bent out of shape, the ends covered with tin foil.

Indonesians soon appeared from the cracks of the jungle to watch the fight. Most of the guys sat cross-legged on the tiled floor of Made's crowded living room, though Weaver and I were given special V.I.P. seats. Other than Made, nobody spoke English, so we all just sat there and smiled at each other until the start of the show.

A slim guy in a blue sarong passed between the TV and us viewers, hunching over as he walked by. It looked a little odd, because his slight duck obstructed our view even more than if he'd just passed upright. But I didn't think much of it until the next person hunched in the same way, holding his position until he'd completely cleared the crowd's view. Then I noticed that everyone did it.

At first I thought, *That's strange. Why are they ducking? It's not like they're even close to getting out of the way.* I later learned that this was custom. No one was trying to "get out of the way." They had bent down as sign of respect, like saying "excuse me."

* * *

Weaver and I stayed at Made's house for a week and rode our motorcycles to the surrounding surfbreaks. Surfing there, I learned how to hold my composure while driving through backside barrels over a shallow coral reef, one of the trip's major thrills. For the first time in my surfing life, I had the opportunity to ride tubes that funneled with machine-like precision.

My first few waves at one particular spot were especially memorable. I arrived late in the afternoon and paddled out through the warm emerald-green water. My blood rushed through my veins. These rides were going to be all about maneuvering in and around the tube. When a set came, I stroked hard and took off smoothly into my first ride. The wave heaved out, creating a cylinder. I readied for the barrel by crouching and grabbing a rail, an approach known as pig-dogging.

As soon as the wave swallowed me, my brain threw out warning signals that something was wrong. My eyes perceived the surrounding green watery walls as a threat. My legs wobbled and I flew off my board into the dryness of the open barrel. Then I hit the water, body surfed a bit, and got sucked up by the soup. Tumbling in the whitewater, I tried not to penetrate too deeply. My arms protected my melon in case it slammed into the reef. Luck was with me; I surfaced unscathed and made my way back out, analyzing what went wrong. *The wave hadn't knocked me off. No, I had freaked out and jumped.*

Ride number two: The wave pitched and bowled, creating a clean surfable tube. I pulled in and kept my eyes focused forward. I held on for a second, but my mind wouldn't accept that my body could stand up safely while engulfed in a moving room of water.

Again I flung myself from my board. *Damn. I'm blowing it!* This time I vowed to hold on, come hell or high water—pardon the pun. The third wave I caught was a little bigger, and I hungered for a successful tube ride. The wave did its thing, and my hand clamped onto the rail. I gritted and promised myself not to let go as the lip threw out and over me.

All I had to do was go straight through the watery tunnel, which you'd think would be easy enough. I held my line just on the heels of an almond-shaped window surrounded by green, swirling water. I could see every drop.

My mind tingled and sharpened. Gliding along inside the wave, I chased the window as it progressed down the reef. Suddenly, the opening seemed to halt its forward motion and appeared to be spinning in place. I, however, kept traveling, aiming my board for the wave's open door. I popped out into broad daylight, my whole body buzzing. I couldn't wait to do it again.

The next wave was even easier. From then on I grew increasingly comfortable in the tube, doing my best to stay in there as long as possible.

* * *

The reef had a lot to do with what made the waves we were surfing so great, but its sharp makeup also made walking on it difficult. In the summer months in California my feet had sometimes grown calloused from walking across the sun-heated pavement, but the soles of the islanders' feet were thicker than my tennis shoes. While bootie-protected foreign surfers hobbled slowly along the jagged reefs, I watched in awe as barefoot locals glided effortlessly over them at whatever speed they wished.

Beyond the healthy dose of culture contrast, I saw a cool species of red ant almost big enough to have a conversation with. If you messed with one he'd take it personal, stopping in his tracks to confront you. If you continued to threaten him, he'd spit a thin stream of acidic fluid about eight inches long from his mouth. It was the most interesting thing I'd ever seen an ant do. Interrupting his day to test his muscle, I popped a twig between the mandibles of one of these creatures. An incredible tension formed between his mouth and my fingers. In our tug-a-war, I pulled harder on the stick as the ant valiantly stood his ground. Yeah, ants lift a million times their weight, but wow, this guy held fast to the ground and felt super-glued to the twig!

Although I didn't hurt them, the ants got their revenge for my rude disruption of their daily routine. As I was strolling through the forest a few days later, I accidentally stepped my flip-flopped feet into a hidden mess of the buggers. My exposed feet and ankles took a sudden hit of intense, fiery bites. The unexpected pain sent me into an unmanly dance, and I swiped at what looked like the same type of ant. Their infantry didn't sweep away as easily as you might expect. I practically had to grab each one by his little neck and rip his grip from my flesh. My skin wasn't jungle tough, and the burn from the bites lingered long into the night, teaching me to respect all the creatures of paradise.

* * *

I learned other things, too. For one thing, Weaver and I discovered that besides our three surfboards each, we had both over-packed. A toothbrush and some flip-flops would've done the trick. Well, not quite, but we realized that our inflated duffle bags were unnecessary and cumbersome. Anything forgotten from home could've been picked up there, with the exception of a few specialty items.

Another thing we learned first-hand about was "Shiva's Revenge." Weaver had the worst case after we hopped a ferry and had our first taste of the rickety bus system that carted us across the islands. During a rest stop on the island of Sumbawa, he bought some soup from a roadside food cart. Fortunate for me, I passed.

As the bus continued into the night, Weaver's bowels began to quiver. He gripped the bar of the seat in front of us, the veins in his wrists bulging as he folded over in agony. He didn't speak, just sweated and groaned, "Ohhhuuummm."

I felt sorry for him. He'd been so enthusiastic about trying something new.

"Hey J.J.," he'd said, all cheery, only forty minutes earlier, "I'm gonna try this place out. Wanna come?"

"No thanks," I'd said. "I'm good."

Glad my own guts were settled, I could do nothing but sit there and sympathize. For a while, I thought he might explode. But then, in a stroke of luck, the bus broke down. Weaver hurried to take advantage of the situation by disappearing into the dark jungle. Twenty minutes later, he returned to his seat shirtless and wearing a face that spelled relief.

They eventually fixed the bus, and we carried on. We were dropped off nine hours later at some bamboo cabanas near a white-sand beach.

We were having a phenomenal trip.

* * *

I learned another lesson to remember: A fool and his surf-board are soon parted. More than once, if he's a slow learner.

The first time happened not long after our arrival. Weave and I hiked along a beach backed by high cliffs. It was afternoon, and we'd left our boards behind to go exploring. Sure enough, we found some nice lefts peeling out past the low-tide-exposed reef.

"Hey, we need to hit it early tomorrow," I said. "This spot looks fun."

"Sure thing," he said. "Just get me up, and it's on."

The following morning, in the cool six o'clock air, we arrived at the trail on the cliff high above the same patch of ocean we'd seen previously from ground level. When we looked down at the waves, though, it was a whole different slice of nature than we remembered. The waves were bigger and messier, and the reef was now submerged under a higher tide. Each swell collided with the jagged volcanic cliff.

I looked at Weaver. "Looks sketchy, huh?" Then we spotted two other surfers in the distance, looking like sea birds among the tireless swells.

"I'll bet they paddled out from that beach down there. C'mon."

We followed the well-defined footpath down the cliff to a sandy beach far to the right of the breaking surf. Neither of us had any idea what we were doing.

We paddled a long way to reach the waves. Two Australian guys were already on it. When we reached them at last I made a snide comment about being sorry we'd congested their empty waves, only to have one answer, "No worries, mate. Actually, glad ta see ya. We just saw a good-sized tigah shaak swim by."

Tiger shark, huh? Of course.

Wouldn't you know it? My first wave closed out and ripped the stupid leash right off my ankle. My brand-new board took a kamikaze run straight for the cliff face, and I swam there alone thinking about what that Aussie bloke had just said.

A good two-hundred-yard swim separated me from the nearest beach. I was still flanked by an open ocean and the high cliff that got continuously pounded by the surf. I took my time with the swim, figuring that if I ended up as something's breakfast, so be it. However, I did try not to vibe anything on.

Now mere specks in the distance, the other three surfers sank out of view.

Weave later admitted his concern over my disappearance. "I got a little worried when I saw you swimming out there," he said. "The waves kept coming in, and we were pretty far from the beach."

Oh, I made it to shore alright, but my board suffered an ugly fate, repeatedly slammed by the surf against a sharp lava cliff and pulverized. Luckily, I had reserves.

The second time was plain-ass foolhardy.

On a tiny island we awoke to the sound and sight of a fresh swell—a big swell. The main surfbreak was empty. From the beach I saw large waves warp the horizon and unload onto the reef. Unable to gauge the true size of the surf from land, I went ahead and hired a local boat to take me and my board across the lagoon. Weaver was wise enough to pass on the session, along with every other surfer on the island. But I didn't care. I couldn't pass up the challenge. I'd traveled to the other side of the planet to ride waves and wasn't about to let those suckers break without me. I had those darn videos reeling through my head.

The waves already looked big from shore, but as we motored closer they became fearsome. I wanted to believe I had the courage to tackle the situation alone, but it was a tough sell. Nervous, I jumped off the wooden skiff and stroked slowly toward the rumbling swells.

The boat turned and headed back.

Being far from shore with no one else around was a little creepy. My equipment could have been better, too. A thick 6'10 had been my gun of choice in Southern California, but here it wasn't nearly enough. I soon found myself in over my head. Literally.

I skirted the channel, trying to reach the lineup. But the waves seemed to break farther and farther out. I kept paddling, watching triple overhead faces crash just to my right.

When the sets had calmed for a few minutes, I eased over to where I thought was the take-off zone and waited. But I had terribly misjudged. In reality, I rested dead in the impact zone. Before I knew it, an angry set reared and began to plow over me. A tall wall of water blocked the sky. It rose, pitched out, and exploded before my eyes. I took a deep breath, bailed from my board, and dove for the bottom.

Unlike the darker ocean waters of home, this water was clean and clear. I opened my eyes to confront the turbulence that was sure to send me tumbling. Grey clouds of rolling bubbles siphoned me up and sent me cartwheeling upside-down and back-wards. Then the wave lost its grip, and I surfaced to face another chunk of ocean. Back under I went.

I couldn't believe it—getting slaughtered just as the session began. But so much damn water was moving around that I couldn't pinpoint my position.

The second wave had its way with me before I surfaced again to the snap-crackle-pop of the wave's leftover froth. After the third wave steam-rolled me, the ocean gave me a break. I reeled in my board and made progress toward open sea.

As I paddled out, a medium-sized wave appeared. I went for it. Though not as potent as the sets, the wave still had lots of juice and stood high above my head. The thing jacked up and I paddled like mad, committing to the drop and throwing myself over the ledge. My rail barely clung to the vertical face and I miraculously made it to the bottom. At the same time, the lip pitched out well down the line.

Uncomposed at the foot of the wave and speedless from the wild takeoff, I stood impossibly deep and had to abandon ship. I dove into the gaping barrel and got ragged around. I surfaced, only to take another wave on the head. That was when an incredible tug came from my right ankle, followed by a dreaded lightness. My leash had snapped.

Déjà vu. Again I treaded water in the middle of the bloody ocean with no board. I let the next set of waves push me over the reef into the safety of the lagoon, then slowly made the long swim back to shore. Glad my beating was over, once again I had to relinquish my ego and bow to the sea.

* * *

The most important lesson I learned on the trip was probably that world travel could be surprisingly affordable, even for a high school pizza delivery boy. In six Indonesian weeks I dropped only six hundred bucks. That included two-dollar bungalows, fifty-cent meals, ten-dollar inter-island ferries, one-dollar all-day bus rides, sixty-cent massages, cheap souvenirs, and many free mind-bending waves.

The grand total out the door, with air fare . . . fifteen hundred smackers even.

During my senior year, I'd saved over seventeen hundred dollars from wages and tips from satisfied pizza lovers all over the Anaheim and Garden Grove area. So I had money to spare.

4

BAJA, MEXICO

Down in the Desert

A few months after returning from Indonesia, I made the inevitable move to Huntington Beach. I inhabited not only the same rundown apartment building my buddy Malavar once lived in, but the same unit. I felt very much at home. The circus of my downtown Huntington Beach life began once again.

Four dudes occupied the drafty dwelling. I shared my tiny room and paid one hundred eighty dollars a month in rent. Our front door was for wave checks, and usually remained wide open. The busy sidewalk made for non-stop entertainment as many faces passed, peeked in, and stopped by. Our stereo blared incessantly, friends telephoned for surf reports, and girls would magically appear in the living room.

Roommates moved in and roommates moved out. Weekend parties were guaranteed. People would lounge in our living room and get jacked up on cheap malt liquor. During one rager, the small potted pine at our doorstep was spray painted, puked on, used as an ashtray, and decorated with crushed beer cans.

This display of debauchery reminded me of the days at Weaver's old pad a year-and-a-half earlier. However, this time my innocence could not be salvaged. Anytime I wanted to shoot a game of pool, I had a friend's old identification card in my wallet, so I could get into the bars on Main Street, literally a hop, skip, or stumble away. If you weren't in the mood to go out at night, someone else would be, and they'd drag your lazy ass off the couch.

Nah, I didn't head to Main Street too terribly much. Shooting pool was cool, but I'd usually play a few games, chat with some friends, and head home to bed. My first priority was to get up each morning and check the surf. If the surf was firing, I'd be on it like a cop on a jelly donut. If the conditions were average, or needed a tidal change, I'd stretch my legs with a casual walk across the street for a closer look. On crappy days, I'd go straight to work.

* * *

While I was growing up, my father had occasionally taken in and employed a relative who'd been down on their luck, or who needed a change. Something tells me I'd been standing in line to do a stint since the day Dad went to work for himself. With him, I saw the pros and pains of running your own show. I loved the bendable hours, but realized that if you failed to finish your tasks your mailbox would have nothing to eat.

I didn't want him to pay me much; I preferred he subsidize my income with surf time. My work schedule depended more or less on the quality of the surf. The better the waves, the later I showed up. Our agreement seemed to work for both of us. I never missed a good session, and he got a flexible employee for a hundred and fifty dollars a week—a nice, low, guilt-free figure I came up with so I could enjoy the surf with a clean conscience.

As long as I covered my rent and my share of the utilities and had enough for pasta and tomato sauce for the month, I was fine. I lived happily on the bare minimum, an occasional new board or (wet) suit being my only vice.

* * *

When summer rolled around again, I signed up on a budget road trip to Cabo San Lucas, Mexico, a journey devised by Malavar himself.

"Hey, man, I just bought a Volkswagen bus for nine hundred bucks," he said. "Runs great! I'm cruising to Cabo . . . You're coming, too."

Mal wasted no time breaking her in. He'd bought the van from a mechanic friend, and he planned a maiden voyage in the vehicle while the last few bolts to whatever problem she'd had were being tightened.

My luggage consisted of little more than the clothes on my back—boardshorts and a tee-shirt—two surfboards, an extra tee-shirt, a toothbrush, an oversized jar of peanut butter, and a fiesta-sized bag of pretzels.

* * *

With Malavar's girl, Nina, in tow, we set off. From Mal's apartment near Golden West Street in downtown H.B., we made a left on P.C.H. and got as far as the Huntington Beach pier before the prized bus conked out. Mal was about as handy with an engine as I was. When we first heard a strange rattle coming from somewhere, we tried our usual fix-it method: we turned up the radio. But this time that old trick didn't work. Good thing we were strong pushers!

The mechanic friend probably knew what the problem was before the vehicle broke down. He repaired the Volkswagen that evening, and we left the following day.

"Okay, gang, let's try this again," Mal said.

In retrospect, leaving for Cabo in an aged four-cylinder, air-cooled V.W. in July without some kind of practice run might have been somewhat hasty. But our excitement to hit the road outweighed good logic.

The bus made it to the Mexican border and through Tijuana, Rosarito, and Ensenada, and kept on truckin'. With a thousand miles of desert in front of us, we rotated behind the wheel, vowing to drive only in the safety of daylight. Creeping along at fifty m.p.h., we broke this promise by traveling late into every night. We wanted to get there.

Desert mice scampered back and forth in our headlights as we rolled along the depleted Mexico Highway 1. We'd eventually turn off the road into the desert darkness, where we'd sleep until the morning sunlight popped our groggy eyes open.

Halfway down the dry peninsula, we fueled up a couple of extra jerry jugs and turned off the main road onto one of Baja's many washboard dirt tracks. We were hunting for a hard-to-reach surf spot we'd heard about. Mal drove and drove down a road that became progressively worse the farther we ventured into nowhere. He stayed easy on the accelerator as the bumpy road deteriorated.

Under a blazing sun, the bus started taking abuse. Soon the track got so bad we swore we'd lost the trail and were crossing raw desert. We maneuvered around tumbleweed and gaping ruts.

The bus hobbled over unavoidable rocks. Sometimes Mal really had to gas it to push up and over the bigger ones, spitting sand and pebbles from the rear tires and making the vehicle bounce over the soccer-ball-sized stones. I expected the bus to snap an axle as it labored across the harsh terrain.

We should've been in a 4X4, not a V.W. bus.

When the road finally became decent (but still dirt) again, we made some time, almost reaching the coast. Then an impassable obstacle blocked our path: deep sand. Our wheels slowed, then sank, imprisoning the bus in its tracks.

"Oh, man," said a disappointed Malavar. "We've come too far to turn back now. The surf couldn't be far too away, right?"

"Yeah, but look at that road," I said.

The stretch of deep sand reached farther than we could see. I felt his pain, but continuing forward wasn't an option. We had no choice except to back out, and we had a heck of a time doing *that*. First we tried to get out in reverse, but our bald tires spun in place and we made zero progress. Then Mal and I hopped out and started to dig with makeshift cardboard shovels. Sweat stung our eyes in the hundred-degree heat.

Nina cheered us along from the sidelines. "Hurry up, guys, it's flipping hot out here!"

A half-hour later, we'd finally managed to claw our way out of the mess. Forced to forfeit our hopes of surfing the area, we carried on down the Baja peninsula.

A couple of afternoons later, we arrived in Cabo and camped in a sun-baked beach parking lot. The days scorched, but the nights were pleasant, and at bedtime I'd drag a blanket across the sand and sleep just above the high tide line.

Less than a week after we got there, the bus broke down while we were scouting the area for waves. Mal's shifter started doing the mambo on the open road and wouldn't slip into gear. We coasted to a stop. He and Nina stayed with the bus while I stood at the side of the road with my thumb out. A cool, aged Mexican cowboy in a brown station wagon gave me a lift to civilization.

In town, I talked an ex-pat with a beer in his hand into giving us a hand. His fee for the effort? "Just some juice for the boys." So I bought some beer. Don't forget, buying alcohol in Mexico is a hundred percent legal at age nineteen.

In his big Ford pickup, the ex-pat drove me back to the Volkswagen and roped the two vehicles together, tow fashion. Nina jumped in with the ex-pat while Mal and I hopped in the bus.

The dude pulled away without warning.

"Hey, Mal, he's pulling away."

"I see that," said Malavar, fidgeting with his key to break the stubborn steering wheel lock.

"Uh, Mal. The dude's dragging us."

"I see that."

The guy tried to U-turn us, but our van only wanted to go straight. At a forty-five-degree angle, the Ford yanked harder on the Volkswagen and made its unsteerable front tires slide slightly on the gravel. Then the crazy dude punched it. His tires started spitting dirt, and screeched when they reached the pavement. Once the Ford had a grip on the road, his increased pulling power dragged our still-in-the-dirt front end through the loose gravel and onto the two-lane highway. The tow rope stretched to the tension of a finely tuned guitar string.

Things got hairy when we caught sight of a full-sized passenger bus hauling butt around the oncoming bend. The nose of our steering-wheel-stuck van was half-dragging and half-rolling toward the center of the road, and the highway's other side had no shoulder for the big approaching vehicle. Soon we faced the monster head-on.

Honk, honnnnnnk! it hollered.

The Ford pulled relentlessly. While Mal argued with the controls, I braced in the passenger seat and awaited our doom. We were on a collision course with this horn-blasting Goliath, with three seconds to impact!

But my friend didn't quit. At the very last second, something clicked and the steering wheel gave way. Malavar spun the front tires, and we narrowly escaped disaster. Mal and I looked at each other, wide-eyed but relieved.

We were towed back to our beach parking spot, where we remained stranded in the searing heat for the next week. We cooled off by surfing all day in the waves out front. Our ex-pat friend helped again by providing a mechanic.

"I know this guy, Hector, who can fix anything," he bragged. "The problem is, he goes on these cocaine binges and is hard as hell to get a hold of."

After several no-shows, we finally saw the face of flakey Hector. His broken-tooth smile said it all. All the same, he shocked us by completing the job. The vehicle's stick shift was back in its socket, and it worked.

Malavar traded an old surfboard for the repair job, and from there we limped the thousand miles back home.

The amazing thing was that Mal's wheels not only returned us to California, they continued to serve him faithfully for another decade. He drove that thing until gaping holes rusted through the floorboard, providing a clear view of the street. When the holes got so big your foot would fall through them, Mal said, "Oh, that's only cosmetic," and covered the holes with thin rubber "Welcome" mats.

* * *

A few months after returning to my shared apartment in downtown Huntington Beach, I grew restless. The surf bum lifestyle felt natural, but the same ol' rotating scene wasn't entirely fulfilling. The cliff-top temples, racing *bemos*, burning incense, and hollow waves of Indonesia still hung hot in my memory. With no debt or obligation anchoring me, I plotted to return.

Working with my dad allowed me to scrape enough income for food and rent, but to save a decent cash sum would require a second job. A friend in my apartment complex delivered for a Pizza Hut in Seal Beach, and I moved right into an "if pizza's financed an Indo trip once, it could do it again," attitude. At nineteen, I wouldn't have to lie about my age to get the job. My neighbor put in a good word for me, and within days I was ringing doorbells and collecting tips. The extra work didn't bother me. My shifts were always at night and the job was fun, especially with the help of the flirty phone-order-taker girls.

Weeks flew by, and time created a small chunk of money.

5

INDO

Heroes in Paradise

No two trips are the same. If I doubted that, my second visit to Indonesia would prove it to be true. Having been there before, I would've felt comfortable going alone, but my old buddy Weaver had been enduring honeymoon hell and bickering with his new bride. When I mentioned that I was "outta here!" he rushed to buy himself a plane ticket to Divorce City and joined me.

The day after my twentieth birthday party and a two-hundred-person late-night rager that rocked my parent's house, Weaver and I left for our second trip to Indo. This time, other than my boards, I brought only what I could carry in a regular school backpack.

During our first encounter with Bali, Weaver and I hadn't had a clue about Kuta's wild nightlife. We hadn't given it much thought, since Weave had had a serious girlfriend (his new ex-wife) at home, and I'd been obsessed with my quest for perfect surf. This time was totally different. With a week and a half before our bud Malavar was to join us from the States, Weave and I found a cheap *losmen* and stumbled upon life in the late night streets of Kuta. We did the only logical party-town thing two young bachelors could do: drank beer and chased women. In a one-eighty from our first visit, we slept in the morning, surfed in the afternoon, and partied all night. I had never seen so many consecutive sunrises.

We made a new Aussie friend, Sean, at our *losmen*.

"Hey guys, I reckon we should hit a pub crawl tonight," he said.

"Pub crawl? What the heck is that?" we asked.

Sean looked at us like naïve children. "Mate, that's bar hopping through the night in a bus with a bunch of other crew. It's heaps of fun!"

"Let's do it," we said.

That evening, after our usual few Bintangs at our *losmen*, we hopped aboard a bus-type vehicle with a crowd of cheerful partygoers. We fit right in.

I eventually lost contact with Sean and Weaver in the continuous mingling through the clubs and bars. One of us would tune in on a girl, or we'd get caught up in a wave-provoked bar stool conversation with another surfer. Late into the night our trio began to dissolve, and by two in the morning it was every man for himself.

I bumped into a fun group of Australian girls that night, among them a stunner, Samone. She had dark, wavy hair, golden brown skin, soothing green eyes, and the body of an Olympic figure skater. Her short, loose-flowing skirt showed enough to rouse my imagination. Though I struggled not to look, her smooth legs were like eyeball magnets.

The girls and I socialized in the party atmosphere of a club.

"Hey ya, mate," Samone said over the loud upbeat music. "Luv ya accent."

"That's funny, I was thinking the same thing about yours," I said.

They were all touchy-feely girls, sliding a hand across my shoulders when explaining something or rubbing my arm during a laugh. The difference between Samone and her friends was that when she touched me, every inch of my body shivered with electrons. Flirtatious like her friends, she tore my heart open with her delightful smile. Is that too sappy? Being the only male among the close-knit group of friends, I hesitated about hitting on her. We all carried on until the wee hours of the morning, when I finally said goodnight and strolled alone to my *losmen* in the quiet post-party streets.

* * *

Two nights passed, both spent laughing and hanging out with Brooke, a gal I'd met on the beach the day after the pub crawl. On our third night out together, she, her sister, and I were shooting pool at one of the many happening clubs when I cruised up to the D.J. to request a Pearl Jam song. As I waited to get the D.J.'s attention, someone tapped on my shoulder. I spun around.

Oh, baby! I was staring straight into the shimmering green eyes of Samone. Not sure what to say or do, I stood there like a dork and gawked at her.

She cracked a sweet little smile and said, "Et's me last night."

I had a pretty good idea what she meant, and suddenly felt like the luckiest chump in Kuta. Wait a minute—I was too lucky.

My mind raced back to the pool table. "Are you kidding?" I said. "There's a girl over there waiting for me!"

It seemed this chick didn't plan on being merciful. She shook her head lightly and repeated, "Et's me last night."

I had to stop and think for a second . . . POOF! A little devil appeared on my left shoulder. 'Hey, buddy, check this out,' he tempted. 'She's back. Now's your chance!' Then, POOF! The angel to my right came in with, 'No, no, you can't just blow off a nice girl like Brooke. That would be messed up.'

'Ahhhhh,' snickered the devil. 'Brooke will be fine. And besides, you'll never see her again anyway. We're in Kuta for crying out loud!'

With that I weakened, and the little devil leaned across my shoulder blades and socked the angel hard in the nose.

"Alright, meet me out front," I said.

Samone twirled around triumphantly and slipped into the crowd and out of sight.

In typical male pig fashion, I snuck away toward the front door. I deliberately avoided the pool table, cushioning as many people between it and me as possible. I felt extremely guilty dodging Brooke, but decided to let my conscience deal with it later.

That night, my attention belonged to Samone.

Outside she awaited me, smiling all cute. I approached her without a word. We grabbed hands and burst into a playful run to her place, a swank hotel that made my run-down *losmen* look every bit the price I'd paid. Balinese paintings and hand-carved statues decorated the walls, and a hint of sandalwood scented the air. The bed appeared inviting, but at first we couldn't quite make it that far.

Samone led me to the middle of the room and turned around. When she pressed herself into me the silky heat of her body turned me to mush. My hands pressed the thin skirt along the curve of her hips. We tangled in a kiss, and she pulled me to the ground. I tucked my hand under her head to protect it from the tile floor. Every now and then I'd grip a fistful of her hair during bursts of intense passion. She seemed to like that.

I couldn't tell whether I commanded her, or vice versa.

* * *

Next morning, sunrays beamed through the open windows. I lay there relaxed in a mess of white sheets while Samone packed for her departure. She wore a bright green bikini that complemented her auburn skin. Her dark hair was still messy from the night, and looked rather sexy. But I could tell something was wrong. She wasn't moving with the same grace as earlier. Finally, she stopped and turned to glare at me. "Well, I guess they's no point in givin' ya me numba, et's not like ya eva comin' to Australia!" Her accent rang heavily through my ears while her eyes burned through my very soul, the same soul that was still in hock for even being there.

At first I was speechless. Then, not knowing what to do, I shrugged and muttered, "Guess not."

She rolled her eyes and continued packing.

A moronic move, for sure. Little did I know that eight months later I'd be heading to the land down under. Not only that, I'd be passing right through her corner of the country.

* * *

In the days preceding Malavar's arrival and our subsequent jump off the wacky, wonderful world of Bali to islands beyond, our new mate, Sean, enticed me to check out his world in Oz. "Ya need ta get your arse to Australia, mate," he said.

I didn't need tons of persuading to get fired-up. Heck, yeah! I thought, a light bulb going off in my head. Then a fuse blew. Samone! I didn't have her number!

As the concept of Australia brewed in my mind, I convinced myself it was better that I wasn't able to contact Samone. If I were unlucky, lust might have transformed into something more powerful, and that could've led to a cruel chapter of careless lies and broken hearts. Worse yet, a relationship might've chained up precious travel time just as I hit a roll. Besides, life had been good without that gooey romantical stuff.

Of course, the karma connected to this kind of logic would eventually come back to bite my ass.

* * *

Weaver and I were stoked to meet up with Malavar on the other side of the world. We shared what we'd learned and headed together to the island of Sumbawa to surf some good breaks. But Weaver and I didn't stay long. We'd been there before, and itched to explore Sumba, an island new to us.

"Well, Malavar," I said as Weave and I departed for the ferry, "have a good time."

"Thanks, man. I'll see ya back in the States," he said. He was enjoying the waves so much he wanted to kick back and do more surfing, and he remained on the island of Sumbawa while

Weaver and I made our way across the heart of Sumba.

One fine morning, before he had the chance to down some breakfast, he found himself committing a selfless act of heroism. A giant swell had kicked up overnight, and Mal woke early to the thunderous rumble of the sea. He sensed that the surf was pumping. Like they did every morning, he and his girlfriend Nina got out of bed and started their leisurely stroll toward the beach for a routine wave check. Under a calm blue sky, they made their way past the row of small wooden bungalows that flanked the wide dirt path of the surf camp.

The reef directly in front of the camp's warung had two distinct surf breaks, Lakey Peak and Lakey Pipe. Separated by a wide channel in the reef, the two breaks produced quality waves on the fringes of a small inner lagoon.

"When I passed the warung on the left and got to the beach, I remember seeing the waves," he told us later. "And they were big."

Huge Hawaiian-sized waves were crashing that morning at Lakey Peak and Lakey Pipe. The channel between the breaks, where a boat or a surfer could normally sit safely, had become a fast-flowing river. The enormous surf washed over the reef and flooded into the shallow lagoon, and the high volume of water forced its way back out to sea through the channel, turning the once safe reef pass into a rushing waterway.

With Nina at his side, Malavar watched in awe as the massive waves exploded, one after another. He'd never seen surf of that magnitude. Although surfers from all over the world were present to witness the awesome display, there were no takers.

"The sheer power of the wave hitting the reef from out of deep water—it looked crazy," he said. "So much water was moving. The current was ripping through the channel. No one was out." Surf wise, he wrote the day off, figuring that all the surf breaks in the vicinity would be breathing too heavy.

Standing on the beach, Mal noticed three local fishermen setting up one of their boats on the shoreline of the lagoon. He first thought, that's kinda crazy. Are they really going out in this? Those swells are big.

Then, as he turned to walk back to his bungalow and sip some tea, he saw the boat easing away from shore. "I was kinda tripping on them," he said. "It just seemed weird to me that they were going out in those conditions. But I figured they've lived there their whole lives and knew what they were doing."

Letting the fishing boat slip from his mind, Malavar returned with Nina to their bungalow patio to relax. "Well, Nina, I guess nobody's surfing today," he said. "I think I'm just gonna kick it and enjoy the palm trees. Maybe lie in a hammock with a good book. Hey, would you mind giving me a little massage?"

The mellow morning had only lasted a few ticks when Rob, a guy Mal knew from around camp, rushed up, pleading for help. "Hey Malavar, there's some guys in a boat in trouble! My friend grabbed a board and went after them! I'm going, too! We need extra help. Grab a board and let's go!"

Malavar ran into his hut and armed himself with the longest board he had, a 7'5. He charged toward the water to team up with Rob and Toki, a Japanese surfer Rob had recruited.

The fishermen's outboard had apparently sputtered and died

early on, and their disabled boat was being sucked out to sea by the powerful currents. In their panic to get the motor started, they had failed to drop anchor on the inside of the reef, where they would've been safe—mistake number one. Then, when they finally did drop the hook, they anchored right at the edge of the reef at Lakey Pipe. That was their unforgivable second mistake.

Most days, they would've been okay. The waves typically broke to the left of where they were. But on this day, with an oversized swell in motion, the larger waves were breaking farther out and deeper in the channel than normal, and the unfortunate men had fastened the boat onto the outlying corner of the impact zone. It was only a matter of time before another huge set would come in and wreak havoc.

Malavar appeared on the beach in time to see a gigantic dark blue wall of water loom up behind the doomed boat. Rob's friend, the Australian who had paddled out after the fishermen, was now in the boat and hollering at the three Indonesians to abandon ship. He knew they were about to get seriously plowed. Frozen in fear, none of the men budged.

As the giant wave bore down on them, the Aussie grabbed one of the fishermen by the shoulders and heaved him into the water. Seconds before the wave swallowed the vessel, the other two guys jumped for their lives. The wave steamrolled the boat, flipping it over and scattering the men in the sea like ants.

In the frothy aftermath the Indonesians scavenged for gear tossed from the boat, clinging to anything that would float. At the mercy of the currents, the three men were now being sucked out to sea.

Wasting no time, Rob, Malavar, and Toki started paddling out to help the distressed fishermen. "We were being pulled out by the current and paddling, so we were getting out there fast," he reported. "The Australian guy was gone, and all I could think about was reaching the Indonesians. By then, I was on pure adrenalin."

The three surfers bravely paddled their boards past the capsized skiff and thunderous waves toward the drifting men. Toki and Rob each aimed for a man, and Mal stroked hard in the direction of the third guy, who was hugging a red plastic gas container. Paddling out through the churning sea, farther and farther from land, he grew concerned about getting back. But Mal had already committed himself, and wasn't about to turn around.

"I was way behind the breaking waves when I finally got to the fisherman," he said. "I paddled up to the guy with the plastic can, and when I looked at him I could see the terrified whites of his eyes. He wasn't yelling for help in Indonesian or anything. I honestly think he was too scared to speak."

Still clutching the gas can in one hand, the petrified fisherman wrapped an arm tightly around the back of Malavar's waist, practically sinking him.

"The way the guy grabbed me, I couldn't paddle or anything. He was just so panicked and hanging on for dear life. I was like 'hey, hey,' but it's not like the guy spoke any English. So I had to show him what to do."

If Malavar couldn't paddle, both men would be swept out to sea. At first the fisherman resisted unlatching from Mal's body. Knowing that a frightened man could be less than rational and might cling to his rescuer with a grip that would prove fatal for them both, Mal was careful not to act as if he would leave him.

Finally the Indonesian relented, and Malavar guided his hand down to the surfboard's leash and showed him where to hold on. By the time they were in a tugboat position that allowed Mal to tow the guy through the water, they'd drifted so far out that the backs of the huge swells now appeared small. "I'm paddling, and paddling, and looking back to make sure the Indonesians' alright. The backs of the swells are getting bigger and bigger, so I know I'm making progress. And my arms, you know, are starting to burn."

For the next twenty minutes, Malavar labored to inch his way toward the waves and reef, doing his best to navigate around the bastard of a rip current.

Not far from Mal, Rob was pulling his shipwrecked fisherman, and the two were now regrouping just behind the surf at Lakey Peak. Toki was towing the last victim, but farther down the reef. All three surfers were growing tired. Dragging the men behind them was hard work. They began to wonder how they were going to get back to shore. Returning through the channel against the current was hopeless, and for miles in either direction the reef was being pounded by enormous waves.

Then Rob noticed the Aussie guy across the channel at Pipe. He had no surfboard and was treading water right in the surf zone when a big set approached. Rob pointed out the lone swimmer to Malavar, and the two watched in amazement as the Australian hurled himself into a monster wave in a desperate maneuver to get back to land.

"Rob said, 'Look over there! There's the Aussie!' I looked and saw this little head on this huge fricking lip, and the guy just went with it." Mal chuckled. "Ha, the thing just threw him! Man, after he went over the falls, he was under water for a long time. We were like, 'Where did he go?'"

Both Mal and Rob kept their eyes on the area where they guessed the Australian would surface. They waited and waited, peering into the churning foam of the broken waves. Then they saw him. Ragged from the thrashing, the Aussie stood up on the reef on the inside. He'd made it.

"We were like, oh my God! And now I'm thinking to myself, that's how we have to get in . . . damn! And we've got the fishermen, too. I'm not happy about this."

To make matters worse, Mal realized that while he and Rob had been watching to make sure the Australian made it to shore, the backs of the waves had become small again. The current was swiftly dragging them back out to sea. "So now my arms are tired," Mal said, "and I got a guy attached to me and we're drifting way out all over again, and I'm thinking, Ah, hell, we gotta do this again? Then Rob looks at me, and I can tell he's exhausted. And I say, 'look Rob, focus. We're gonna do this together. We've got to make our way back and take a wave in. We have no other choice. We're taking a wave in with these guys. And he's like, 'Okay, okay.'"

Pulling the fishermen behind them, Rob and Mal paddled with all their strength and slowly but surely crept up behind the waves at the Peak. They'd lost sight of Toki, but were in no position to do anything about him anyway. Now in pure survival mode, all they cared about was getting to the beach. Towing the fisherman, they couldn't paddle much longer. Knowing he couldn't attempt to ride in because he had to take the Indonesian with him, Mal mentally prepared to throw himself over the falls of a giant wave. There was nothing more he could do.

"At first I was pretty nervous," he said. "I mean, I'd surfed good-sized waves before, but nothing like this. But then I was like, *okay, that's cool, whatever we gotta do*. You don't think about it anymore. You're not scared anymore. You have to do it. I knew there's one way in, and that's the way in. And I'm thinking, alright, this is the first time in my life I'm going to have to tackle something this big."

They almost got to the breaking waves when all of a sudden a Zodiac appeared out of nowhere. "I don't know where it came from," Mal said, "but I guess one of the guys on the beach had a Zodiac. Rob and I look at each other, and we're like, *oh my God, no way, a guy's coming out in a Zodiac!* We were so relieved."

The Zodiac driver had to be extra careful passing through the rough rip current. He pulled up next to Mal, Rob, and the two fishermen, and one by one the fatigued men crawled into the boat. By that time, Toki had appeared, doggedly paddling up with his guy. But after his guy got into the zodiac, water from the choppy rip started spilling into the boat. They were on the brink of overloading, and there was absolutely no room for Toki. The driver instructed the surfer to grab the boat's side. Mal recalled, "Yeah, I remember Toki, the Japanese guy. I've got one arm, Rob's got his other arm, and he's just holding onto the boat, getting dragged and taking water in the face."

The loaded Zodiac beat sluggishly against the roaring rip and inched back through the same channel that had spat everyone out in the first place. Miraculously, all the men made it safely to the shore of the lagoon.

"When we got to the sand, the fishermen's legs just fell out from under them," Malavar said. "Their family members ran up and were hugging and kissing them. They were so happy to see their husbands and fathers alive. I mean, they were stoked. And then the family members started coming up and hugging us and thanking us in Indonesian, 'Terimah kasi! Terimah kasi!' Everyone was so grateful. And I remember being on the beach, too, and being grateful."

Acknowledging that Rob, Mal, and Toki had risked their necks to save the lives of the local fishermen, the surf camp owner came up to the surfers and said they could have their meals for free for the remainder of their stay. "We had free fish dinners every night after that," Mal said cheerily. "It was great!" Then he paused to reflect on the true depth of the ordeal. "But I'll never forget that guy's face when I paddled up to him. I can still see the whites of his eyes. I mean, if we hadn't paddled out there, they were dead."

Sumbawa is third world territory. It has limited resources as far as sea rescue goes. If the surfers had not paddled out to the help the fishermen, they would've disappeared behind the horizon. The half-hour the paddlers fought to keep the other men close to land made the difference between life and death.

Rob, Toki, the Aussie, and Malavar not only saved the three fishermen's lives; they most likely saved a lot of hardship for their family members, too. Over and above being relieved of the emotional sorrow, in a tough world where people are lucky just to put food in their stomachs, those families still had their providers.

6

AUSTRALIA

Mates and Snakes

After two months of island hopping in Indonesia I returned to California, where I moved with five friends into a big house a few blocks from my old Huntington Beach apartment. I was further away from the beach now; the waves that used to take one minute go get to now took five.

At first I shared a room upstairs for two hundred dollars a month. Later, I relocated into our huge garage, which I shared with my friend, Mitch, for a hundred. Actually, I dug living in the garage better than in the house.

Mitch, who masterminded the garage scene from the start, had the place electrified and pimped out. Neon lights clung to the walls, carpet covered the concrete floor, Bob Marley posters looked out from above the beds, and a huge checkered blanket partitioned the secret room from the outside world. The only thing missing was a disco ball.

Once I came back from surfing to find Mitch and his girl smooching under the glow of a red light bulb. Mood music drowned out any hint of my presence, and I backed out respectfully. "Nice work," I said later.

"Thanks." Mitch knew I meant the room. "Heck, I mean

really. The beach is three blocks away. For a hundred bucks a month what more do we need?"

I returned to delivering pizzas and saved every cent I could. Six months later, I boarded a jumbo jet bound for Oz.

* * *

Australia became my first true solo journey, cushioned at the airport by one extremely hospitable Sean.

"Welcome, mate. We'll drop ya gear at me place then head ova ta me mum and dad's for a bah'bee. They's looking forward ta meetin ya."

"They're looking forward to meeting me?" I was touched.

I threw my long black board bag into the back of his red Holden, and we were off. We drove around the outside the city for a view of the skyline. Unlike in L.A., smog did not cloud the atmosphere, and sunshine bounced off the bright buildings. The clear air made Perth feel exotic.

When we got to Sean's parents' house, his dad handed me a bottle of strong home-brew. His bronzed face smiled. "Cheers, mate." He treated me like a relative, one he liked. Before I'd sipped down the first beer, he handed me another, and Sean's mum emerged from the kitchen with a cheese platter. I was their guest of honor.

The warm "no worries" feeling I got from Sean's family struck deeply. I doubt they realized the profound impact their welcoming vibe had on my young life. They were genuinely happy to have me over, which in turn made me happy. It was easy to see the joy that followed from being nice.

* * *

Sean skipped work to take me on safari. We drove his Holden several hours south of Perth to a campground along a lonely tree-studded coast. The next day at breakfast, he toasted bread over our campfire's morning embers. He spread it with butter and Vegemite. "Heeya go, mate. Breky." He handed me the tar-covered toast.

I'd tried the stuff before, in Indo, and yuck, it tasted funky and bitter. But to humor my friend, I ate the bread slice he handed me. Um, not as bad as I remember. Not that I found it good, just . . . interesting. I finished the toast and the taste left my mouth, and soon I craved another piece. Two pieces later, I was hooked. The flavor grew on me, and I now loved it!

We were hiking through the woods after breakfast when I focused on a strange figure camouflaged in the brown and red colors of the surrounding shrubs. "Holy crap! Sean, look, look—a kanga-friken-roo!"

Sean wasn't overly excited "Yeah, mate, and look ova theya."

Far to the right of the first 'roo, two others were half-hidden in the bush. I scooted closer to the wild animals. They looked cute, but unpredictable. I refrained from getting close enough to take a punch. After that, I saw kangaroos everywhere—in the woods, near the beach, darting out onto the road in front of the Holden.

Before he returned to Perth a week later, Sean dropped me in the ultra surf-zone of Margaret River. He left me in a campground with his tent, a jar of Vegemite, and a contingent of local boys I had met previously in Indo. The guys gave me rides to the surrounding breaks. We had barbeques, and on weekends we visited the local pub.

West Oz is known for its wild blue surf, and there I faced some of the most challenging waves of my life. Adapting to the fierce energy of the water forced me to become increasingly aware of my own personal nature, and of nature in general. Living in the tent in Australia's clean and raw environment, I found a new peace with the world.

The way I viewed the earth began to change. Our planet was no longer an oversized playground for my plunder, its pleasures and treasures to be fondled and forgotten without thinking of preserving its purity. I now envisioned the world as a dynamic ball of energy spinning through space, with all of its magnificent colors, tumultuous weather, and fascinating eco-systems. More than ever, I respected the Earth as a place of immense beauty—a place to protect.

* * *

After almost two months in Western Australia, I pinned up a sign on the caravan park bulletin board:

> **Twenty-year-old male
> (traveling with boards)
> Looking for a ride to the East coast.
> Will share petrol expenses.
> I'm at tent site 43.**

The next day I came in from surfing to discover a note tucked in my tent zipper. Some guy named Tony had left his phone number. Three days later, we were in his station wagon driving across the Nullarbor Plains, a part of Australia's vast arid desert where few live and little grows.

The sun-beaten road went on and on and on. We stopped to rest at a two-hundred-foot cliff overlooking the Southern Ocean and the Great Australian Bight. I got out of the wagon and stood at the edge to soak in the awesome sight.

Below an ominous layer of dark clouds, huge waves thundered into the cliff-side. A stiff, chilly breeze from the latitudes known as the Roaring Forties raked the seas. From the safety of dry land, I peered out toward the temperamental belt of ocean that had been many a sailor's nightmare.

* * *

We drove through endless kilometers of barren desert until we saw smoke shoot up from the cracks of the car's hood. Tony's station wagon was having issues. Lucky for us, a British Petroleum service station had been planted not far up the road. But time crawls in the desert, and service can take forever.

"Sorry, mate, this could take weeks. Ya might as well go on without me."

I untied my boards from the roof of the wagon and moseyed into the rest stop for a twelve-hour cup of coffee. At last, I hitched a lift with a cocaine-snorting trucker who had stopped to gas up. At first he declined me the ride because my large board bag wouldn't fit in the truck's already over-packed trailer, but then he relented and let me strap my boards under the truck.

"I'm warning ya, mate. If a tire blows, it'll tear that thing ta shreds."

"That's cool, I'll chance it. I'm tired of being idle."

Although I felt glad to be moving, the way the trucker passed other vehicles almost gave me a stroke.

Late in the night he radioed his big-rig buds and arranged to rendezvous at the next truck stop. He disappeared for a while, and returned red-nosed and sniffling. After that, he drove even crazier! I closed my eyes, wishing I could get out and walk. Ten edgy hours later, he dropped me off on the city streets of Melbourne, Victoria.

From there, I hopped a train to the nearby town of Gee Long, where I was greeted by Laura, a pretty, sweet-hearted gal I'd met a month earlier in a West Oz pub. She had issued a warm invitation to her place. "I leeve close ta Bells Beach. Ya'd absolutely luv'et out theya!"

She took me on a grand tour of her quaint countryside home and back yard, where she pointed to a large shrub that hugged the back of the house. "Look," she said.

Um, I'd seen printed artwork of the familiar bush on tee-shirts, bumper stickers, and tattooed bodies, so I knew what it was. "Wow, that's one massive marijuana plant. I need my camera." I handed it to her and posed next to the pungent plant.

Laura had a regular daytime job, and I dropped her at work and took her car to explore the surf. Right-seat driving took a little getting used to. Heading to the beach I unwittingly drove on the American side of the road until oncoming traffic brought me swerving back to Australia.

* * *

On the weekend, Laura did an excellent job as my tour guide.

"Hey, mate, ya wanna go see the penguins on Philip Island?" she asked.

"That sounds terrific!" I said.

"Sweet. We'll be cruising down Victoria's Great Ocean Road, too. It's beautiful."

She took me to the Twelve Apostles, towering pillars of natural limestone formed by the ocean's incessant gnawing surf.

I visited Laura for a week, and after that I jumped into the cab of another truck, a ride to the Gold Coast that had materialized through Laura's connections.

Pete, yet another helpful soul I'd been acquainted with back in W.A., had given me his parents' number, just in case. "If ya eva head ta the Goldie," he'd said like a true mate, "me mum and dad are real cool. Just show up and tell'em you're a friend of mine. They'll take ya in."

The trucker steered inland through green rolling hills from Melbourne to Brisbane, and ultimately let me off in Burleigh Heads, only blocks from Pete's parents' house. "Theya go, mate. Good luck," he said, and drove off.

Following the directions on a piece of paper that Pete had given me, I ambled up the road to a nice condominium-type set-up and knocked on the door.

"Hello," said Pete's mom. "Pete said a young American might be stopping by. C'mon in and have some tea." She made me feel right at home. Pete's parents were helpful, and let me stash my boardbag in their garage. From there, I tucked a single board under my arm and took a bus south to Lennox Head, where I discovered that not all Aussies were friendly to outsiders.

Although I'm in awe of the legendary Steve Irwin's hands-on approach to studying Australian wildlife, I had no intention of rubbing skin with any deadly reptiles. My main attraction crashed along Australia's shores. But on the world's biggest island, you never know who you might meet. After lucking into a mellow koala bear kicking high in a eucalyptus tree and bumping into countless kangaroos, I eventually found a close encounter of the wrong kind.

I met David, a friendly gospel American who lived near Lennox Head with his pretty Australian wife. We decided to go surfing. From where we parked on the road, a dirt footpath wound through thick, belly-high grass to the rocky beach below. David and I were halfway down the trail when we crossed paths with another surfer heading up. We stopped on the narrow path so the guy could stroll by. The second he passed us, a wicked snake sprang up in the middle of the trail. He let out a mean "Hsssss . . ." and exposed his sharp fangs less than a meter from our stomachs. He blocked our path as he prepared to strike.

"Whoa, Whoa, Whoa!" David froze.

Shocked by the proximity of the snake, I stiffened. Although I was grateful to have any type of barrier, my surfboard provided little solace as a shield between me and a nasty bite.

"Hssssssss . . ." We waited, swallowing our breath. Three, five, nine, I don't know how many seconds passed in the standoff. Finally our startled foe slipped down onto its belly and scurried away. David and I looked at each other, our hearts pounding.

"Wow, that was intense!" he said. "That was a king brown. If he sinks his teeth in you, you're in serious trouble."

I wasn't sure what "king brown" meant, but it sounded venomous. I don't know about David, but after Mr. Brown bailed I remained skittish as we continued down the trail. Every sound and stick in sight sent me flinging off in the other direction.

I later found out that a king brown is one of the world's deadliest snakes.

* * *

During my last few days in Oz, at a lush beachside campground in northern New South Wales, I was inspired by two South African surfers traveling in an aged orange van. They'd bought it good and cheap. I secretly admired their wheels, and yearned for their ease of not having to lug gear on their backs, pitch a tent, rely on a bus, or hitchhike, as I had to. All they had to do was jump in, start the thing, and go. After a half-hour chat, these guys had me aching to visit their homeland. They raved about South Africa's unspoiled countryside and fine waves.

"There's more surf spots than surfers, Bru," they said. "At most breaks you'll be looking for someone to paddle out with. And South Africa's beautiful, bountiful, and your U.S. dollar goes really far over there."

Now I was really fired-up.

I glanced over at their van, knowing darn well I was gonna get home, save a grip of cash, and go back out again into the world somewhere. Then I thought, hey, I know. They bought a vehicle here in Australia. Why couldn't I buy my own wheels in South Africa and drive myself wherever I wanted?

As I sat on the flight back to the States, the whole idea soaked into my brain like good music.

7
SOUTH AFRICA
Dolphins and Dead Men

In the past, I'd considered all types of off-the-wall strategies to make a fast buck. For example, one time my friend Mitch had wanted to haul me away with him to Alaska to risk ripping off our fingers in the nets of the commercial fishing industry. We were having a beer in the warmth of his living room when he'd pitched his chilly idea (This was before Reality TV).

"Dude, I've been thinking a lot lately about going to Alaska," he said. "And even though I've heard working in the Arctic's like a frozen Hell, they say the money can be great! Wha-da-ya think?"

"Um, yeah, I guess that sounds alright. If you go, count me in."

We never went.

Another time, while sipping black tea in a dingy Malaysian café, a suave European had suggested I accompany him on an epic journey up East Asia to Japan to become gigolos.

"You like to make love to women, don't you?"

"Ah . . . well . . ."

"Of course you do. And why not get something extra out of it? There's lots of money in Japan," he beamed. "And the

Japanese like Westerners. I know someone who did very well consoling a lonely widow. Join me, my friend. Let's leave on a train tonight and we'll be halfway up into China by next week!"

He had spit out long numbers to entice me, but it didn't matter. I never took the guy seriously. I wasn't the type to pimp myself out. Seeing no virtue in the venture, I declined.

Sometimes an unorthodox moneymaking scheme had got me thinking, and on occasion, even packing. However, nothing had gripped me enough to chase down any of these escapades.

When I got home from Australia, I called my long-time friend Keera in the resort town of Park City, Utah.

"Hey, what's up, Keera? I'm looking for work, and up for whatever."

"Okay, I'll keep my eyes open," she said.

A cool chick with lots of friends, she hung up, made one phone call, and scored me a waiter job in a busy pizza restaurant. She rang me back fifteen minutes later.

"Okay, J.J., I got you a job."

"Really?"

There was a plane leaving L. A. X. on Christmas night, 1994, to land an hour later at Salt Lake City International Airport, and my snowboard and I were on it. Keera was there to greet me when I landed.

"You ready for snow?"

I crashed with Keera's family for a few nights, and then found a place of my own. For one hundred seventy bucks a month, I bunked with a bunch of bong-toking ski bums in an old snow-covered house at the top of Park City's Main Street. I shared a small, light-starved room and slept along the side of the wall on a stack of blankets and pillows.

Within a week, I had three jobs. A property management company hired me part-time for their weekend graveyard shifts, and I found two separate waiter gigs, the one at the pizza joint and another in a restaurant at a local mountain resort.

My schedule was so whacked I sometimes forgot where I was supposed to work next. Possibly due to a lack of sleep, or maybe to the high altitude, I always felt a little light-headed. On Fridays, I'd finish at the resort around ten in the evening and trudge two blocks through the snow to catch one of the town's free shuttles to my front-desk graveyard shift. Vacationers would show up at random wee hours of the morning. I was lucky the door bell dinged loud enough to wake me . . . .

Going to a ski town to earn money for a surf trip may seem back-asswards, but everything worked out well. One Park City perk was my free employee lift pass (the reason I had sought a job at the mountain). Although I wasn't the sort of rider who risked snapping a femur blasting Olympic-sized airs, I savored the pleasure of riding in Utah's fluff powder. And in two months I banked three thousand dollars.

* * *

I thought I'd be flying into South Africa alone, but at my server job at the ski resort I worked with the enthusiastic young girl who had traveled a lot locally but had been craving something more daring, more international. As we chatted while riding the lifts one fine powder day, Pam asked whether I would mind if she joined me overseas.

At first, I didn't take her seriously. "Sure, as long as you don't mind living in a beat-up car on a barren beach," I joked.

That didn't faze her. "Even better," she said. "Let's get outta here!"

Pam wasn't messing around. A couple of months later, on a bright April afternoon, we met at L.A.X., and together we boarded the lengthy flight bound for the Dark Continent . . . Africa.

* * *

We arrived around dawn on a cool, grey morning and hopped on a bus out of the airport and into Jo-burg (Johannesburg). Right away we entered rough urban streets where homes and shops were fortified with solid metal bars. As we passed graffiti-covered walls and littered alleys, I noticed that the only people roaming about at that quiet early hour were black. My butt slid to the edge of the seat. All the hype about racism was starting to psych me out.

I hadn't a gripe against any ethnic background. I'd grown up where many different colors blended together in a peaceful kaleidoscope of humanity. My high school was mellow. Asians dated whites, who dated blacks, who dated Hispanics, and most guys would have loved to date this one hot Arabian chick.

Also, in my travels, the great majority of people I'd come across had been friendly, regardless of their skin tone or language. However, in South Africa, I soon discovered that you didn't have to be racist to feel racial tension. When Pam and I stepped off the bus in an area I wasn't too sure about, my nerves tightened. From the mugging stories I'd read about, it seemed even our relatively small backpacks made us prime targets.

We set out on foot in search of a hostel. Across the road, two men walking parallel to us cast suspicious stares. Then they ducked down an ally. Though I was traveling in dull clothes and shouldering a worn-out pack to appear less alluring to thieves, I couldn't help but grow timid. Pam didn't look overly flashy, either. Still, my uneasiness increased. Not wanting to freak her out, I refrained from blurting out my insecurities and just stayed alert as we walked. Soon, however, feeling a little too vulnerable, I thought, *Screw it!* and hailed a taxi.

* * *

At the hostel, Pam and I slept hard from our two full days of time-warping travel. When we finally awoke on our dorm bunks, I suggested we go to Cape Town A.S.A.P. (a twenty-four-hour train ride) so we could relax and buy a car. But when we went to the station the following day, we found the train's second class full. We couldn't board.

I got antsy, but this wasn't a major setback. Another night in Jo-burg would be tolerable.

We showed up at the station the next day and were once again denied a ride. Man, that bummed me out. I wanted to get outta Jo-burg's grip, bad.

Two men stood between us and the train: a white man with a very cool mustache—the kind that flipped up on the sides and was long enough to curve into nearly full circles—and, wearing the same conductor uniform, his black colleague. Only the white guy addressed us; his co-worker was busy with something else.

"Sorry, the train is full. You'll come back again tomorrow," he said with a South African bite.

I couldn't fathom the idea, and watched with envy as people with tickets filed into the train.

"Well…. What about third class? Is there *room* there?"

The guy looked at me like I had a death wish. He glanced over at the black man, who had stepped far enough away that he couldn't hear us. The white man's eyes narrowed and he half-whispered, "Look, it's all black. They will harass her." He flashed his eyes on Pam. "And if you are lucky, they will only steal from you. I strongly advise that you wait for tomorrow's train."

After he made his point, I wondered whether it could really be that darn cutthroat.

"Well," I said, "is there *room* in third class?"

The man paused, then gave a reluctant nod.

"Look, sir, I'm anxious as hell to get going, like to-day. Please put us on that train."

Shaking his head at his inability to get through to me, he sold us two third class tickets.

I was excited to be leaving Jo-burg and heading for Cape Town.

* * *

As soon as we boarded, my enthusiasm dwindled. People squeezed into each other on the hard bench seats that lined the aisle. The air felt humid from too many humans breathing and too little ventilation. Every face was black. What did I expect? We stuck out like Eskimos at the equator.

Most people quieted when their eyes landed on us. I walked in nice and smiley, but I wasn't feeling the love. It felt more like everyone was seeing a swastika tattooed on my forehead. My tune stayed bright, however, though I had to fake it. I hoped Pam was experiencing a more favorable sensation.

Apartheid had recently been scratched off the law books, but it hadn't been erased off the psyche of those it had suppressed. And who could blame them? After all, regardless of the law, most blacks were still cramped and suffocating in third class.

Sweat gathered on my brow. Most of the windows were either barely cracked or jammed shut. Whether it was so many bodies overcrowding the car or my growing uneasiness that caused my temperature to rise, I couldn't tell; all I knew for sure was that the skin under my jeans was sweltering.

Our first task was to organize a spot on the crowded luggage rack above the seats we'd scrounged. My mind dropped to the money belt around my waist. I hoped that lifting my bag over my head wouldn't cause my tee-shirt to rise above my hips and expose the bounty strapped to my belly—a passport, $2,800 in traveler's checks, and a stack of green twenties.

I did my best to keep my arms as low as possible while stuffing my bag above, making up for lost height by tip-toeing. Although the urge was strong, I resisted peeking down to see whether or not I had succeeded in keeping the loot a secret. The last thing I wanted was to bring unwanted attention to my mid-riff.

There was another area of concern. Next to me, Pam was rearranging baggage with raised arms. She was an attractive and busty girl, and through the thin white cotton of her V-neck tee-shirt I could plainly see her big, perky breasts jiggle with her every movement. *Oh, crap,* I thought. *These other men in the car must be seeing this, too.*

In her usual good mood, Pam turned her head toward me. Trapped in thought, I didn't realize I was blatantly staring at her tits. I couldn't stop thinking about who else might be checking out those puppies. My feelings about the whole train ride completely derailed as I scolded myself in secret for leading this innocent gal into a potentially hazardous situation.

I hoped it was mere paranoia.

From the get-go, I wanted to show everyone in third class that I viewed people as people. And if that were the case, then why did I feel so darn threatened being around just plain ordinary . . . people?

Maybe I had picked the wrong place to start.

The presence of other women in the car made me feel a little better. But would they help us if we were attacked by a mob of men? Or would they just fight for a slice of the stolen bread?

The train began to roll.

* * *

Pam and I sat squished together, sometimes jabbering softly. The majority of people around us didn't exactly appear to embrace our presence. And honestly, by this time I was over third class.

The train moved along smoothly, but the minutes dragged. A few hours passed, and Pam needed to use the restroom. At first she attempted to use the ones in third class. But after one look at the neglected facilities, she shunned them and headed toward second class. Boy did that make me feel better. I don't like to say it, but there she would be able to roam freely without being questioned simply because of her skin color.

Once Pam left, a man of around forty came over and sat beside me in her empty spot. His clothes were worn but clean; his smile, however, was a little shady. I told myself not to judge.

"Tell me, where are you from?" he asked, his accent almost too thick to understand.

I didn't want to tell him the truth for fear of being labeled rich. Yet compared to him, I was, and we both knew it, so I figured lying would be more trouble than it was worth.

"America."

"Oh, I see. And how do you like it here in South Africa?"

So far, I had only been to a crummy part of Johannesburg and inside that particular train car.

"It's beautiful."

"Can I ask you a question?"

"Sure."

"How is your American Negro (that's how the South Africans referred to African Americans) different from a South African black?"

He had broached the one subject I absolutely hoped to avoid: race.

I didn't know the answer. After all, he was the first South African black I'd had a real conversation with. We all know the tragic truth about how the American blacks had originally been brought to the New World in ships as slaves. However times had changed drastically. From what I'd seen in South Africa thus far, his brothers across the sea had it better than he. But I wasn't about to tell the guy anything like that. Besides, I hadn't seen enough to make an educated judgment.

"Well, you speak very differently," I said, stating the utterly obvious. I knew he knew I knew that wasn't the answer he was looking for. As to philosophical differences, I had no clue.

I reached for my clear plastic water bottle and unscrewed the lid. It was important to me to offer the man a drink, hoping the act would symbolize a perception of equality. He accepted my gesture and put his lips lightly to the bottle's end, tilting some water into his mouth. Once his thirst was quenched, he handed the bottle back to me. Making sure not to wipe the spout after his use, I followed with a swig of my own. Unlike Pam's boobs swaying in the wind, this was something I *did* want everyone to see.

After we talked awhile, the man got up and disappeared.

The train's hypnotic steel-bump-roll triggered my lingering jetlag. My heavy head lowered until my chin rested on my chest. I fought the urge awhile before I drifted into a deep sleep.

Pam was still out and about.

* * *

"Wake up. Wake up, J.J. . . . *Dude, get up!*"

Pam gave my shoulder a hard shake. She'd returned from her walkabout all fired-up. "Hey, I met a couple of really nice guys who want to buy us lunch. One of them said to bring our bags when we come up. Come on, let's go check it out!"

Her words took awhile to sink into my groggy brain.

"Oh, man, how long was I out?"

"How would I know?" she whispered. "I've been gone

awhile. I was kinda worried. I mean, I really had to shake the crap out of you to get you to wake. I thought maybe someone had done something to you." She took hold of my hand to pull me up. "Now, let's go!"

Asking where we were going was pointless. I just did what I was told.

* * *

What a difference! We walked up the clean, cushy aisle of the second-class dining car. Compared to third class, this place had the look and feel of a multi-star hotel lounge. The fresh and ventilated air dried my sweaty neck.

Pam led the way to the seats of two men she introduced as Steve and Andy. Directly across from them were two empty seats, which they offered to us.

We sat down.

Steve gave us a brief rundown on himself. He hailed from Cape Town, and his business involved transporting cars. With the help of his mate, Andy, and four hired colored men (in S.A. coloreds are not blacks, but brown-skinned people such as Indians, etc.), he had relocated six vehicles from Cape Town to Jo-burg. Now they were railing back home.

He could guess our story: clueless tourists.

Leaning forward in his chair, he folded his hands and explained why he'd summoned us from the depths of third class.

"We saw you board in Jo-burg," he said. "I knew you hadn't the foggiest idea what you were getting into. Look, you're not safe back there. You may be fine during the day, but come night things will happen. Things you don't want to happen."

His words sparked my darkest imagination: *Four men have me pinned to the floor, and a knifepoint is piercing my jugular. Three others are dragging Pam away, laughing wickedly and clawing her shirt. She is pleading. I struggle to break free, but can't. Why did I bring us here?*

I snapped back to reality when Steve spoke again. "Listen. Just hear me out. I've already spoken with the conductor and gotten the okay. And I have talked to my men, and two of them have volunteered. Now what I want to do is have our two guys up here trade places with you two in third class. That way, you can have their bunks up here."

I couldn't believe that Steve, a stranger, had been so concerned for our well being. With nothing to gain, he'd mapped out the strategy of our escape. We had little reason to doubt the sincerity of his generous offer. But I couldn't just jump on it. I'd paid for third class. Even though Steve had totally freaked me out with the idea of spending a night in the train's poorest sector, I had to consider his hired men and how un-cool it would be to displace them.

"Wow . . . I'm not sure what to say . . . except that I don't want to put anyone out."

"The guys will be fine. They'll be in their element. You won't, if you stay there. And besides, they'll probably get drunk and have a good time back there. Trust me."

Deep down, I wanted to say, *Hell yeah, you're awesome, and where do we sleep?* But sitting across from Steve and Andy, I felt naïve, humiliated, humbled, and plain-ass lucky.

"Okay, if it's really alright with your guys, it sounds good to me . . . and thank you."

Steve had just relieved the gnawing stress I'd felt since we'd boarded this nasty ride. But really, I would never deny that it was Pam who was the true hero.

With my mind now off imminent danger, the passage became pleasant. As we catapulted past huge wine vineyards, my anxieties fizzled. The locomotive had taken on a strange romantic allure.

* * *

Night fell. The air grew downright cold in our mini-cabin as I curled up on my hard, narrow bunk. Still fully clothed, my toes felt soggy; the socks inside my Docs were putrid from my nervous sweat. I shivered, but smiled inside, unharmed and listening to the train travel through the darkness.

Second class boasted hot showers. In the morning, after a marvelous high-pressure, near-scalding soak, I slid fresh socks onto my thawed feet. My toes had never felt so happy.

* * *

Once in Cape Town, Pam and I hoofed it toward a hostel we'd been told about. "Check that out," I said. "The mountain really does look like it's been sawed in half."

We had a clear view of Table Mountain, the famous peak that marks the city and creates an unforgettable backdrop for the Victorian architecture of downtown. Cape Town was going to be an easy place in which to chill.

Next morning, I grabbed the local paper and a coffee and headed to the hostel's second-story balcony. Flipping through the classified section, I spotted an ad selling a red '78 Ford Cortina station wagon for $4,000 *rand* (roughly U.S. $1,600.00). I dialed from a phone booth near our hostel. According to the guy who answered the phone, the vehicle was still available. He gave us his address, and a couple of hours later Pam and I boarded a bus to a suburb on the outskirts of town and showed up on this guy's doorstep. Parked curbside next to his front lawn, the old red hatchback looked like a dandy traveling machine. We test-drove, liked, and negotiated.

The wagon's owner had a daughter backpacking through Europe, and so for karma's sake he gave us two young travelers a smoking deal. He gladly settled for 2,300 rand (about $900.00 American dollars). Pam and I split the bill, and *bam!*, we were mobile.

We named the red Cortina wagon Tina, and drove her straight to a surf shop where I picked up a brand new board for two hundred sixty bucks (The South African guys I'd met in Australia had told me boards were inexpensive in their home-land. Since I was due for new equipment anyway, I'd flown without the hassle of carrying boards, planning to buy a couple when I got there (I had, however, brought a good wetsuit from home). I later bought a decent used mini-gun (longer board) for meatier waves.

From the surf shop, Tina took us to a thrift store where we geared up to flee Cape Town: a sleeping mat, blankets, a cook-ing pot, a wooden spoon, and a cracked but working guitar—the basics.

Just hours before we left town, I was strolling alone down the street to stock up at the food store when something caught me by surprise. From the doors of a tall glass building, a robust man in a suit and tie strode assertively into the middle of the crosswalk clutching an automatic rifle. I did a double-take at the odd scene. The man stopped under a traffic light and put the entire street under siege. The light flicked from red to green, and the few cars waiting at the light didn't budge. The combination of the man's weapon, his stature, and his business suit gave him the look of someone who'd gone over the edge, not unlike Michael Douglas in *Falling Down*.

At first I feared he would blast bullets at anyone unfortunate enough to be in range. I ducked behind a brick wall and peeked around to watch what the mysterious man and his killing machine were up to.

The man held his center-street position with his finger on the trigger. Moments later, another business-suited man toting two big white bags came out of the same glass building and strode across the avenue. He safely entered an adjacent building, with the gunman confidently following.

A money exchange between banks, I guessed. Although the transaction had been successful, I couldn't help thinking that a wire transfer would've been easier.

* * *

Driving through the countryside in our own wheels gave us the freedom to step on the gas and roam wherever we wanted. This was as enjoyable as I'd hoped. Pam and I sang and danced in our seats as I steered Tina south under blue skies on the two-lane highway out of Cape Town.

We twisted through hilly, rocky landscape laced with green-leaved shrubs and purple flora. Soon we stumbled upon an open-country, sort of free-for-all vacant campground. The isolated setting exaggerated my sense of uncertainty about being in this foreign environment. Predators, man or beast, were free to stalk our lonely site. I did my best to man-up.

"Hey Pam, whaddaya think? Looks . . . free."

"Um, yeah, sure!" she said cheerily. Before embarking on this little safari, she'd said she'd be up for anything, and she'd kept her word. I valued her dauntless high spirit. Her mood remained good no matter where I dragged her.

We prowled the grounds in silence before pulling into a spot to camp.

As the sun sank behind the nearby hills, I lit a fire and fixed a pot of oxtail soup. Now I felt like a real cowboy, stacking the fire ring stones so the pot simmered evenly over the flames. Bright stars sparkled in the southern-hemi sky as Pam and I reclined against a blanket-covered log, savoring both the oxtail soup and the Wild-West-like moment.

After finishing dinner, we crawled into the back of Tina to sleep. Though I kept a tire iron close at hand, and despite my current look-over-your-shoulder disposition, peace prevailed through the night.

Come morning, we brewed coffee over smoldering embers before leaving to find some waves.

We rolled down the coast near the Cape of Good Hope, where the Atlantic and the Indian Oceans' deep blue waters converge. I stopped at a long sandy beach where head-high peaks—the rights a bit cleaner than the lefts—poured in. The lineup was dotted with a handful of other surfers. A healthy dose of sunshine warmed the air. The water, on the other hand, was Cape-cold.

I wasted no time suiting up, waxing my virgin board, and paddling out through the chilly breakers. Within a minute a nice wave reared up before me, a right. I dropped in, sprung off the bottom, and arced high on the blue face, feeling out the new board under my feet. I raced a fast section and blasted the lip on the inside. That was when it hit me that I'd finally arrived at my first surf session in South Africa.

Afterward, we called Andy, Steve's friend from the train. He invited Pam and me over to meet his family and have a *braai* (a South African B.B.Q.). We drove to his house, in a clean cheery neighborhood.

The food hadn't yet hit the fire when we heard his phone ring. He picked up the receiver.

"Hello, Andy speaking…uh huh…uh huh…alright then, I'll be there as soon as I can."

Duty called. Andy's main job was photographing crime scenes for the police. A black cop had committed suicide, and they needed Andy to photograph the scene.

"Hey, J.J., would you like to go for a ride?"

"Sure, a ride sounds fun!"

Pam stayed with Andy's wife and two toddler daughters.

Andy stepped on it. He charged across the open highway and then blazed through a maze of ratty neighborhoods, flying through the stop signs.

"You don't stop around here, bru," he said, noticing my perplexed look.

After driving around in circles awhile, he grew frustrated. "Oh, bloody hell, I can't find the place. We're gonna have to make a quick stop. There's a cop shop not far from here."

Andy reached into his glove box and pulled out a big Dirty Harry handgun. He cocked the thing and jammed it between his legs! I didn't need to ask what the hell the gun was for; I found out soon enough. The cop shop Andy headed to sat dead-center in a shanty town. In case you don't know, a South African shanty town is absolutely no place for you if you're white. And about now, my half-Mexican semi-tanned skin seemed to gleam like polished ivory.

My long sun-bleached ponytail began to curl.

Rows of single-story ramshackle houses pieced together from weathered plywood and beaten corrugated tin lined the littered streets. Through the false security of my rolled-up window I observed men, women, and children walking around in clothes that needed a good scrubbing. The very air had a grubby dirt-under-the-nails tint to it. This place reeked of destitution.

On the other hand, to my surprise, the town functioned like any other community, albeit much more run down. We drove past a gas station that had seen better days, and booth-size shops that probably sold everything from Coke to cocaine.

Then I saw the cop shop.

A chain-link fence topped with spiraling barbed wire encompassed the box-shaped station, which was about the size of a Dunkin' Donuts shop. The sandbags at the base of the fence were dotted with bullet holes, as was the building itself. Most of its windows were broken, or at least cracked.

We pulled up and parked. I had to wait in the damn car while Andy disappeared for a brutally long five minutes. I kept the doors locked and the windows up. Through the glass, three men eyeballed me as if daring me to open the door and step into their world.

No chance.

In this environment I was no conscientious objector. I would've felt safer holding one of those handy-looking firearms my friend was packing. This hardened society made an American ghetto feel as safe as an amusement park. And I couldn't tell who wanted out more—me, or those who were spying on me.

Andy returned with directions to our destination, and we sped off to see the deceased.

Police cars had pulled up to the brown lawn of a sun-beaten home that would have been considered gloomy on an American scale, however, compared to the flimsy structures of the shanties, it was a legitimate house.

Uniformed policemen were trotting back and forth doing this and that when we roared up to the scene. Andy walked straight into the house with his big flash-ready camera. I followed, navigating from one room to the next as if I belonged there. Scant on furniture, the living room and halls had bare walls and a slight smell of toe-jam.

Then I saw him, belly-up on a bed in a room brightened by sunlight beaming through yellow curtains. The gun, still in his hand, rested on his bare chest just above his bloated belly. His head was tilted back, so I could see only the underside of his chin and open nostrils. This was okay by me; I wasn't about to walk around for a closer look. All the gore I needed to see had spattered across the yellow curtains behind him. He'd blown his brains out.

My first thought was, *Couldn't you have worked out your problems?* But for all I knew, this guy could've been bad news and wouldn't be missed by his community. Because I'd never know his real story, I pretended he'd tried to be a good guy and mourned his grim end. Evidently his life had been unbearably miserable, and there'd been no one nearby who cared enough to seize the pistol and console his troubled soul. I wondered what his last twenty-four hours had been like, before he'd squeezed the trigger.

We didn't stay long enough for me to ponder life and death. Andy snapped some pics of the carnage from different angles and we headed back to our braai.

* * *

Pam and I spent the night at Andy's, and the next day we said goodbye to the Cape Town area. Tina followed the coast eastward over gaping gorges and through some cool, lush, sparsely populated holiday towns on a stretch of road known as the Garden Route. This enchanting corner of earth dialed deep into my spirit. Everything pulsated—the flowing rivers, the salty sea, and the wind-filled sky.

Sometimes we'd park Tina, then Pam and I would do our own thing. I'd hike alone down a beach, sit on a rock, and look long at the waves roll in from the blue nothingness. I couldn't have been happier. Each day was a great gift, and I knew I should live it up. I felt truly lucky to be thoroughly enjoying life.

* * *

Here is where I had an encounter with South Africa's thriving sea life. I'd already read lots about S.A.'s abundance of sharks, particularly the Great Whites. Their haunting reputation had always chewed at the back of my mind.

One windy, overcast afternoon while surfing a lengthy stretch of beach with five other guys, my peripheral vision caught a large, grey, fish-shaped tail break and then plunge back down below the water's surface. The splash startled the living crap out of me, and my legs automatically lifted onto my board.

A few seconds later, a curved dorsal fin popped up, with a simultaneous blow from the creature's head. *Oh, freaking good,* I thought. *It's just a dolphin.* Another one spouted, followed by another. Swish, swash, they swamped the place. The animals had caught me by surprise, but the real shocker was their numbers—like, thousands! Probably tens of thousands were speeding by. I couldn't tell whether they were chasing or being chased. Like us humans, dolphins apparently have sexual intercourse just for fun, but it didn't look like the boys were after the girls. Either way, the other surfers and I were bobbing in the direct path of mammal madness.

Actually, I had trouble locating the other guys in the water because the sea was so thick with frenzied dolphins. Fins, tails, and spouting blows darted past. Some would leap. Everywhere, out to the horizon and inside toward shore, the ocean surface frothed. Let me tell ya, I'd been in the water with dolphins plenty ... *plenty.* But never had I seen anything like this. They streaked past so close I expected to get clobbered. Yet I didn't get hit.

Then, as fast as they'd arrived, the dolphins faded from sight. With a clear view now, I could see the other guys were tripping, too. We looked at each other, our jaws in our laps.

Suddenly, up the coast, the ocean boiled again. Another army bore down on us. We couldn't believe it was happening a second time. This time we were ready, but that made the stampede no less spectacular. Once more, thousands of heads, fins, tails, and blows splashed the water. I sat back and enjoyed the show. By the time the second huge flow of dolphins had gone by, we surfers had been herded into a group. Whereas we'd started out fairly far apart, all six of us were now sitting on our boards close together in a circle, smiling. No one said a word.

To top off the wild experience, a large gull came out of the sky and started diving at one of the guys. The bird squawked at our mate, but did nothing more than make a loud wing-flapping scene. We laughed hysterically, still high from the dolphins. The nutty bird only bothered to antagonize one of us, and flew away. Then all the animals were gone. Mother Nature had just regaled us with one of her many magnificent spectacles—the great annual sardine run.

* * *

Jeffery's Bay, to which most surfers who might be reading this will require no introduction, was one of our destinations. Pam and I shared a room there for twenty rand a night (U.S. three dollars each). For about three weeks I scored epic waves in and around the area.

After that, Tina took us up the east coast, past the Transki, and to Durban, Natal.

There, in a hopping dance club near the beach, Pam and I toasted my twenty-second birthday. She laughed because I didn't want to turn another year older just yet. She was already twenty-four.

In Natal, we stayed almost every night with friends we met through Sharon, a soulful white woman who lived on a tree farm and played a soothing guitar. She hadn't a sliver of prejudice in her, and got raving excited when we went to the theater to see a movie about Jimi Hendrix. "Look at those long beautiful fingers," she said when the huge screen showed Hendrix sliding his hand coolly down the neck of his guitar. By example alone, Sharon taught me a lot about loving thy neighbor.

One friend would introduce us to another, and we ended up crashing on six or seven different couches. We slept in Tina less than I'd anticipated. The bulk of our tab ended up being fuel and food, and surprisingly, Pam joined me most of the time for meals of inexpensive rice soaked in pots of oxtail soup. She was surprised I could live on the road happily for a hundred bucks a week. She was even more shocked to find that she could, too.

After a few months, we sold Tina and went our separate ways. Pam stayed in Natal with friends while I headed back to Johannesburg and jumped onto a jumbo jet.

* * *

I didn't just go home. My flight from South Africa back to California stopped in Kuala Lumpur, Malaysia. Not excited about having to catch the connecting fight two hours later, I'd coaxed the travel agents into extending my layover for two months. I made my third jaunt to Indonesia by jumping on a ferry across the Straits of Malacca and biting into the archipelago from northern Sumatra.

It felt great to be back in Indo. I sat on a bus that bounced past jungle villages scented with smoke from trash-burning fire pits. I'd always loved that smolder aroma mixed with the thick humid air. And when our bus passed by these villages, without fail the children would immediately spot my Western face and run smiling toward the bus from their huts, waving and shouting the only English words they knew: "Hello, Mister!"

They made me feel like a king on a parade float.

In those parts of the world, life's pace was slow. With my brown boots crammed deep into my backpack, I joined the islanders in their flip-flop ways.

* * *

My traveling habits had changed from my first Indo trip. For one thing, I now deliberately immersed myself as best I could in the indigenous culture, studying my *Bahasa* Indonesian pocket phrase-book and practicing the lingo with whoever wanted to chat. Another difference was my attitude toward the roadside food carts: on my first trip, I had steered clear of them. I'd dabbled in them on the second run. And by this time, they were practically the only places I ate (I still avoided the soups, though). Also, I had by now fully accepted and partook in the traditional Indonesian paperless butt-wipe system (when in Rome, you know). I'd even say that I started to prefer their ground-level squat toilets to the up-high sit-on style back home.

Also, in preparing for my first Indo trip, I'd gotten shot up with every recommended vaccination in the book. But in the years since then I'd favored a more natural path, and no longer took those types of precautions. I shunned anti-malaria pills. Instead of absorbing "anti" pills into my body, I favored a more direct method of dealing with mosquitoes, the don't-get-bit method. Covering up with jeans, socks, and long sleeves at dawn and at dusk became my insurance policy against a thirsty mozzie injecting my bloodstream with a strain of the dreaded disease.

* * *

After traveling down Sumatra, the largest island of the Indonesian chain, I came to Java, the most populous. My bus dropped me in Jakarta, a huge city clogged with traffic congestion and air pollution. To get out of the bustle, I lugged my surfboards down the hyperactive city streets toward the railway station. Cars honked and honked and honked. Buses blasted clouds of black exhaust. On the sidewalks, run-down vending cart owners fried rice or noodles in their big woks. Every single vendor I passed tried to sell me at least one soda pop. It looked like a hot, sweaty hassle of a way to make a buck. I felt bad that I felt glad I didn't have to make a living like some of them did.

I managed to find the rail station that helped me out of the Jakarta jungle.

The train ride was crowded and unpleasant, though my own discomfort paled as compared to that of some of the more desperate people of the city. As the train filled up at a station stop, a man and a melancholic young blind girl boarded. Solemnly, she walked down the isle, singing a wretched, echoing tune through a portable karaoke machine. Her male partner walked around collecting money in a tin can. They left the train before it took off. I couldn't help but wonder how the girl lost her sight and had a sick feeling that she was sabotaged to create a pitiful scene. This sort of thing did not rest well in me, but I fought to make some sort of reason out of it.

Then, the train passed what I called "the slums of Jakarta." Far from peaceful village life, this was a squatter settlement built much like the shanty towns of South Africa. But this place looked worse. I think it had something to do with the weather. The tropical air tended to make things go septic. Plus, this particular ghetto festered on the banks of some putrid water. The stench was bad enough, as though downwind of a rotting carcass, but watching a woman scrubbing clothes, another washing a large pot, and yet another bathing her baby in the moat really stunk. What a tough way for the infant to start life. All my tooth-fairy, Easter-Bunny, trick-or-treat, Ho-Ho-Ho childhood privileges sank painfully into my gut at the sight of this ugly reality.

My playgrounds as a youth had been places like Disneyland and the beach. When my parents would say life wasn't fair, I had no idea. All over the world, millions live in slum communities where things like shampoo and toothpaste are expensive extras. Seeing real poverty on a television program was one thing; having its rancid scent dissolve in your every breath was quite another.

The train rolled away from the God-forsaken impoverished dwellings and into fresher air, leaving the others behind, for all I knew, a lifetime.

The stock on my lifestyle skyrocketed.

* * *

I had an urge to shed the guilt that had taken root inside me. At first I tried random acts of kindness, like buying candy from various small shops (to spread the wealth) and passing it out to children. But that wasn't good enough. I had to dig deeper. By the time I arrived at the next beach, I'd begun to deprive myself. Normally, after a morning of surfing I'd go on a long walk down country roads to soak in my surroundings. Now, however, I'd depart hungry and without water. The warm, salty ocean alone was enough to dehydrate a man. Combine that with trekking hatless in the tropical midday sun, and I would acquire a terrible thirst. I wouldn't relieve my dry throat until evening, when I'd pour a glass of water and drink it slowly, one small sip at a time. Breakfast I skipped, and lunch and dinner were small—mostly plain rice—and spaced so that my hunger never subsided. Surprisingly, my energy levels remained relatively high.

After a few weeks, I eased into eating more satisfying portions. In a strange way, I think the fasting had made me more aware . . . of lots of things.

I couldn't possibly emulate the lives of those with next to nothing, nor did I wish to try, but I had a need to set aside my Western mentality and attempt to see life through their eyes. I squatted as the locals did and paid close attention to the way they communicated with one another, and to how they smoked their cloves. Sympathetic, empathetic, or just plain pathetic, in my mind I had turned into a man from the third world. Except that I had a deep, dark, secret: almost two thousand U.S. dollars tucked safely in a bank account. And plenty more where that came from.

I couldn't fool the cows that pulled the plows. I was rich.

My sister, Christy, and I at
Huntington Beach '78

My First Surfboard, age13

Summer of '89...just turned 16 and completely surfstoked!

Indonesia '91

Weaver always made friends easily. Mexico

Weave and I shelled out the equivalant of 3 bucks each for this bungalow in Indo.

West Java

Malavar, Nina and I with his
prized bus, Cabo San Lucas

Living in Scott's closet, H.B.

J -Bay, South Africa

With my roomate
Miguel in the
Canary Islands.

I got a lift for
over 1,000 kms
with this friendly
Aussie trucker.

Great
Australian
Bight

A close up of an elephant brawl, South Africa

Camping along Cape Peninsula, South Africa

Leaving 17th St. H.B. for Costa Rica.

Somewhere along the Baja

Resting with the Israelis in the mountains of Guatemala

Surfing Costa Rica

Venezuela

Sailing with the locals in Bequia

Crewing across the Caribbean Sea

Hitching in the Southern Hemi

Dropping in

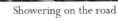
Showering on the road

Sometimes surfing hurts

8
MEXICO
Bailing on a Bike

In September, I returned home in time for my sister's wedding. The change from trotting barefoot in muggy jungles to standing tuxedoed in a Southern California beachside church was a major dose of culture shock. Happy to watch Christy exchange vows with Ty, her new husband, I was glad it was she who stood at the altar and not me.

* * *

Traveling excited me now more than ever. Waves had without a doubt guided my path, but I became hooked on the entire on-the-road experience. I began to dream up another more extensive trip before I'd returned from the one I was on. Ways to flee California had consumed my consciousness back in South Africa. One day, while driving my little station wagon along the Natal coast, a motorbike zipped around me and sped off into the distance. Watching him, I knew I'd get home and be raring to split again. Right then I came up with a gripping idea.

To get out of Cali promptly on the cheap, all I'd have to do would be slip south of the border on a motorcycle. It made perfect sense. After all, a used bike could be cheaper than a plane ticket, and bikes were great on gas. Plus, I could go in any direction with a mere pull of the throttle. If I wanted, I could ride all the way to South America.

My imagination drifted like currents in the sea. I envisioned riding to Brazil, hopping a freighter to Africa, and then motoring up through the Sahara and into Europe. Then I could sail to the U.S. Eastern seaboard and cross my own country on the way back to the West Coast. But I got carried away, and it all began to sound more like work. I'd skip the Sahara.

It would be easier to stop short of the Darien Gap, a hundred-mile stretch of thick jungle, gushing rivers, and marshy swamp that separates Panama from Colombia. A road had never been built linking the North and South American continents, partly due to expense and partly for environmental reasons. Expeditions have successfully traveled through the area, but its lawlessness attracts fugitives, smugglers, and anti-government guerrillas. Kidnappings and murders are all too common. Crossing its wilderness is a formidable challenge. Although I found its lore intriguing, I would admire the Gap from afar. That place is hardcore.

There is a way around the Darien by boat. But I had an uneasy feeling about riding a motorcycle alone through Colombia, with its thugs and drugs. I boxed my original plan with its deterrents and focused on a ride to Costa Rica.

* * *

Now that I was back in my old Huntington Beach haunt, I needed to get busy with some employment and beef up my kitty.

I'd recently bumped into a childhood chum, Scott. These days he had a son, a real job, a strong sense of responsibility, and a place three blocks from the beach. For a hundred fifty bucks a month I slept in his walk-in closet.

That's when I met Janie, the roommate of one of Scottie's friends. When I cruised through the door Jane happened to be kicking back on Scott's living room couch, looking good. In our brief conversation I mentioned something about job hunting. The following morning, Scott's answering machine relayed a message from Jane. She worked a few miles up the coast in a seafood restaurant that needed a busboy, she said, and I should come apply.

After catching a few waves, I checked out the restaurant. I walked through the door, my long hair twisted by the morning surf and tied back into one woven lock. Soft, wavering light from electric brass lanterns gave the dining area the feel of being inside an old wooden ship. I met with the forty-something blonde female manager and told her I was a friend of Jane's. She gave me and my app the once-over.

"Can you start tomorrow night?"

"Sure."

There I became friends with other surfer busboys in a mold similar to my own, most notably Matt and Zack. They schooled me in Busboy 101: how to fold linen napkins into flower shapes, where to sneak a bite to eat, and which servers tipped out best.

Matt and Zack lived one street south of me and just happened to be buddies with a guy named Dave, whom I'd met a month earlier in Indo. Dave was considering riding with me to

Costa Rica. As I passed him one afternoon on the stairway to Matt and Zack's apartment, I hit him up.

"So, are you coming with me?" I asked, hoping he was still keen.

Dave paused and let out a sigh. "Hey, bro," he said in his deep, surf-like drawl, "You know, that's pretty gnarly, riding motorcycles through countries like Nicaragua."

He didn't need to elaborate. I got what he was getting at. I'd had the same feeling about Colombia. He wasn't going anywhere. Not with me, anyhow.

Some people thought my idea was dumb. But I blew off reactions like the one from my Peruvian friend, Miguel: *"What?! Are you crazy?! Your Spanish sucks! You don't know those countries like I do! You're going to die!"*

My response: "Nahhhh . . ."

Over the years, I'd heard all kinds of nasty bandito stories. But I also knew not everyone found trouble south of the border, and besides, I was on a roll. I ignored over-reactive pessimists who said dreadful things like "You can't do that!" Even so, apprehension wasn't entirely absent in me, and in a futile attempt to round up a two-man posse I had a little heart-to-heart with Weaver.

"Look, man, I've got the coolest idea!"

He'd become too wrapped up in his education to take such a break. I'd sensed it all along, and finally had to face the facts: finding another rider wasn't happening. I was going solo.

* * *

In addition to bussing tables, I took on a couple of midweek graveyard shifts sweeping floors in a pet hospital. Ray, a fellow janitor who also moonlighted, worked during the day installing carpet. Ray knew my plan, and strangely enough, it was he who discovered the machine that would propel me into the heart of Latin America.

Laying carpet in Laguna Hills for a relatively young doctor, Ray had noticed an off-road motorcycle in the garage. He asked the doc if he'd consider selling the bike. Doc said maybe, and Ray handed his phone number to me.

Three days later, I showed up at Doc's house with little expectation. He buzzed his garage door open and there she was, in a corner: a 1982 Honda 500 XL. Showing her dusty red fenders, the street-legal dirt bike begged me to ride her home.

"This bike's been good to me." Doc wiped the seat and gave the old girl a few solid kicks.

Pu, pu, putt. Pu, pu, putt. Pu, pu, Varrrrooomm!

He revved her up and looked at me. "Hop on."

I jumped on the back.

We were in a hilly residential area. Doc pointed straight up a hill, and, to prove what his bike could do, shot out of the garage like a slug from a forty-five. We didn't just climb; we rocketed up the hill! *Waaaaaaaaaaamm....* The tires gripped the pavement. My butt nearly flew off the seat and I grabbed on to Doc, despite the fact that he was a dude.

WOW! I thought, *this thing is jamming with two of us on her back!* Trip or no trip, I wanted her.

Back at Doc's house, I tried not to seem so fired-up.

"Well," I said calmly, my face still flushed from the ride. "It's pretty much what I'm looking for."

Doc knew where I planned to take her, and thought it would be an exciting chapter in his prized bike's life. He wasn't hurting for cash, and after a little negotiation we agreed on a price of three hundred and fifty bucks. I was stoked. Between Doc and Ray, I had my ride outta Cali. It's amazing how some people will go out of their way to help you.

* * *

The months flew by, September to December. Now that I had the bike, other preparations fell into place. In my dad's garage, I bent, hacked, and drilled into pieces of metal flat bar. My Uncle Benny came over with a portable welder and tacked a simple support for the flat bars onto the bike's frame. The end result: surfboard racks. I made sure they would allow enough room for my left leg to move comfortably between the board and the bike, that they were removable, and above all, that they would hold a surfboard.

Grabbing an old board out of my folks' storage shed, I mounted it carefully on the racks. Excited for a test run, I left my helmet behind and tore through my old neighborhood, spurring her up to fifty-five m.p.h. to study the board's reaction to the wind. Everything worked beautifully. If my surfboard and I couldn't handle a ride around the block together, that would've been troublesome. I wasn't about to travel without it.

I bought a can of black spray paint and coated the red fenders and gas tank so I wouldn't stick out as much south of the border. Surely, no one in Mexico would notice the long-haired *gringo* carrying a surfboard on a black motorbike!

To minimize potential legal problems, I made an appointment to get a motorcycle license. This would have been a few degrees easier had I not run into a little glitch while toying with my bike. Because I was a lousy mechanic and knew jack about motorcycles, I had a friend who loved to tinker with engines help me with an oil change. Now, my mechanical friend was human—if that makes sense—and like anyone, he could make a mistake. Well . . . he blew it.

He'd taken off the engine cover to do his thing, which was fine. But then, as he was putting it all back together, he tightened a bolt too hard and cracked the cover at one of the bolt holes. Not a huge crack; in fact, the bike still ran. But it dripped barrels of oil, and my riding test was later that same day. He cursed and apologized. I said not to worry about it, that I would fix it later. I had to get going.

Knowing they check that stuff before the test gets underway, I showed up at the D.M.V. hoping the riding performance judge wouldn't bar me for having a motorcycle unfit to ride. Drip, drip . . . My bike and I both sweated as the examiner inspected my brake lights.

"Okay now, show me the hand signal for turning right," he said. "Okay, left."

I did my best to keep his attention away from the pavement underneath my idling bike, which was now stained by a silver-dollar-sized pool of black. He told me to get ready.

Riding a motorcycle wasn't new to me. But riding as fast as you can is a heck of a lot easier than riding as slow as you can. I hadn't realized the test was all about the latter. I followed the painted yellow line in a slow circle, and did pretty well, I thought.

"Do it again," he said, "slower." I slowed to the point of tipping, and accidentally put my foot down, but resumed. Other than being nervous about the foot thing, all went well. I guess he never noticed the oil.

"Okay, you're done."

The man penned his clipboard quietly for a full minute, until I couldn't take it anymore. "So how'd I do?" I blurted. "Did I pass?"

He kept his eyes on the clipboard and nodded. Yes!

To fix the cracked cover, I contacted a hard-core metal smith, my dad's master-welder friend, Fuji. He mended the piece beautifully and, to be nice, only charged me five dollars. The bike looked as good as ever.

Other pre-departure business included my new *Chas* surfboard. By the end of December, it was shaped and ready. I'd requested a thick stringer and heavier-than-normal glass job, and ordered it a bit longer than my standard Huntington Beach break shortboard. I didn't want to be undergunned when the waves grew overhead and hollow, the conditions I craved most.

Jumping from the Stone Age into the Space Age, I traded my old traveler's check routine for the convenient debit card. Although I had a trust issue with computers, I was cool with this transition toward the technical world. Besides, I still had almost a thousand dollars in traveler's checks from the Africa/Indo run, which gave me a nice diverse mix of currency, including the worldly popular, thief-luring, indispensable, unmistakable U.S.

dollar.

* * *

New Year's Eve, 1995, was my last day of work (I had for-feited the janitor gig a week earlier). The restaurant's lounge overflowed with festive patrons boozing and schmoozing. Bal-loons clung to the ceiling, tied to colorful streams of ribbon that draped the scene. By the time the clock struck twelve, I'd bussed my last table. When everyone hollered "HAPPY NEW YEAR!" I agreed. That warm fuzzy final-day-at-work feeling tingled through my body.

While everyone screamed and blew their kazoos, Janie, the girl who had helped get me the job, celebrated with me. Her slender, tender body felt sensational when she pressed against me to get a kiss. We'd been hanging out ever since we'd started working together, and in those few months we'd developed a good friendship. She wrapped her arms tightly around me.

"Be careful when you go," she said.

"I will. Thanks for everything. I enjoyed being your busboy."

* * *

On New Year's morning, 1996, Huntington Beach pumped with swell (actually, the waves were firing on New Year's Eve, too, which had caused me to be late for my final shift at the restaurant). Armed with the longest board in my so-so quiver, I cruised to the surf via Matt and Zack's place to join them in greeting the New Year by surfing big peaks with an offshore wind. We paddled out and hooted each other into waves. A big set approached, and Zack stroked for it with everything he had. He dropped steep and deep into a meaty left. As I scratched up and over the mounting sea, I looked down saw him racing just ahead of the pitching lip.

It's almost as much fun watching a buddy take the drop as it is doing it yourself . . . almost! This energizing wave fest provided plenty of surfer camaraderie.

After the session, I went to my room (Scott's closet) and stuffed just about everything I owned into a couple of boxes the size of a microwave oven. I had hardly any clothes, no bed or other furniture, and in the last year had sifted several times through my belongings and weeded out all but the absolute necessities.

Several nights later, I stashed the boxes in my folks' storage shed, where they'd hibernate till I returned. Since I intended to leave for Mexico the following day from Scott's pad, I also said goodbye to my parents. We visited in the living room, and the scene felt unusually quiet.

"What a long, horrible ride," my mother sulked.

"Don't be silly, Mom, the ride's the fun part."

"You're not normal J.J. You know that, right?"

"C'mon, Mom, do you know anyone who's normal?"

My mom couldn't understand what compelled me to take this trip. I'm not so sure I could, either. But I had to go.

Around midnight, following promises to be careful, and passing out hugs, I kicked the Honda into gear and started back toward Huntington Beach. I felt my parents' eyes on me as I motored out of their neighborhood and into the darkness.

In the chilly January night, I took a route seldom ridden. The occasional car lit up the lanes in the late hour. Then, as I neared the coast, I rode directly into an incredibly dense fog bank. In a blink, the weather changed from semi-clear to thicker than clam chowder. My eyes were blinded by the white. Fearing something would slam into me from behind, I made my way over to the side—wherever that was—and removed my helmet.

I couldn't believe it. I'd been creeping myself out with thoughts of masked thieves and unsympathetic government employees when I knew damn well from years of swimming in the ocean that my first concern should've been sweet-talking Mother Nature. She had total control over my progress, and was giving me a little taste of awareness by stopping me in my tracks. At her mercy, I paced around in the cloud for at least an hour before it shifted enough to set me free.

Back at Scott's place, I couldn't sleep. Daydreaming shouldn't be done lying on a couch at night. My heart spun with feelings of pure freedom interrupted again and again by an underlying sense of anxiety. Around five o'clock I passed out from thinking too much.

By eight in the morning I was up and about, compulsively checking my money belt for my passport and various forms of *dinero*. With these items, I could lose the rest and still press on. Although it was my goal, it wasn't mandatory that I ride all the way to Central America. If the engine blew up along the way, I would ditch the wheels and hitch for thrills . . . or hop a bus.

Tinkering with the bike in front of the apartment, I looked up to see Zack and his girlfriend, Tamara. They'd cruised over to say hi. I'd been fumbling with a bungee cord, trying to secure my backpack to the back of the seat.

"Hey, why don't you strap it on top of the gas tank," Zack suggested.

I did, and the bag held snugly in place.

"Good thinking," I said. "Well, hey, I'm gonna do a test run with all of my gear. I'll stop by your place on my way out, okay?"

I headed back into the apartment and grabbed my most important piece of luggage: my surfboard. It would travel inside the fading but faithful cloth board bag I had bought during my first Indo trip. I intended to use the long, narrow bag as a makeshift sleeping bag. A month earlier, I'd taken it to my Aunt Connie's house for a little modification. She'd cut a slit halfway down the thing, and, using her sewing savvy, she'd hemmed the edges with strips of Velcro. The cover hung loosely around the board, and I wrapped it with a thin rope, pulling the floppy fabric taut and creating an easy-to-carry disguised object.

With all my gear in position, including the board on its racks, I ran the first fully loaded test run along the streets of downtown Huntington Beach. My bag presented a slight hindrance to maneuverability, but not too bad. Other than that, I was good to go.

For some reason, I kept stalling, burning time. The bike waited patiently. Valuables strapped to my waist, breakfast digested, gas tank filled to the rim, a can of fix-a-flat lashed to my rear fender—after an hour of dilly-dallying I came across my reflection in the bathroom mirror and said, "Now, go!"

I took one last look around Scott's place, laid the key to the apartment on the kitchen counter, opened the front door, locked it, stepped outside, and closed the door. From there, I rode one street over to Matt and Zack's pad. They lived on the second story and were upstairs on the balcony with a group of friends, leaning on the railing, looking down. I pulled up on the driveway and took off my helmet to chat, but remained seated with the engine idling. My body buzzed with nervous excitement as the conversation sped to necessities.

"Do you have any duct tape?" Zack asked.

I confessed I didn't. He disappeared, only to re-emerge seconds later with a grey roll. I pulled my gloves off and he tossed the tape down into my jittery hands. Ripping open a section of Velcro, I slipped the roll into my board bag.

After a few minutes of chit chat, I delayed no further. "Well, I'll see you guys in about a year!" I put on my helmet.

Everyone above began to hoot, whistle, and cheer. Uplifted by this unexpected encouragement, I gave the throttle a few good twists of the wrist in reply. My friends' genuine enthusiasm for the ride fired me up. Their support continued as I backed out, turned my wheel, and eased away.

I rode carefully toward the ocean and turned left on to Pacific Coast Highway. Passing the Huntington Beach pier, I took a final look at the familiar landmark before the road demanded my undivided attention. My first concern was whether riding along with the big eyesore at my side would be reason enough for the cops to stop me. I knew I'd be cool all day long in Mexico, but in Newport and Laguna Beach, where the law enforcement is notoriously strict, I didn't want them to spot me. I rolled down the coast without incident.

Southbound on Interstate 5, I loosened up. It felt great to

maintain some speed for a change. Buzzing through traffic, I saw kids in cars pointing fingers, probably at the board.

* * *

I had two pit stops in mind: Malavar's place, in Oceanside, followed by Marty's house, near San Diego, where I would spend the night. I'd known Marty since my high school pizza delivery boy days. A few years older than I, he had been the assistant manager at our Pizza Hut, where we had become amigos. These days, he worked as border patrol along the dusty divide between the U.S. and Mexico.

When I got to Oceanside I knocked on Malavars door. He and Nina were expecting me. As always, Mal popped in a surf flick as we chatted on the couch. Nina threw some leftover pizza into the oven.

"How funny," Malavar laughed. "At home, everyone's worried about you, and here you sit eating pizza and watching surf videos."

"I'm telling ya, man, that's how it usually is."

Really, a brush with disaster happens from time to time, no matter where you are. Let's face it: driving in Los Angeles has got to be one of the most dangerous acts around. It's got to be far riskier to ride a motorbike on a metropolitan freeway in the U.S. than on some lonely road in rural Mexico. That's my theory, and I'm sticking to it.

Malavar walked me outside.

"So, you're really going, aren't you?" he said, checking out my wheels for the first time. He stepped back, shaking his head. "Well . . . if anyone can make it, you can." His words filled me with courage.

* * *

After I left Malavar's, I watched the road under my tires and realized I was not turning back. The cold January afternoon crept in through the cracks of my clothes. Living at home for several months, I'd grown comfortable knowing where my head would lie each night. In fact, my reluctance to leave Scott's apartment earlier in the day had led me to question whether I had grown lazy. But the liberating sensation of riding my bike down Interstate 5 made me quit digging pointlessly into my thoughts.

The sun was fading fast as I approached Marty's house in the eastern suburbs of San Diego. I hadn't seen Marty for some time, so it was great to catch up.

"Hey, bud," he said when he opened his door and saw my ride. "So you're on another mission, huh?"

I rubbed my bike's seat, "Yeah, well, I picked up this here pretty Philly and want to know how far she'll go."

We hopped into his pickup and cruised to a local pool hall for a game. There I got the true sense that the trip had begun, probably because I was so close to Mexico I could smell it.

While I shot pool, my brain kept running through the game plan for the next morning. Given the fuss my mother had made about the whole motorcycle thing, I'd promised her I'd check out the possibility of taking the train from the border town of Mexicali, Mexico, to Guadalajara, over a thousand miles to the south. At first I wished I hadn't said anything to her; after all, I had the motorcycle so that I wouldn't need things like trains. But after some thought, the idea began to appeal to me. I wouldn't be surfing the winter waters of northern Baja anyway; I hadn't packed a cumbersome wetsuit. Hypothetically, if I could throw my bike on a train's caboose and rail the opening chunk of the trip, I'd skip past the frigid surf zone and coast right into tropical Mexico.

But first, I'd have to ride to Mexicali, roughly a hundred miles east of San Diego. I figured that if I left San Diego by four in the morning I'd reach the border town around dawn, giving me a brand new day to beg my way onto the train. In theory, it sounded good.

In practice, it was a bitch.

* * *

Falling asleep at Marty's that night was damn near impossible. By the time I finally passed out, my night's sleep ended up as a half-hour nap. Marty had set his alarm at my request.

"Wake up, J.J. It's 3:30, time to fly," I heard through the blurry walls of a dream.

If you're from some other part of the country, don't be fooled: Southern California in the winter, in spite of its temperate reputation, can get cold. Under my denim jeans and jacket I wore longjohns, two tee-shirts, a flannel, two pairs of socks . . . everything I'd brought with me. Walking out of Marty's house to the driveway, I knew I was in for a polar experience.

I pulled on my flimsy rawhide gloves and slid my hand across the seat to wipe off the condensation. It took a hundred kicks to get my bike motivated that morning, but eventually she woke, too. The sound of the engine igniting exploded the silence. The whole neighborhood must have been upset by the tremendous commotion. I said thanks and goodbye to Marty, and made my way through the mellow early-hour streets toward Highway Eight, the road to Mexicali.

Not ten minutes after leaving Marty's, I stopped before entering the highway on-ramp. Pulling the towel from my bag, I rolled it up and tucked it around my neck and under my jacket. The frosty air had already made its way to my skin through the cracks in my clothing.

I was lucky Interstate Eight was free of traffic, because the morning was so darn bitter that I slowed to forty-five m.p.h. to reduce wind chill. Even then, I stopped after twenty miles to thaw my legs and blow heat through my fingers to kill the cold. The road headed east out of San Diego and into a barren desert, cutting through a stretch of high, sandy dunes. The piercing cold had me shivering as I motored on, but my nerves were surprisingly settled by the steady hum of my Honda.

* * *

Out of nowhere, the quiet highway turned into a scene out of *The Road Warrior.* As I was cruising along in the darkness, minding my own business, a strange chill rushed down my already cold spine. Curious, I glanced into my mirror. At that very moment, a bright beam of light bulleted toward me from behind like a speeding comet. The beam rocketed up within inches of my tailpipe and then swerved away, leaving a ghostly streak of fading light in my rear-view mirror.

The comet that had nearly struck me turned out to be a midsized sedan blowing by at over a hundred miles an hour. Now in front of me, the car abruptly launched into violent speed wobbles, and then started full-on fishtailing. The tires screeched as I watched the vehicle whip back and forth on the roadway.

The driver appeared to struggle for control, but it looked as if he had accidentally missed the brake and hit the gas. The car did one last wild tail slide and then shot diagonally across the pavement, sped off the road, and accelerated up a large sand-dune embankment. It climbed higher and higher, to a point where the bank became so steep that something had to give.

I hoped the damn thing would stay up there, but way high on the slope gravity overwhelmed the sedan. It began its decent in a crashing roll. My eyes were fixated on the drama. The whole scene was bizarre. The sound of my engine disappeared, and I heard nothing but the crushing of the car's roof and sides as it bounced down the hill and rolled back down toward the road—toward me.

I could no longer feel myself riding forward. Instead, I had the sensation of just watching the show in a trance. When the car neared the bottom of the bank, my brain switched back on and I instinctively veered to avoid getting tangled in the wreckage. I counted myself fortunate that the car's awkward rolling momentum petered out on the wide dirt shoulder.

In an instant, I grasped what had just happened.

Fearing that someone might've been severely injured, I pulled over, ripped off my helmet, and ran back toward the accident as fast as my frozen legs would take me. A cloud of dust surrounded the vehicle, which I could now make out resting belly-up on its half-sunken roof. The damage to the vehicle was veiled in the shadows behind its still illuminated headlights, which beamed through the haze in two completely different directions. One lamp shone in my eyes, making it difficult to see. But before I reached the wreck, a silhouette appeared hurrying toward me from out of the dusty cloud. A man came into view, shouting frantically, "ARE YOU OKAY? ARE YOU OKAY? ARE YOU OKAY?"

"Yeah, I'm okay. Are you okay?" I replied, for it was he who had just rolled over and over in his car. The instant he knew the only damage had been to himself, his hysterics halted. Silence overtook us as we turned to eye the mess.

I looked at him. "What the hell happened?"

The guy didn't look back, but after a shameful pause he said, "I fell asleep."

Yep, that's what I got for riding at four in the morning. My mind still numb to the facts, I blurted out, "Did you just almost kill me?" I don't know why I said that.

He didn't answer. Now that reality had kicked in and he'd been tossed out of dreamland, the guy appeared to be in shock from the tumble. He had no doubt been wearing his seatbelt, because although his car had been absolutely totaled, the dude didn't seem the slightest bit hurt. We kept staring at the wreck.

Less than fifteen seconds and not one word later, a passing big rig roared up and stopped at the site of the accident. The guy left my side and ran up to the truck's passenger door. He turned to me and said, "Don't worry, my girlfriend lives in the next town!" and climbed into the cab. The truck clanked into gear and vanished. I didn't even get the guy's name.

I now stood alone in the dark, returning my gaze to the demolished auto as the last of the displaced dust settled on my shoulders. *So this is how my trip starts?* I thought. *On this entire stretch of highway, how could a sleeping driver have happened to blindly charge up behind me, full throttle, only to suddenly wake at the last second to avoid snuffing me out?*

This may have put a dent in my whole "safe on a lonely road" theory. I wondered whether some people had been right after all when they'd called this ride foolish, or too dangerous. And I hadn't yet placed a toe in Mexico. I took a deep breath and collected myself. After a moment of silence, I walked solemnly back to my motorcycle and continued toward the border.

Mile after frigid mile passed under my wheels, and soon I noticed the sky brightening to shades of purple, promising dawn's arrival. The idea of a new day excited me, and I rode on without making my usual stops to rest and relieve my frozen limbs. My hands could barely grip the handlebars by the time I finally made it to Calexico, America's answer to Mexicali. There I pulled into a mini-mart gas station to take a good, long break. My bike needed fuel, and I craved a hot cup of Java. It was time for a little celebration . . . and contemplation.

The stint from Marty's house had only taken a few hours, but it felt like days.

The warmth and bright lights of the mini-mart seemed odd after the cold and lonely ride through the dark desert. My icy hands felt a pleasant sting when I placed them on the hot glass of the self-serve coffee pot. When my fingers could move easily again, I poured a cup.

Back out in the graveled parking lot, I paced slowly by my

bike and sipped the bitter black brew. My numb toes, double-socked in my Docs, regained feeling, and the deep chill that had penetrated my bones began to fade. The sky grew lighter. Although the air was still cold enough that I could see my breath, I removed the towel from my neck and stuffed it back into my bag. By the time I'd completely thawed out, the sun was shining in the east.

The sight of the big aged "Mexico" sign at the border entrance pumped me with anticipation. Traffic was minimal in the early hour, and when I rolled up to the mustached officer at the booth he nonchalantly waved me through.

Mexico! I thought, as if I'd never been there before. My first aim was to find the train station. Now that I was actually here riding down the worn streets of Mexicali, the whole train idea seemed lame. But I stuck to the plan, passing through the heart of town looking for signs of life. A few people were just starting to stir. I pulled over next to a leather shop, where a man was pushing open the retractable iron-rod front gate. As I sat on my idling bike, a strong smell of rawhide jumped into my nose. The guy looked at me.

"*Hola. Dónde está el* train station?" I said in perfect Spanglish.

The guy looked confused at first, then answered rapidly, "Blah, blah, blah, blah…blah, blah" and pointed over my shoulder.

Although the Mexican in me wanted desperately to understand all that he'd said, I was clearly dominated by my *gringo* culture; I couldn't comprehend a word. "*Gracias*," I said, pretending to get it, and took off in the direction of his gesture.

Within minutes I was lost. Hearing a mild clunking sound coming from behind me, I turned and saw that my taillight was dangling. One bolt had disappeared, and the red plastic cover had cracked at the base of the other bolt. I grabbed the duct tape my friend had so wisely given me and circled a couple of laps around the seams, securing the cover to its original spot. But though I'd reattached the light cover, it no longer glowed. It occurred to me that the light had died only hours after it had saved my life. Testing the useless light, I didn't know whether to feel lucky or freaked out. I felt both.

I finally found the train station, quiet and empty. A long, weathered, tired-looking locomotive rested on its tracks as I sat and imagined a scene busy with eager travelers anxiously awaiting their turn to board and migrate toward expectant friends and relatives. I parked and walked around for several minutes, finally sitting down on an old bench to relax. Evidently I was early, very early. No train was leaving anytime soon. After some time, I learned that the train wouldn't depart until that evening. I'd have to wait all day to find out whether I could get on the thing. I bailed.

I chose to wait on the U.S. side of the border, where I'd noticed a tourist information center that looked like a good place to gather information. For the second time that morning, my wheels crossed the international border, this time to leave Mexico.

At a little café in Calexico, I ordered a plate of *huevos rancheros* and sat in an empty booth. I slowly forked at the food, but inside I was antsy. Although there was no rush, I felt delayed.

The time came to click into travel mode and forget the clock, with the exception of having to be at the train depot that evening. I mulled around Calexico until late afternoon, and then headed back into Mex.

* * *

People hung around the station as the daylight fizzled out. Exploring the crannies of the train, I eyeballed a spot between car and railing where my bike could easily fit. The hard part would be persuading the boss man to agree with me.

A short round man in uniform approached.

"*Mira aquí, para mi moto.*" I pointed to a possible area for my bike.

The conductor shook his head, "*No es possible.*"

"*¿Por qué?*" I argued softly.

"*Porque* blah, blah, blah, blah" he rattled off.

I'd had enough Spanish practice. "Okay, wait. Do you speak English?"

"Where you want go?" he asked in broken English.

"Well, I'm headed to Costa Rica. But I'd like to ride this train as far south as I can."

Boy, was that a mistake. The man grimaced.

"Huh? Go where? I never hear this. It is impossible. You cannot ride your motorcycle to Costa Rica!" He slapped the back of one hand into the palm of the other. "Where is the permit for this vehicle?"

"Permit?" . . . Crap. I had totally spaced on the fact that I needed one. I'd driven to Mexico a hundred times and had gone as far south as Cabo San Lucas; never before had I ever got no stinking permit.

"Where do I get one?" I asked, pleading ignorance, which wasn't difficult. By this time I hoped the conductor would feel sorry for me and agree to let me ride the train.

"At the border," he said smugly.

"If I go get one, can I ride on your train?"

"NO!" He felt about as sorry for me as a homeless guy feels watching a billionaire's mansion burn. After denying my request, he left to attend to other business.

I quickly got over the whole train thing and didn't kick myself for trying. After all, I'd only burned one day. Besides, leaving without a permit could've caused unnecessary hassle down the line. So, in a way, the train idea had helped.

I left the station and cruised through the dark streets of Mexicali and back to my homeland. Fortunately for me, a security guard patrolled the parking lot adjacent to the entrance to Mexico, so I wasn't too worried about leaving my bike briefly unattended. I slung my bag over my shoulder, grabbed my board off its racks, and walked to a small office at the border.

With its faded baby-blue paint and a long, bare, chest-high counter, the room resembled a version of a back-country United States Post Office. Inside, another *gringo* sat working on a permit of his own. But he left in a flash, apparently in a rush to get somewhere.

The two men in the office turned their attention to me, and a very simple process took place. I handed one of the officials my passport, the bike's pink slip, and ten U.S. dollars, the price of the permit. He stamped my passport twice, one for me and a different one for my bike. He scribbled the bike's info on the stamp and gave me a shiny little sticker to stick someplace visible on the bike's frame. I could now legally ride to any corner of Mexico for up to thirty days.

When I stepped out of the office, my skin got a dose of the dropping temperature. Although I now held a vehicle permit, I faced the onset of a brand new night—not an ideal start. I wasn't about to fork out thirty bucks for a motel, but attempting to ride into the Mexican darkness would've been lunacy.

Near the parking lot, about thirty feet from Mexico, a small patch of grass under a huge floodlight looked nice and cozy. I pitched my small coffin-sized bivy tent and crawled inside. Like the night before, I put on every article of clothing in my bag—longjohns under jeans, under walking shorts, under boardshorts. I slid the cover off my surfboard and stuffed myself into it. The board took half the space in the cramped tent, but she was sleeping with me, safe from thieves. Prior to that, I'd never snuggled a piece of fiberglass before in my life, I swear. Unfortunately, it didn't keep me any warmer. It didn't take long for my toes to begin to stiffen.

Night crept on, and I realized that sleep was to be no more than an elusive fantasy. I tried to keep my eyes shut, but the same floodlight that had originally made me feel safe now began playing pranks on me. Strange faint shadows would appear on the nylon walls of my tent, and every so often I unzipped the door and peeked out, only to find nobody there. I hadn't rested for three nights, and my sleeplessness played havoc with my imagination. After hours of lying there freezing, I got up and packed my bike before dawn had a chance to crack.

Pacing in the parking lot to try and circulate cold blood gave me time to think. I had to make a decision. At this fork in the road, I could either continue heading east toward the Mexican mainland or go south, down the Baja.

I was drawn to the Baja peninsula because it was familiar territory, and once at the bottom I could take the ferry to Mazatlan. It seemed like a good way to break myself in. The only hang-up was that I'd just ridden a hundred miles inland from good old Mexican Highway One, the only paved road that traverses non-stop from northern to southern Baja, where the Gulf of California and the Pacific Ocean collide.

Mexicali happened to be directly above San Felipe, where the black line impersonating a road on my crappy tourist map of Baja California ended. There was on the map, however, a distinct grey line crossing the heart of the Baja desert and connecting the road from San Felipe to Highway One.

Hmm, must be a decent enough road to bother putting it on the map, I thought. A rough estimation with my thumb and index finger suggested the distance of the grey line couldn't be much more than a hundred miles. It was a dubious choice, but I decided to tap into Mexico through the Baja peninsula.

Leaving the parking lot, I crossed the border and motored confidently through a quiet and sleeping Mexicali. Within minutes the desert opened up to a landscape wide and precarious. Huge boulders and cacti lay scattered as far as the eye could see, and a hazy outline of low mountains in the distance resembled a cardboard backdrop set in some cheesy 1960s Western. I finally had the impression I was getting somewhere.

The sun peeked over the horizon and instantly killed the chill in the air. I breathed new life, thrilled to be pushing forward. Just motoring down the highway listening to the engine and watching my front tire drive me across the open desert felt action-packed, as though I were riding in the days before they sank a bullet in the last buffalo on the American frontier.

Traffic on this stretch of highway was nonexistent, and the solitude heightened my senses. My mind bent to the contorted pitchforks of the cacti, and my body felt the road's every dimple under my wheels. Now it was just me and the Honda.

Forty miles down the road, a red-stained Pemex gas station came into view in the lonely desert. Because you never knew how far it would be to the next one, I had vowed never to pass one up. The morning had already heated up, and I disappeared around the back of the station keeper's shack to strip off my longjohns, top and bottom. After I returned to the bike, the mustached man who ran the place asked the old standby question.

"*Adónde vas?*"

I had learned from the train conductor's reaction that revealing my final destination was unnecessary and could be confusing. And who in Mexico cared, anyway? To keep things simple, I just blurted out the name of the next big town on the map.

"San Felipe." It was the absolute truth.

At the Pemex, my confidence level rose with the quantity of gas in my tank. I felt a certain ease after the fuel-up, as if I'd given my horse a much needed drink.

A gentle breeze started to groom the desert floor.

As I adapted to riding in this raw environment, my mind wandered. Suddenly, the harrowing incident of two nights earlier replayed in my head like a broken DVD—the car on Highway Eight that had almost wiped me out and the stigma it would have left had I been killed. Mom and Dad would have been pissed, calling my stupid dreams a worthless waste of life. As for me, peering down through a cloud at those reading the obituaries in the paper, knowing my fantastic journey hadn't lasted two lousy hours out of San Diego, I'd have been, well. . . *embarrassed.*

My thoughts returned to the road, and I noticed that the breeze had increased. Soon, sand lifted and tumbleweeds rolled. Over the next hundred kilometers the wind grew stronger and stronger, until it became a force to be reckoned with. I had to lean into the sudden gusts to avoid being blown off the road.

This combat with nature diminished my speed. My speedometer read forty-five, thirty-five, twenty-five miles per hour and falling. The surfboard on my side wasn't helping. As my light bike succumbed to the bullying of my other mother, Mama Nature, I wished for a heavy Harley Hog.

The wind was as relentless as a fire-spreading Santa Ana howling through southern California's Cajon Pass. The sand pelted my jeans as I watched it blast across the desert surface. Occasionally, I'd stop and place both feet on the ground to stabilize, inching forward between violent gusts.

I was in desperate need of shelter.

Then, in the distance, I saw a sign. Not from God, but planted by Mexican entrepreneurs hunting for tourist dollars. "Camping, 8 kilometers ahead."

Oh, good, I thought, and with new optimism I crept forward.

It took me almost an hour to cover the eight kilometers, fighting to make my way through the unfriendly blow. I finally arrived at the so-called campground, only to find nothing more than vacant desert on the shores of the wind-frothed Sea of Cortez. There wasn't even a stinking outhouse to hide behind. Maybe I had missed the holiday season? The sight of water was a good sign, though, indicating that I was closing in on San Felipe.

Several hard-earned kilometers later, a decrepit trail led to an oasis—a neglected-looking cement house. Something told me to investigate. I couldn't pass up an opportunity to retreat from the wind.

The struggle to reach the lee of the abode,—or should I say, adobe?—had me sweating and cursing in my helmet. The sand was softer than I'd expected; the further I rode down the trail, the deeper my wheels sank. I had to punch the throttle and kick up mountains of dirt to make progress toward the weather-beaten structure. My laborious trudging paid off when I reached my refuge of a wonderfully shaded and wind-shielded cement slab patio. Boy, I couldn't have felt more relieved.

I mocked the wind from the safety of shelter and turned to inspect an entrance that at one time had boasted a door.

"Whoa!" The entry led into a dungy living room, lit only by the sun's rays creeping through two tattered curtained windows. Piles of broken furniture and shattered glass littered the floor. Debris crunched under my boots as I searched each room to make sure I was the only tramp prowling the grounds.

I found an old mattress in one of the closets and drug it into the kitchen, the brightest spot in the house. The adrenalin faded from my exhausted bones. A peaceful breeze slipping through a busted window made me drowsy, and the fatigue from the past few sleepless days hit me all at once. Taking off my denim jacket and rolling it up for a pillow, I laid my body down on the mattress and passed out, hard.

My eyes eventually opened to a setting sun, and I was surprised to see that the raging winds had subsided to a delicate breeze. The sand had settled, and a bright orange color lit the western sky. It was turning into a nice evening. I spotted San Felipe in the distance and guesstimated it at a distance of roughly five miles. Close enough to fetch dinner and get back by dark. I stashed my gear deep in a closet and headed for the dry streets of the small desert haven. This time I knew to expect the quicksand trail, and rode on the harder ground along the side.

For a hoot, I looped around the main drag before parking next to a roadside taco stand. A chubby cook in a white apron was catering to three locals eating at a long wooden table. I sat unsociably on the bench seat at the table's far edge, hoping for a quiet meal and quick return to my hideout.

My stomach rumbled from not eating all day, and the savory smell of fresh fish and garlic made me even hungrier. The cook acknowledged me, and I flashed a peace sign. "*Dos, por favor,*" I said, ordering a couple of tacos. He grilled some seasoned fish till it sizzled and placed it on to two warmed tortillas. Then he squeezed a lemon wedge over the steamy chunks, wetting the meat with its juice. Next he sprinkled on chopped onions and cilantro. Finally, he added diced tomatoes and jalapenos, and topped them with guacamole-type saucy stuff. He put the plate in front of me and said, "*Buen provecho.*" That meant "Enjoy."

They were almost too beautiful to eat. In the end, I put away six of them.

I hadn't a clue as to what to expect the following day, but judging by the map and what I'd ridden through thus far, I had the notion I'd see stints with little to no civilization. My gut told me to carry extra fuel. Fortunately for me, an auto parts store was open for business just across the street. After dinner, I bought a one-gallon gas can.

I made it back to my hangout right at dark.

The breeze stayed light and steady as I attempted to fall asleep. This would've been pleasant, had I not been squatting in such a spooky and accessible place. During the night, I was startled several times by what sounded like footsteps trying to sneak lightly across the cluttered floor. *Crunch, crunch.* I'd tell myself it was nothing until I couldn't stand it anymore. With the largest blade of my Swiss knife ready in one hand, and my mini Mag-lite flashing in the other, I crept from room to room to make damn sure no one was lurking in the dark. I found the same thing every time: a torn curtain whispering in a breeze that sounded a lot different close up.

Awww, stop freaking yourself out, man. You're only losing sleep.

While not as restful as my long afternoon power nap, I finally got some *siesta*.

The early morning air was crisp and quiet until I fired up

the Honda. At the gas station in San Felipe, I began to regret my decision to travel down the Baja. If I had started down the west side of the peninsula on Highway One, like I should've in the first place, I'd have been fine. However, since I'd hastily left Mexicali and taken Highway five, which ends in San Felipe on the Gulf of California, I now had to sniff a route across a crude network of shoddy dirt back roads to meet up with Highway One and my link to La Paz. *What if I couldn't find the main highway? What if the road dead-ended? What if I rode in circles?* I had to be optimistic. *Maybe the road's good. Maybe it's even paved. After all, they bothered to mark it on the map.* With my tank topped off, and a spare can to boot, I hopped onto my bike and headed south.

* * *

The highway was much better than I'd expected, the pavement dark and new. A couple of miles later the surface became faded and slightly more rugged, but the ride was still pretty smooth at my steady fifty to fifty-five m.p.h.

My pace slowed when the pavement ended, but the dirt road remained smooth enough for easy, enjoyable riding. Small waterside communities hugged the seaside, with new ones under construction. Future *gringo* vacation homes, I imagined.

The road stayed good for a surprisingly long time. Every now and then, I'd pass a small team of guys building. The stretches of nothingness between neighborhoods grew. About twenty miles south of San Felipe, I stopped at the work site of a half-built house. Men were stacking cinder blocks and bags of cement in the morning sun. They worked at a relaxed pace, without any particular urgency. I noticed a large gasoline drum in the bed of an old Chevy pickup. I thought it a good idea to top off my tank, just to play it safe. The men smiled at me when I rolled up and parked next to the truck.

"*Hola*," I said happily to the whole crew. "Puedo comprar poquito gasoline?"

"*Sí*," said one of the guys. Without another word, he hopped into the back of the truck and handed me the end of a black rubber hose. I unscrewed the cap and held it over my tank while he cranked the circular hand pump on the large drum. Glorious gas poured in.

"*Bien*," I said when the fuel reached the brim.

We'd pumped only a half-gallon or less, so the man didn't want to charge me anything. But I forced him to take ten *pesos,* the equivalent of a dollar, a small price to pay for my peace of mind.

The sun beat down stronger by the second, and I took a short break to shed my longjohns.

After the fill, the dirt road worsened a bit. The background grew increasingly barren before it wound past the last speck of civilization—a farm house. I stopped to discover that this lone outpost served meals in a shaded open patio. I must have missed the morning rush, as I was the only customer sitting at a round wooden table. A short lady with long black braids served beans, rice, and eggs with fire-crisped corn tortillas, charging me an affordable twelve *pesos*. For the first time that morning, I relaxed. The rustic setting and breakfast cooked by an authentic Mexican woman made me realize I was traveling farther from home. The

U.S. of A. was behind me now.

Any comfort I derived from people or shelter dissolved as I rode deeper into miles of treacherous sun-dried desert. I couldn't help but notice my bike beginning to buck on the rapidly deteriorating road. The Honda's gauges shook and vibrated at sudden clashes with wheel-sinking crevices. I slowed.

The contour of the land changed from flat to slightly hilly, and the road dipped in and out of my view. Some of these hills were steep, and maneuvering my heavy-laden bike to the tops through the annoying ruts required total concentration.

I summited one such hill to an odd and daunting sight. The winding dirt track descended in a large half-moon shape, only to be obstructed by a manned roadblock in the distance. It looked military. I cringed. They must have been looking for . . . coyotes or drug traffic? They were right in my way. I had no choice but to confront them.

The barricade consisted of two green canvas-covered trucks and roughly fifteen armed soldiers. I motored up cautiously to the men flanking the track and pulled off my helmet. The commanding officer, who wore enough pins and stripes to make it obvious he was the head honcho, demanded I hand over my passport and vehicle permit. No other words were exchanged as the gentleman eyeballed first my photo, and then me. He ran his stare down the length of my covered board and back before his eyes settled for a moment on my bag. He looked up at me. I sweated nervously under my denim jacket.

I expected to get searched. I was already anticipating the guys foraging through my gear, scrutinizing my reasons for being there.

"*¿Adónde vas?*" asked the man.

"Cabo San Lucas," I lied. If the officer knew anything about tourism, and he should've, he could have guessed the thing at my side was a surfboard and made the connection between it and Cabo's surf culture. That would have made me simply look like an innocent tourist, which I was.

The officer thumbed through the pages of my brand-new passport and studied my bike permit. He looked intently at me again and made a joking comment in Spanish to one of his comrades. The whole company chuckled, and he gathered the documents in one hand and gave them back to me. With an affirmative "*Pasa,*" he waved me through.

I couldn't believe it had been that easy. The other men stepped back as I rode by, oh, so politely. I didn't care why they were there, as long as it wasn't to mess with me.

I laughed at the paradox: I was more bothered by the thought of being detained by human beings than by being totally imprisoned by this wasteland. Common sense told me I had made a bad decision in taking this road. But I'd ridden too far to turn back.

A couple of hours after passing the military check point, things were looking grim. Dry weeds crept up from the ground, and the road branched out in so many places I sometimes wasn't sure which trail to follow. I had little choice but to drive deeper into the sandy vastness.

The midday sun beamed down with a vengeance, and the uneven track made handling the motorcycle a workout. My skin under my jeans grew damp with sweat as I crawled pitifully along, mile after difficult mile. Every time I reached an area that produced a vista, I felt a splash of hope. I wanted so badly to see the elusive Mexican Highway One etched out in the desertscape, with cars rolling merrily along its fine pavement. But the hopeful feeling dried up when I repeatedly faced the same forbidding expanse of endless sand and rock against outlying mountains that stretched as far as my eyes could see.

Just when I thought things were looking bad, they got worse. During a break to relieve my sore rear and exhausted arms, I noticed that the back of my seat where I kept the spare gas canister was wet. The jolting of the bike on the murderous road had split the can slightly at the seams, causing fuel to seep out. I hurried to pour what was left into my tank. Fortunately, the leak had been slow, and the can was still heavy with fuel when I picked it up to add the remaining gas to my tank. Gas was important. I had no idea how many miles I still had to traverse.

What may have worked in my favor was my drag-ass pace. Slow motoring probably kept fuel consumption down to a minimum, although it wasn't the best for making time.

As the afternoon sun leaned toward Japan, I wondered whether I'd taken a sidetrack or a wrong turn somewhere or whether this road would connect with the main highway. I had no way of knowing. Lost in the heart of the inhospitable interior of the Baja peninsula, I cursed my foolishness. Swallowing the last drop from my small water bottle, I wondered whether I'd end up sucking cacti under a hot, cloudless sky. But kicking myself for getting into this situation wasn't going to help me a lick.

I would have to be patient. My only recourse was to stay light on the throttle and let my wheels spin haphazardly in the direction of the descending sun. Oh yeah, and try and stay positive.

Time ticked away. There were moments when I felt like trading in my straining motorcycle for a more conventional camel. Well, that isn't entirely true. My Enduro was in its element, alright, and I would've been plenty comfortable had I come across a damn GAS STATION!

I knew that sooner or later I'd ride up to a sign that read "Hell, next left."

I doubted that this stupid stretch of desert ever got patrolled by the Green Angels, Mexico's version of the AAA Club. Regardless, my bike pushed faithfully forward. And with each bumpy mile, my confidence in her grew stronger.

* * *

As the afternoon progressed, I noted that my ride was feeling less strenuous. The dirt road had actually began to improve. Oh, boy! In the hazy distance a wooden shack appeared, a hint of civilization. I couldn't believe it. I was getting somewhere! My heart orchestrated a beat of hope. Just then my bike sputtered and coughed. I stopped and switched my fuel line over to "reserve." Whatever happens, happens, I thought.

The road led me around a rocky outcrop to a wide-open view of the glorious sight I'd been looking for. Far away, across the landscape, a vehicle traveled steadily down a long paved road. Highway One? YES! All the sweat and worry had paid off!

The dirt track got better and better as I approached the highway, and I rode faster to meet it. At last, after hours of bumpy riding, the weathered Mexican One lay like silk under my dusty wheels. I had no idea where I was on the map, and didn't care. The despair of not having my bearings in the middle of nowhere was gone.

The sun was due to set soon. A few miles up the road, on my right I spotted a large clearing in the desert. A mobile home— some sort of headquarters, I judged—sat far to one side of the property, and alone on the other side sat a large deluxe model R.V.

I rode onto the property and parked close to the R.V. A man who looked to be in his early sixties stood tinkering with the dune buggy that sat on a trailer attached to the R.V. Figuring this guy knew what was up, I went over to say hello.

"How's it going?" I asked.

"Good. How are you?" replied my fellow *gringo*.

"I'm really good," I answered honestly. "I'm guessing this is a campground?" I looked around at the bare piece of property, apparently an overnight spot for transient vehicles.

"Yeah, there's a lady in that place over there. She'll help you." He glanced up to indicate the house on the other side of the grounds.

I walked over and knocked on the door. An old woman opened it. For nine *pesos*, she welcomed me to camp out on the hard-packed desert ground.

Just being there, well, I couldn't have been happier.

The sun dipped below the horizon when I began setting up my tent, and a cloudless lavender sky added to my sense of re-lief. It must have looked like I'd had a rough day, because the door of my new neighbor's palace on wheels flung open and he emerged gripping two *Coronas*.

"I thought you could use one of these," he said with a smile. "I'm Bill."

"Thanks, Bill. Boy, if you only knew." The beer in my hand was icy cold, my parched mouth as dry as a foxtail. I took a long pull. The *cerveza* sizzled down my throat like cool water cascading over a red-hot tailpipe. It went straight to my head.

"My wife's inside cooking. Will you join us for dinner?"

"That'd be great."

"Just come over when you're ready."

He went inside while I finished with my tent . . . and my beer. Fifteen minutes later, I was tapping on the screen door of the R.V.

"Come on in and have a seat," the wife said kindly. She served me a healthy dish of steamy pasta covered in a garlicky red sauce and set a fresh *Corona* next to the plate. "So, how far you going?" she asked.

"Costa Rica," I said. "If things roll a little smoother than today."

They liked the idea, which didn't surprise me, as I could see they were doing some exploring of their own.

I had some appreciation for the joy of traveling around with such creature comforts as they had: lights, heat, air conditioning, fridge, stove, shower, and toilet. No packing and unpacking, no sleeping on lumpy floors. I certainly wasn't biased against other types of transportation, especially given how at ease the home-like setting made me feel. Riding the Honda was fun, but sitting there admiring the plush R.V. setup made it easy to picture myself packing a healthy quiver in a similar huge motor home and remaining comfy for months at some sweet out-of-the-way surfbreak.

We finished dinner, and I thanked my hosts for their warm hospitality as I stepped back out into the crisp air to go lie on the hard surface of my tent floor. I felt lucky to be there, and very much appreciated my escape from the bowels of Baja.

Though I slept horribly on the rock-solid ground, when morning broke I loaded my bike with vigor. Not only had I found a real road, I'd been told by the R.V. couple that a gas station was within reach. My poor bike gasped on fumes when I coasted up to the pump.

A *gringo* in a pickup heading north cruised up to the pump beside me. He looked to be in his early thirties, and took an immediate interest in my bike.

"Cool, man. Where you headed?" he asked.

"Umm, Central America," I murmured.

"No shit? That's wild!" And then, after a pause, "What's your name?"

"Uh, J . . ."

"What, like in James Bond?" he joked, his eyes fast on the motorcycle.

"Not exactly." I felt anything but heroic. In fact, if I were going to be compared to some action hero, I'd have to say I felt more like an Indiana Jones than a James Bond. Whereas Bond used his wit and skill to get himself out of (or into) sticky situations, Jones, it seemed, relied more on pure dumb luck, often taking a good beating in the process.

Still, humbled by my experiences of the preceding days, I kept my conversation with this dude short. I didn't see any reason to burst his bubble and reveal what a dork I had been.

To be on asphalt again with a full tank of fuel and a realistic destination felt nothing short of spectacular. For the first time since I'd left home, the road made sense. After all, with only one lane to follow, I couldn't miss. With the desert whizzing by and my front tire playing its Rough Rider act, I had no doubt I would cover some real ground.

I stopped for breakfast at a small sunlit café in Guerrero Negro. The smell of refried beans and coffee grounds took me back to being a kid sitting with my cousins at my grandmother's kitchen table. She would be cooking and chatting with my aunts in Spanish with a few English words thrown in here and there, but I had rarely understood any of what she said.

Shaking the urge to head south as fast as possible wasn't easy. I figured my friends would be thinking that by now this cowboy would be sipping *Margaritas* in a hammock under a tree in some picturesque village. But it didn't matter; I was the only culprit monitoring me. Delays don't exist when you're not on a time schedule. With the sun's rays warming me through the window, I relaxed and reminded myself not to rush.

The highway traversed the peninsula and Baja's mountainous spine. Eventually I found myself back on the gulf, where serene fishing towns perched along crystal blue waters. Late that afternoon I arrived in Mulege, where I stopped for the night. All my anxiety had faded away, or maybe I was just too damn tired to be wound up. The last few nights had offered little sleep. In desperate need of a good recharge, I splurged on a room. Twelve bucks (in *pesos*) led me to the softest bed I've ever sunk into, and a night of sleep I may never forget. My beat body didn't wake once in ten solid hours of slumber.

In the morning I woke eager to chalk miles, and easily reached La Paz before nightfall. Riding down the streets, it was easy to spot the cheaper lodgings by the condition of their signs. I found a place near the heart of town and lugged my gear through the main entrance. Across the brick-floored lobby, a blonde *gringa* played contently with what appeared to be the house monkey. He'd been chained to a post with enough slack to be interesting. The girl held the little guy like a toddler while his long, black-furred arm reached mischievously for her honey-colored locks, his other arm wrapped tightly around her shoulder.

After dropping my stuff in my room and pushing my bike through the lobby to park it close to my door, I trailed back through the corridor toward the entranceway. The girl I'd seen before walked right up to me.

"Did you see that monkey over there?" she asked. "He's really friendly."

"Oh, that's cool," I said, at a loss for words.

"I think he's a spider monkey," she said.

"Um, yeah, I bet he could be a spider monkey."

"So, you came in today?"

"Yeah . . . I, um, just got here." I didn't know why, but her bright eyes and outgoing approach rendered me uncharacteristically shy.

"I'm Solina. I've been traveling with my dad."

"Good to meet ya."

Solina was tall, sociable, sixteen but could have passed for nineteen, and had a face that made you look twice. She came from the Pacific Northwest and had taken many a trip with her father to Latin countries. Her Spanish was far superior to mine. She invited me to enjoy a "sunset *cerveza*," as they called it, with her and her dad. I said I'd catch up with them after I gathered some info on the ferry to Mazatlan.

I strolled through town to the ferry booth and learned that the ferry departed La Paz three mornings per week. One had left earlier that very same day. I bought a ticket for the following trip, which would give me two nights in La Paz to chill out. I didn't mind the break.

The sun had already set when I arrived at the *cantina*. Solina and her dad, Cole, were sitting at a patio table enjoying the perfect weather. No wind, no bugs, not hot, not cold. I said hello to Cole, a chiseled man in his early forties who sported a five o'clock shadow and a silver hoop through one earlobe. He spoke intelligently and looked like a modern-day pirate—a cool combo in my eyes. The two were traveling in an old Kombi van. I noted an open, free-flowing communication between father and daughter and imagined the wonderful bond they must've shared living a little left of the pack. We chatted over a one-dollar beer and free baskets of tortilla chips. When we finished, I thanked them for the company and left to turn in early.

Sleep became my best friend. Out of the cold at last and into a comfortable bed, I made up for lost dreams, sleeping the whole night through, the second time in a row.

The morning air felt fresh, yet noticeably warmer than up north. The sky looked clean and clear. Rejuvenated, I walked down into the heart of La Paz. Not five minutes later, at a street-side café, I again ran into Solina sitting at an outside table with a guy named Tony, whom she had just met. They asked me to join them for coffee, and I did.

Tony, only two years my senior, was making his way back to the States from Cabo San Lucas. Like me, he traveled on min-imal funds. On arriving in La Paz, he'd found a five-dollar room. When he told me that, I got excited. The eight dollars I'd spent for the previous night's room sounded expensive in comparison. Every dollar counted, and I later relocated to his habitación and saved three bucks. Changing rooms paid for sunset *cerveza*.

Having no agenda for the day, the three of us voted to hang together. First we went to the beach and played some volleyball. Then we strolled to the music store to find parts for Solina's gimp guitar. After that, we philosophized over lunch about the many ways to "live." We unanimously agreed that life was a great adventure, and holding back on your dreams would be a shame. I chalked that up to the fact that being far from home gave us added gratification.

The day whizzed by, and before we knew it the time had arrived for another sunset *cerveza*. Again we met up with Cole, who'd spent the day working on his van.

Tony was contemplating his move the next morning. "I'm not sure whether to take a bus or hitchhike," he said. Turning to me, he asked, "How was the traffic heading south?"

"Well," I said, "I saw plenty of U.S. plates. If you are planning to hitch, I'd be happy to give you a lift to the main drag."

The way I saw it, taking Tony the few miles out of town to the intersection of good old Highway One would give him a healthy jolt of ride-generating potential. Not everyone who went to and from Cabo turned off the main highway and into La Paz. It felt good to offer a helping hand, especially since I knew what it was like to travel toting gear without a vehicle.

After our sunset *cerveza*, Tony and Cole wanted to see a movie at the local cinema. Solina and I, on the other hand, felt more like having another beer and playing guitar. Tony traveled with one of the six-stringed instruments, which he had loaned to me. It happened to be sitting in my room.

Solina and I split up from the others and stopped by the store to grab a couple of long-necks before heading to my room to strum some chords.

Solina loved music, and hoped to cut an album of her own some day. She sat atop the small table with the guitar in her lap, her feet resting comfortably on a chair. I took a seat on the bed with my back against the wall and one foot planted on the floor, listening. Under the faint shadows of a cheap light bulb, her cords blending together in sweet harmony behind a pleasantly soft and steady riff, she became absorbed in her own rhythm. She began to sing with poetic depth and beauty, and by the end of the first chorus she had captivated me with a passionate song of young love I had no choice but to believe in. She played as if no one were watching. But I saw her, alright, and secretly fell for her charm.

Solina finished her song and reached for a swig of beer.

I began to think. Here I was, sitting with this girl. I hadn't been under the impression that her father was absent-minded. Why then would he knowingly let his cute daughter of sixteen sit in a small, dimly lit room and drink beer alone with a 22-yr-old—or any-year-old—guy?

Before an erotic thought could pop into my head, I heard a solid knock, knock, knock, on the door. Aha, I knew this man would be keeping tabs on his girl! Cole obviously hadn't spent a heck of a lot of time at the cinema. He entered the room smiling, collected his daughter, and bid me a polite goodnight.

* * *

The next morning, I left my helmet and jacket behind for a lackadaisical run to Tony's hitchhiking post. He clung to the back of the seat of my bike as we rode toward the main highway. The morning air was fresh, and the cool wind brushed against my skin. When we arrived at the crossroads, Tony hopped off and we shook hands. He took a long, admiring look at my ride.

"Good luck on your adventure!" he said.

"Thanks. You, too." I figured he must be expecting a little of the unexpected, himself.

After returning and paying for my five-dollar room, I loaded my gear for the ride to the Mazatlan-bound ferry. Before I set off, a familiar figure walked down the sidewalk toward me. Just as she'd said she would, Solina showed up to say goodbye. My bike idled as she wished me well and gave me warm hug.

"Be careful out there," she said.

"Thanks, I will. Good luck with everything. And keep writing those songs."

She then turned and strolled away. Not once did she look back. Sometimes that's how it is when you make friends on the road. You find that your time is up, often prematurely, and, as this girl had, you simply turn and walk away.

Nearing the southern tip of Baja on the desolate ride to the ferry, I enjoyed the clash of desert and sea. The ferry terminal loomed large, jutting up from the barren landscape, and I stopped at the manned gate leading into the dusty parking lot. In front of the terminal, I saw two other motorcycles decked out with travel gear baking in the mid-morning sun. How about that, I thought. Other riders.

A tall, broad-shouldered guy in a heavy-duty motocross outfit stood near the bikes pinching a lit cigarette. He had a burly air about him. The dude looked like he could ride through a hurricane! He spotted me at the gate and we exchanged a biker-to-biker wave. At first, I didn't see his fellow rider seated on the shaded steps of the terminal, a guy with a shaved head who sat licking an ice cream cone.

The man working the gate checked my ticket, and I rode straight up to the other bikes and parked. Pulling off my helmet, I gave the lead rider a cheery "Hey there!"

He smiled. "Where ya headed?" He spoke with an accent I couldn't quite pinpoint.

I set my helmet on my seat with confidence. "Costa Rica."

"Really?" The guy eyeballed my old bike and shook his head and chuckled. "Man, you've got guts going on that thing." The remark was a joke to him, but a compliment to me . . . sometimes I was a stupid kid.

"Maybe so, but I got this far," I said. "What about you? How far you going?"

He turned his head to the south, and with his smoke in his hand he made a swift arc gesture in the direction of the equator.

"Thrrreeewwwt," he whistled. "We're going all the way. Tierra Del Fuego, Chile. It's been my lifelong dream to ride down the Americas."

Listening to him, I had little doubt they'd make it.

His name was Omar, and he'd masterminded their trip, or so I gathered. Motorcycles were paramount in Omar's life. He had raced competitively and was well versed in bike anatomy. He and his buddy, Zachary, were Israeli. Every Israeli must complete two years of mandatory military service, and these boys had had to pay their patriotic dues before considering an excursion of this magnitude.

Omar had rallied up a partner in Zachary, taking care to choose someone adventurous and durable. They'd worked in L.A. to finance their journey, Zachary cooking for cash in restaurants and Omar, appropriately, working as a bodyguard protecting such high-profile stars as Michelle Pfeiffer, whom he described as "a cool chick."

Our dusty bikes were the only vehicles in sight. All the cars, trucks, and buses bound for Mazatlan were waiting in line on the other side of the terminal. The ferry crew had told us to hold till last, which gave us the opportunity to chill.

The Israelis and I clicked right away. Both boys were easy-going and friendly, and we joked and laughed from the get-go. After an hour of hanging out, Omar made an observation.

"You know, there's safety in numbers. Perhaps we should ride together, at least for now."

That sounded sweet, but these guys looked tough to tail. "Yeah, I'd like that. But I can only cruise at fifty-five. Sixty, tops." I didn't want to stress my baby out, though I had a stubborn tendency to crank the throttle. I often had to ease off when I'd glance down and catch the speedometer needle pinned in the red past sixty-five, the last number on the dial. Speed, or rather my lack of it, would be their core objection to riding with me.

"Well," Omar said, compromising, "there's no reason we couldn't slow it down. Besides, it is safer." He knew as well as I that something as horribly simple as a pothole could flip your day upside-down. At slower speeds, the road's imperfections were maneuverable. Not to mention the livestock that roamed the highways—dogs, bulls, and chickens all shared the lanes. You had to be especially alert approaching towns and villages.

We became a team. The fact that we had ended up at the same spot on the same day baffled me. It turned out that both the Israelis and I had originally planned on boarding this ferry several days earlier, but neither of us had gotten the start we'd planned on. While I'd played musical border crossings and hide and seek with the ambiguous highways of Baja, they'd been dealing with a few unforeseen delays of their own. However it had gone down, coincidence or fate, I was happy we'd met.

The ferry was scheduled to sail overnight and arrive in Mazatlan the next morning. I'd been on similar ferries in Indonesia, but never before with my own wheels. After loading the larger vehicles, a ferry worker ushered the three of us aboard with a wave. Finding a secure spot for the motorcycles was our problem. Our trio split up in the maze of parked vehicles, and I tucked my bike in a crack between a truck and an auto. By the time I'd unstrapped my bag and shouldered it, the ferry had departed the dock.

Once at sea, we regrouped on the top deck to enjoy the ride. Amongst the many Mexicans, we ran into an interesting mix of travelers, including a vanload of Italian surfers and a couple of dudes from Arizona sightseeing in a pickup truck. We *gringos*, including the Italians, congregated to flap our gums in English.

The wind increased as we chugged out to open sea. Hours later, when half the sun hid below the horizon, the air grew cold. The flock of *gringos* scattered and fled for warmth. I put on more clothing and headed to a remote part of the boat. The frigid breeze added a dramatic touch as it whipped through my hair and whistled in my ears. I leaned lazily against the railing and satisfied my urge to look down. The rhythm of the large boat splashing over the water's deep blue lulled me into a stony state of mind. I imagined floating high in the sky—really high, where earth's atmosphere meets space—and tried to envision the size of the planet. My flying self rode the thermals in pursuit of the glow of the setting sun as orange clouds and jagged continents passed underneath, and I marveled at the huge curvature of the slowly spinning earth.

When I snapped out of that, I thought of my new biker friends. A comforting thought. The whole safety in numbers concept kicked in. Who wanted to be robbed, beaten up, bike-less, and left for dead in some strange part of the world?

It was day's end, and the sun finally sank below the sea.

* * *

Everyone retreated inside for the night, except us. Preparing to sack out on the deck, Omar and Zachary pulled out their down sleeping bags. They crawled inside and zipped the bags up over their heads. They looked warm. In an attempt to join my new comrades and confront the night head-on, I did my usual "wear every article of clothing I owned" trick and used my deflated backpack as a pillow.

The skimpy towel I used as a blanket provided virtually no comfort or warmth, and as the temperature continued to plummet, I froze. After a long attempt at sleep, I looked up to see the Israelis motionless in their windproof cocoons. Good grief! I knew I wouldn't get any rest in that windy mess. This act of brainless bravado could only last so long. The time came to retire the towel. Defeated by Mother Nature yet again, I rose to my feet and slipped into the main cabin.

What a difference! Within seconds my body warmed up to sleeping temperature.

Dimly lit and quiet, the cabin floor was carpeted with bodies. Chairs pushed together formed makeshift beds, and families snuggled close on the ground. I scooted a small plastic bench to a wall and balanced myself atop it in fetal position. It wasn't a superb night of sleep, but once out of the cold I drifted in and out of consciousness to the rocking of the ship.

By the time I returned to the deck the next morning, Omar

and Zachary were up, packed, and ready to ride.

I looked at Omar. "Damn, you made it through the night!"

He grinned. "We're rough, tough and ready for anything."

I believed him.

* * *

Overnight, the air had turned semi-tropical. Our ferry was nearing land, and the sight of palm trees and lush greenery provided a stark yet refreshing contrast to the dry desert we had left behind. One by one, the *gringos* appeared on deck. Everyone buzzed with excitement when the ferry pulled into port in Mazatlan.

The Israelis and I talked about how we'd ride. Single file sounded safest, with Omar, the most seasoned rider, in front; me, on the smaller bike with a busted taillight, in the middle; and Zachary bringing up the rear.

Getting off the ferry was a crazy mess. We were sucking fumes, and horns blared galore. To top it off, my bike wanted to sleep in. It took some serious kicks in the gut to fire her up. I ended up last off the ferry.

Our first encounter with Mazatlan's bustling traffic saw Omar going head-to-head with a semi. Omar's error. He'd jumped the gun at a traffic light, and then had to slam his brakes as the truck swung left in front of him. He back-peddled cautiously and eased out again when the path cleared. It was scary to watch. The near collusion reminded us that the Mexican drivers don't brake for bikes.

* * *

We had all skipped the foul ferry food, and were starving

by the time we stepped onto dry land. Zachary had made plans for us to dine with the Italians. We found our way out of the city and onto the wide-open highway, where their van came roaring past us. They stopped at a rural roadside *comedor* and grabbed a bench table under a tattered tarp. We pulled up and joined them.

The non-English-speaking cook served us gristly mystery tacos. Our dog-meat jokes would've been funny had there not been several bony mutts skittishly sniffing about, scavenging scraps. We hoped the poor pathetic pooches hadn't been driven to cannibalism. Regardless, we had trouble stomaching the tacos and not one person ate his fill. That's rare for a team of hungry men.

Back on the road, we were once again overtaken by the Italian mob. As they raced by, one of them stuck his whole torso out the window and snapped photos of our trio riding motorcycles. Then the van disappeared ahead of us and out of sight, never to be seen again. To this day, I wish I had just one of those precious pictures.

At our first fuel stop on mainland Mexico, the Israelis and I were resting by our bikes when a pickup truck pulled up on the other side of the gas pumps with a crowd of guys and one girl in the back. The driver got out and headed into the little store. All of a sudden the chica hopped out of the back and focused her utmost attention on our three-man crew. Striking a pose, she hollered in a thick Mexican accent, "Are you bikers? I *liiiiiiiiike* bikers!" She totally knew what I had at the side of my bike, too. "Are you surfers? I *liiiiiiiike* surfers!"

While she was saying all this, the driver returned to his

truck. The flirty girl's male friends seemed annoyed, and the pickup almost drove off without her. The second the truck started to roll, the chica jumped into the back. We laughed at the whole scene. It had happened so unexpectedly.

Back on the road, we came to a toll road that must have been either new or freshly redone. The jet-black asphalt was as smooth as a bowling ball. The road ascended into mountainous terrain, and our course began to twist and bend. Once in the mountains, I found it difficult to keep up with the blazing Omar. He knew his motorcycle well, and throttled through his turns. I lost ground. Behind me, I knew Zachary felt the pace lagging.

At our next break, he made a comment. "J.J., you need to lean into your turns more."

I knew I could no longer blame my conservative riding on the extra weight or the surfboard. These guys carried twice the gear I did. Now that I was traveling with company, riding like a pansy wouldn't do. I'd have to get with the program and ride with some gusto (This may sound like foolish machismo, but hey, I'm a guy, and sometimes I can't help it).

After our break, I studied Omar as he sped around one bend after another, leaning confidently into his turns, and did my best to follow suit. It was time to get into a groove with my motorcycle and dirty-dance with her. With every turn now, I dipped down a little more toward the pavement. The roaring engine and the road twisting under my tires gave me the feeling of racing on a track.

That's when I got carried away.

During one of my efforts to get lower, gravity reasserted

itself as my front tire slipped on the pavement midway through an especially tight turn. I was lucky, though; the tread re-gripped the ground a split second later, saving me from going down. But the slide had scared the living hell out of me. Right then, the race ended. I would have to learn to find my comfort zone in a turn.

I had become aware of a light rattle developing somewhere in my bike. Hoping the discomforting sound would go away on its own, I rode on.

We rode until we came out of the mountains and back down to sea level at a pleasant beachfront R.V. park, a hangout for re-tired Americans and Canadians fleeing the chilly northern win-ters. The spot could've been mistaken for a tropical island. It had all the trimmings: sand, palms, and ocean. For a buck apiece we parked our bikes safely among the motor homes and pitched our tents on the beach.

A few of the old-timers took quite an interest in our wheels, watching as Omar and I inspected my bike for the source of the rattle.

"Look here, the chain is loose." he said. Then he noticed my rear tire slightly off-kilter. "Here's the real problem," he said. "We've gotta straighten this thing out."

The bumpy ride across the Baja interior had tweaked the wheel, stretching the chain out. We adjusted the tire back as far as it would go, but the chain continued to hang limp. We would have to remove a couple of links. We decided to leave that for the following day.

We stopped messing with the chain, and Omar gave me a crooked smile. "Oh, and by the way, your headlight is out."

"Really? I wonder when that happened."

"Don't know," he said. "I don't recall ever seeing the thing lit up in my rear view."

"I probably lost it when my taillight went out back in Mexicali."

* * *

Omar, Zachary, and I were the joint's sole patrons at the small restaurant down the street from the R.V. Park. A *señorita* sauntered over to take our order. The boys remained quiet, so I took it upon myself to speak for the group. "*Buenos noches. Dos cervezas y una Coca, por favor.*"

The Israelis looked at me like I'd just ordered in Hebrew. Zachary said, "You didn't mention you spoke fluent Spanish."

"Huh? I don't," I confessed. "I can order a beer, though. Can't everybody?" I hadn't realized they didn't speak a lick.

"Well, that sounded like Spanish to us," he said.

All this time, they'd been getting by on what English the Mexicans knew. Even so, I refused to pretend to be able to rap the Latin lingo.

"Hey, now, I know just enough to get myself into trouble, that's all."

That didn't matter to them. They appointed me translator until they beefed up their vocabulary. It felt nice to be useful.

* * *

I slept well that night. The warm air, the soft sand under me, and the gentle lapping sound of the ocean combined to make my tent a sleeping haven.

In the morning one of our new Canadian neighbors, Earl,

emerged from his R.V. and walked our way, bringing with him coffee and conversation. We sat down with him on a bench by our bikes.

"I admire you kids," he said in a crackling voice, his short white mustache jiggling as he spoke. "You know, when I was your age I wanted to do something like you're doing. But then I met old Gerta over there, and well, soon after, we got married and had kids and all that business. Life's been good to us."

"That's nice," we said, sipping our coffee. None of us knew a thing about having wives or children.

"Keep it up, boys, you're doing it right." He ogled our bikes as he talked. "Live as much as you can while you're young. The years go by fast. I'm telling ya, grab life by the balls or it'll get away from ya!"

By now, Earl had us gazing at our wheels and nodding in agreement. His speech sounded far better than the "When you gonna get a real job?" speech I once got from my bitter grandfather.

After Earl's pep-talk, I thanked him for the coffee and hopped onto my bike to scout out a mechanic for the slack chain that jangled loudly as I motored down the highway.

I hadn't gone far before I spotted a hand-painted plywood sign along a mellow backcountry road with the word *Mecánico* emblazoned on it. Behind the sign, a lone brown-skinned man plucked weeds from the rich soil of his front yard. He looked up and cracked a friendly smile.

I wasted no time. "*Buenos Dias, Señor. Mi moto está* broken."

The mechanic assessed the damage and blurted something in Spanish. I had little choice but to trust him. He rolled my bike to an oil-stained cement slab behind his house, removed the chain, and grabbed a chisel and a heavy rock. At his bidding, I held the chisel steady while he carefully but forcefully pounded a few links loose. He then rewrapped the chain around the sprocket and properly adjusted the tire with a rusty wrench. The repair looked pretty darn good.

"Un momento," I said, and took off for a quick test drive down the street. Everything worked fine. The rattle had died. When I returned to settle up, I expected him to hike the price for the job. To my astonishment, the man only charged me thirty *pesos*—three bucks.

More than satisfied, I handed him extra for his trouble.

With my bike back in action, I returned to the campground with the urge to hunt for waves. Seeing that Omar and Zachary had partaken in a croquet-type game with the snowbirds, I snuck past everyone, grabbed my surfboard, threw it onto its rack, and zipped away.

Unfortunately for me, the Pacific lacked swell that day. I got skunked. I didn't mind, though; sniffing around deserted beaches was enough to satisfy my inclination to try to find surf. I pulled up to one spot where the land rose from the shoreline, forming a protected cove with a crescent-shaped beach. The scene had the essence of the Caribbean.

I returned to camp at sunset, dry but happy.

* * *

The next day, the Israelis and I continued on our journey

south. As the miles passed, the vegetation seemed to grow dens-
er. Or maybe I just started paying closer attention to it.

After many tiring hours of riding, we arrived at the edge of
a small coastal town in the Mexican state of Colima. I knew of a
surf spot near the town and had purposely led the boys there and
convinced them to stop for the night. Looking across the beach,
I saw the Pacific producing punchy chest-high peaks. My heart
started to pound. I was finally going to get some waves!

The boys guarded our gear while I scouted out a room. A
brisk walk with an occasional skip in anticipation of the trip's
maiden surf session led me to a perfectly shabby beachside inn
that promised a cheap night's sleep. A red-eyed Mexican surfer
dude opened the door to a room with a sheetless double bed and
bare cement walls.

"Five dollars," he said.

"There are two more of us," I said.

"Eight dollars."

I bolted back to tell Omar and Zachary. "Okay, I found a
place. You can have the bed. I'll take the floor. Let's go!"

The Israelis couldn't understand the rush. We parked in front
of the room, and they casually pulled their gear from their bikes.
Not me. I unloaded like a spastic and hurried into the room to
change from boots and jeans into boardshorts. After sliding my
new board from its cover, I bit the cellophane wrapper off my
only bar of wax, waxed up, and sprinted down the beach.

Though it had been but a week and a half, you'd have
thought I hadn't been in the water in years. After a practically
useless two-second stretch of the muscles, I jumped into the

ocean with my new board and ducked under a wave. The warm water instantly massaged my skin. My mind thought of my surfing buddies back home and the frigid California winter ocean temps I knew they were enduring.

Right away, I snatched a belly-high wave and methodically pumped down the line to feel out the new board. The wave grew steeper, so I started to dig into the face to build speed. With a nice close-out section forming in front of me, I dropped down and pushed hard off the bottom and gave the lip a good blast. *Bammo!* I was stoked on the board already. She did what I asked of her with ease. I paddled back out and sat in the lineup. My attention veered to the Mexican countryside and an adventurous feeling gushed through me. Surfing in a foreign land had a rawness that I loved. Like riding the bike, being in the water made me feel alive. I continued catching waves and getting to know my board until dark.

Back in the room, Zachary had boiled pasta on his portable stove, and over dinner we discussed the following day's agenda.

Omar sat with an unlit cigarette dangling from his mouth. "We're taking off for Acapulco at first light," he said. "It'll be a long day's ride." He looked at me. "What do you think? Are you coming?"

The mediocre surf here wasn't good enough to part me from my pals so soon. I enjoyed riding with them.

"Yeah, I'm coming."

"Good. Then let's get some sleep."

* * *

We loaded our rigs to the new-day sound of cockling roosters. But the real ruckus came when we fired up our motorcycles and roared off. After a quick pause to top off our tanks, we didn't stop for a hundred kilometers.

The lengthy stints between rest stops began to take their toll. I'd see Omar up in front stretching out his legs and adjusting his position on his seat. Meanwhile, I contorted into new comfort zones of my own, leaning forward and resting my upper body weight against my bag to relieve the pressure off my sorest body part . . . my *nalgas*.

On long rides, my mind wandered. Hours of paying attention to the road fostered a hypnotic fuzziness that forced me to daydream. Off-the-wall stuff I hadn't thought about in years replayed in my mind: things like banditos, corruption, tacos, tequila, and the time my friend Weaver was out on a date and ended up in a hassle with a much bigger man.

We were kickin' on his front porch in downtown Huntington Beach sipping a Ketel One and Tonic when he told me what had happened. "Yeah, the guy was huge," he said. "His hands were like a lumberjack's. I was afraid he was gonna kick my ass, so I threw him across a table."

When I'd first heard him say that, I'd had to think for a second. *What?* Then I'd remembered who I was talking to. Without trying, Weave had a way of making me laugh with his recitations of life's ironies.

"Yeah, man, it was my third date with this Asian girl, and I really liked her. She was nice. So anyway, I was meeting her friends for the first time. They all went to UCI, and dressed perfect and proper, and drove little BMWs and Mercedes, and wore perfume and bright bracelets, and had manicured nails. And we all met up at the bar at one of those strip mall family restaurants in Irvine."

So now I'd learned that everything had taken place at a family restaurant, in Irvine. In a sick way, that made his story even funnier. At first I'd thought the incident had happened in a place where you'd expect a bar fight, like at a biker bar, not at a sports bar in a family restaurant.

Weaver went on. "Yeah, and when you walk in there's all these booths around, filled with families with their kids. They've got their crouton-covered salads, and their pizza, and lemonades and iced teas and stuff. And it's just super-ultra-conservative."

So Weaver had met up with his date and a few of her friends for a casual drink at the restaurant bar, and so far so good. They were chatting and getting to know each other.

He said, "Everyone's doing fine, just kicking back, when all of a sudden this great big man comes up behind me. He's kinda like looking over, and leaning over, and he's all drunk, and he puts his hand on my shoulder."

In addition to Weaver's group, he said, there were a couple of college girls eating a pizza on the next stools over. Weave told me he'd had his back to the two girls, and the guy had leaned on him in an attempt to flirt with them.

"This big ol' man was leaning over and reaching for the girl's pizza scoop, like he wanted to be funny and serve them their pizza. And the dude's a giant. He's about six-four, and his hands have these great big sausage fingers. He's a monster, and just as drunk as can be. He's leaning on me, holding his balance by putting his hand on my shoulder. The girls next to me are obviously annoyed. The guy's like fifty-five years old, you know, a full-grown man. He shouldn't have been chatting up college girls."

Weaver had gotten irritated with Sausage Fingers when the guy said to him, in his big, robust voice, "You don't mind, do you?" (About leaning against Weave's shoulder.)

"Yeah dude, I *do* mind," Weave had said. "I don't need you leaning on me. You're bugging everyone here. Why don't you just go away and leave us all alone?"

Sausage Fingers didn't completely leave everyone alone. He backed off a bit, but was still lingering around.

"He thought he was some WWF wrestling guy and could do whatever he wanted."

Weaver had asked the bartender to do something about the disruptive dude, but the barkeep had shunned the request. Finally, Weave had asked to speak to the manager.

"So I told the manager, hey, this guy's really drunk and he's harassing these girls, and he's harassing me. Would you please do something about it?"

The manager had semi-blown off the situation and said it was no big deal. He dealt with Sausage Fingers by seating him at the far end of the bar and feeding him another drink.

Oh, that's a great solution, Weave thought. *Sit the intoxicated guy to the side and serve him more liquor.*

Leery of the whole scene, Weaver shuffled seats with his date and her friends so that his back was to the big guy. He didn't want to be involved in any conflict; even though he had a hunch things weren't settled.

Sure enough, just as Weave was starting to feel mellow and resume his conversation with his date, he'd felt this large hand grip his shoulder. It was Sausage Fingers.

"You think you're tough," Saus said. "I'll fight you right now! Let's go outside!"

Now Weave was thinking, *Oh, crap!* "I turned around and looked up and thought, *Oh my God, this guy's an ox.* He was huge. He would've killed me. There was no way I was going to walk outside with him and go toe to toe, no way. And besides, I'm figuring as soon as I stand up he's going to hit me anyways. He's not gonna wait for me to go outside."

Feeling like he had no other choice, Weaver had planted his foot on the footrest of the bar and gathered his momentum. With one fell swoop, he'd lashed up with all of his might and punched Sausage Fingers in the face—right in the middle of the restaurant, with its families, kids, and soft music.

"I hit him," Weave said. "Then he took his giant hand and grabbed my throat, trying to choke me. And I hit him again, as hard as I could, *Boom, Boom, Boom!* And he's not even fazed."

Behind the two scuffling men stood a couple of tables filled with people dining. Their attention now, of course, was on the unfolding drama.

"I got him a little off balance, and I grabbed him. Using all my wrestling knowledge, I winged him around. His whole body came off the ground, and he went sliding across the tops of the tables. Cleaned every table. Knocked all the people out of their chairs. All the food and all the drinks fly everywhere. Everyone's horrified!"

Now afraid he had really pissed off Sausage Fingers, Weave jumped over the mess of food and floored bystanders and started kicking the big guy.

"I was just kicking him and kicking him in the restaurant, praying to God that he doesn't get up, 'cause I know he's gonna kill me, and now I'm just looking for an out.".

Two decent-sized dudes had appeared out of the crowd and ripped Weaver away from the fallen Sausage Fingers, who was struggling to get to his feet.

"I look over and the girls I'm with are just traumatized," Weave said. "They're in shock. They've never seen a fight before in their lives. A few minutes later, the dudes walk me outside, and there's like five cop cars, a fire truck, a paramedic, an ambulance—the parking lot's filled with emergency vehicles."

Weave had watched in disbelief as he saw Sausage Fingers being hauled out on a stretcher. "I couldn't believe it. The guy was *fine*. He was just drunk. He was *not* injured."

While the police were questioning him, one of the officers told him Sausage Fingers might want to press charges. Weave looked at the cop. "What!? Press charges? Wait a minute. The guy was bothering everybody at the bar. First I told the bartender he was hassling me. Then I called the manager over and said he was hassling all the girls and everybody at the bar. And all they did was serve him more drinks. And then the guy came over and called me out on a fight and wanted to beat me up. Did you see the size of that guy? He's a giant! I mean, really, do you think I went over there and picked a fight with that guy!? I'm not crazy."

They had finally let Weave go. The people in the restaurant

had vouched for him, telling the police that Sausage Fingers had started the trouble.

Needless to say, the date hadn't gone very well. Everyone went home, and that was the last time Weaver ever saw that cute little Asian girl.

* * *

Much of the Mexican countryside ride passed this way, just thinking. I wondered what was going on inside the boys' helmets, whether they were experiencing the same sort of introspection. Zachary summed it up during a pit stop: "I've thought of everything I could possibly think of . . . twice."

After half the day had gone by, a warming trend on my lower right leg had me concerned about my motorcycle. I worried that the extended riding had stressed out the engine. But more than anything I wanted to keep up with my cohorts, so I didn't mention my troubles during our short rests. To run with these Israeli soldiers on their tuned machines, my bike and I would have to be tough.

Cruising through villages, we were often chased by over-zealous dogs. Omar, leading the way, always got assaulted first. He would coolly let them charge at him, and call their bluff. We'd already learned that they'd usually stop just short of our rolling motorcycles to bark. At worst, a gung-ho mutt could have bitten a boot, but they never did. On one occasion, a daring puppy ran at Omar with all his might, only to over-attack and knock his noggin on the bike's foot peg. The poor pup skidded in three circles on his belly with all four spread to the pavement, then got up and whimpered away. The skinny village dogs didn't have the ferocity of a pissed-off pit bull, bred and fed in the U.S.A.

* * *

As the hours burned by, I could feel my baby's pain. I knew something was wrong. She'd become lethargic. The excessive heat from the motor's right side was baking my calf, but I couldn't stop because we were closing in on Acapulco.

This is beautiful Acapulco? Entering Spanish Harlem, we saw rows of depressed multi-story apartment buildings strewn with laundry lines and clothes drying over balcony railings. Traffic grime had dyed the ghetto walls grey. Motorists lacked consideration for one another, and the streets were pure chaos. Taxi and truck drivers purposely cut each other off. A large, soot-spitting bus broke rudely in on our fragile line. Up ahead, Omar disappeared and reappeared amidst the honking jumble. I finally lost him completely. Nervous sweat bubbled from my skin. Forgetting about Zachary behind me, I focused on steering, braking, and throttling to avoid encountering an abrupt end to this story.

Maneuvering through the mayhem, my greatest anxiety had to do with my bike's diminishing power and her increasing heat that broiled my Levis. I was having to crank twice as hard on the throttle to produce the same amount of thrust as before. Her limited "go" was particularly unnerving when I had to punch it to race through a gap between two buses. Inside my hot-breath-filled helmet, I shouted encouragement to my baby: "Pleeeeease hold on, just a little longer. We've gotta be outta this soon!"

I knew I'd endured the worst of it when the buildings grew progressively nicer and the street teed off and hugged the coast. Oh, man, what a relief. I saw Pacific blue, and up ahead, Omar had pulled over to the side of the road to let us catch up. I stopped behind him, my leg and engine sizzling. Finally, Zachary appeared out of the mess.

Once across *The Streets of Acapulco* and into a mellower part of town, we hunted down the cheapest hotel we could find. The pickings were slim, and we each shelled out a hefty fifteen U.S. dollars to share a third-floor room with one queen-size bed. That felt like big bucks compared to what we'd paid to camp or to rent a dinky room elsewhere, but we were too bushed to bitch. Besides, this room had clean white walls, sparkling tile floors, two comfortable couches, and a hot shower.

As we unloaded our bikes in the parking lot, I clued Omar in about my engine. "Man, the heat could've seared a steak."

"Hmm, let's have a look." He leaned down to inspect. "Ah, I see."

I couldn't believe it. In one second, he'd discovered the problem. The lid to a thing-a-ma-bobber had opened due to a missing bolt. I'm no mechanic, and I wasn't sure how this mechanical hiccup had caused the extra heat. He explained something about the engine getting too much or not enough air.

Omar reached into his tool chest for some baling wire, clipped a piece, and in two seconds had the part jury-rigged together. Holding up the wire, he smiled. "You don't go anywhere without this stuff."

I made a mental note of that. Doubting that my usual method of sweet-talking my bike back to health would've worked in this case, it would be a complete understatement to say I felt fortunate to have Omar nearby.

* * *

Trashed from the ride, we took turns soaking in the shower. Then Omar whipped out some plastic and announced, "If we go somewhere that takes American Express, my father is buying."

Zachary and I looked at each other as though we'd won the lottery. Cool!

The stressful day now behind us, we could at last enjoy ourselves. Walking down a clean, neon-lit street, we felt the buzz of life in Acapulco. We celebrated our survival at the Hard Rock Café.

The boys planned to stay in Acapulco an extra day to take care of personal business. My business involved getting back into the water. A short day's ride away, Puerto Escondido, Mexico's most famous surf spot, beckoned.

Lazing on the couches in our comfy hotel room that night, I made the decision to leave in the morning.

"I'll be heading out tomorrow," I said. "You guys should catch up with me in Puerto. There's plenty of brown beauties on the loose there." I had to use some kind of bait. To my delight, they were into it.

"Sounds good. We'll be leaving here the day after. Look for us."

* * *

I set out by myself at six the next morning, apprehensive yet primed to ride. I had appreciated their company, but had a dumb urge to assure myself I still had the guts to travel alone. I don't know what it was I felt I had to prove to myself.

The road that led me out of Acapulco swung along an impressive towering cliff that plunged into the sea and overlooked some splendid beaches. Away from the bustling city, I finally understood the area's allure. All the same, I was glad to be outta there.

I motored on as I'd done in the Baja, with no one in front of me or behind. My cruising speed lingered at a steady fifty-five m.p.h. Trying not to daydream too much, I gave the highway my utmost attention. Traffic disappeared completely. After a while, the road veered away from the coast and into an arid landscape. Low hills intermingled with big sections of flat terrain, speckled with clumps of palm trees and shrubs that gave it the look of a bad haircut. As usual, barking dogs chased me through the pueblos as the day heated up.

For a while, I felt strong, bold, daring. My bike and I were the Lone Ranger and Silver. But then my ears picked up a faint rattle from below, and I wanted my friends back. I knew damn well what was happening: the old saggy chain thing again. I took it easy, but the irritating noise underneath grew louder.

Wishing I'd stuck with auto shop back in high school, for the next half hour I breathed encouraging words to my motorcycle. "You can do it, baby. Hang in there. We're halfway there."

For a while, I felt I could make it. My bike kept pressing on, the breeze created by riding cooling me off on this otherwise sweltering day. Then, on a mild turn, I heard an upsetting *clunkity-clunk* followed by a sound like that of sizzling bacon. The bike coasted to a stop.

In the absence of my engine-driven breeze, my spirit melted in the sun. *Of course, the day I ride without a mechanic!* I cursed myself for not having hung the extra day in Acapulco. "I'm a moron!" I moaned.

With the bike still alive and idling, I drew a deep breath and set her on her kickstand. Yep, a quick inspection showed the sprockets bare and lonely. The chain had fallen off and lay limp over the engine casing. This was the bad news.

The good news was, the engine screamed when I reached up and pulled the throttle, telling me that at least her innards were sound. I switched her off, and everything was quiet. The silent sun-baked countryside reminded me that I was on my own. I got to work and spun the chain a full length. It remained intact. More good news.

With nothing to lose, I dug my fingers in and lapped the chain completely over the front sprocket, and then as far over the back sprocket as possible. Maybe I could ride the chain back into place, as I'd done with my bicycle when I was a kid.

Things didn't exactly work according to plan. I stepped hard on the kick start and my bike lunged forward, throwing me off balance. My front foot lodged itself awkwardly under the bike, leaving me precious little leverage. I tried to straighten out by leaning and pulling in the direction opposite the unbalanced machine, but it was no use. Having failed to anchor myself to the sky, I plunged sideways toward the ground, the bike between my legs. It all happened in slo-mo. Laboring with all my strength to lower the bike softly, I reached a bare hand out to cushion the descending load from the impending bounce on the pavement. My palm burned on the hot asphalt. At last, the handlebars thumped against the ground.

Sweat had glued my clothes to my body by the time I scrambled out from underneath the bike and lifted her up. To my amazement, the chain was now wrapped around both sprockets. This time when I kicked her over, she fired up like a dream—no lunging forward to screw me up. Okay, please work. I popped her into gear and released the clutch, and my bike rolled forward. I couldn't believe it. My body went limp in relief when I felt the cool breeze from my forward motion.

The disturbing rattle continued down below, but this boy was more than pleased to be moving onward. Cruising with extreme caution, I rode at turtle speed, leant not one bit into the bends, and hobbled into Puerto Escondido in mid-afternoon.

* * *

Puerto Escondido isn't so *escondido* (hidden) anymore. Once a quiet fishing village, Puerto has grown rapidly since surfers first discovered its awesome waves in the 1970s. Playa Zicatela, the heartbeat of the town's thriving surf scene, is famous worldwide for possessing some of the biggest, cleanest beach break barrels on Earth.

Zicatela's mellow, touristy beach road was strewn with sunlit cafes and hotels, from pricy to dicey. I motored up to an empty, open-air tiki-type bar, parked, and tossed my sweaty denim jacket across a stool.

The bartender approached me and smiled. "*Buenas tardes.*"

He couldn't have known how happy I was to see him. "*Buenas tardes, señor. Una Corona, por favor.*"

Under the shade at the bar, I took a swig and looked at my dusty motorcycle parked a few feet over in the sun. The afternoon sea breeze whisked in and cooled my skin. A wave of relief washed over me—I'd frickin' made it!

* * *

The Spanish word *cadena* (chain) stuck in my head like a bad divorce. Armed with my bike's make, model, and serial number scratched on a piece of paper, I rummaged around the town and its outskirts, tenaciously hunting through Puerto's scant Honda supplies for a new cadena. Helpful auto parts clerks telephoned stores in Guadalajara and Mexico City, but the answers all came back the same: "*Nada*." Mexico was out of stock. It seemed my great motorcycle journey had come to an unscheduled halt.

I walked out of the last store and sat on the curb, defeated and depressed. The Israelis would surely ride south into Guatemala without me. All of a sudden, I found the idea of facing the border alone daunting.

Looking up, I spotted a phone booth across the street. It sparked a thought. *Oh, man, I know. My dear old dad!*

I hurried to the booth and dialed "O" for operator. "Um yeah, I'd like to make a collect call."

Luckily, my dad answered the phone. He was all happy. "Hi, Son, where are ya these days!?"

Without a hello, I said, "Dad, listen. Grab a pen. I need the ultimate favor."

My father didn't mess around. The next day, he bought a new chain from an Orange County Honda dealer, drove a hundred miles south to Tijuana, passed through customs with the goods, and sent the package domestic. He said that would shave off heaps of time by avoiding international shipping. The Mexican post had assured him that it would arrive at the Puerto Escondido airport in about a week, but I wasn't so sure.

Temporarily stranded, I waited. But being stuck near a good surf break is like being forced to kiss a beautiful woman.

* * *

Late in the afternoon the day after my arrival, I felt a strange sensation pulling me down to the beach road. I paced around near the sand, and within minutes heard a rumble so deep it sounded like an approaching avalanche. There, amid a light scattering of tourists, Omar and Zachary roared into view, looking cool to the core. Their bold presence commanded stares, and they weren't even trying.

The rumble of their engines gave me an easy feeling. When they cruised up, I gave them each a "high five." My biker bros were back.

In hopes of sliding the Israelis into a Puerto groove, I'd already scouted out a hovel for them. The place where I was staying had rented their last room, but down the road I'd found the boys a decent low-cost unit. I showed them the way and hung out in their room while they settled in.

"Look, guys," I said. "Here's the deal. My wheels are outta commission. However, I've kicked in a plan to get me rolling again. I hope you're into sticking around a few."

Outside, two fine female tourists wearing Brazilian bikini tops and short skirts strutted by the room's open door. Omar and Zachary looked at each other, and then at me.

"Well," said Zachary, "we're not on a strict schedule."

I smiled. I'd feared my chance to continue with them had

slipped away under my flip-flops, but now it looked more than possible. The cool thing was that it meant we'd established a good camaraderie.

Wearing beach clothes instead of biker gear, we met each morning at an open-air thatched-roofed café with bamboo tables. It struck me as odd that a motorcycle trip felt so wildly different from going on holiday. People vacationed for a break from their jobs and to jellify their minds. An excursion like ours, on the other hand, sometimes called for intense concentration, which could be exhausting. So here in Puerto, taking a break from our ride, we were on vacation. We sipped ginger tea and chatted, relaxed as slugs. Tomorrow would be more of the same.

Although the surf remained only so-so throughout the week, I paddled out a bunch just to get wet and get used to my new board. The fact that the waves weren't firing didn't concern me. I'd already been to Puerto during prime surf season a couple of years prior, after returning home from Australia. It had been an extreme budget trip. My parents had paid for half of the two-hundred-dollar flight into Oaxaca City as a birthday present. From there I'd taken a bus to the coast, where I'd spent a thrifty month living in a small mosquito-infested room, eating beans and oats, and riding warm, tubing, sand-bottom waves.

This trip, my stop here was purely functional. I'd hoped for waves, of course, but I was itching to get into Central America, a place I had yet to explore.

I didn't have the gall to ask the Israelis to wait longer than a week. If the chain didn't arrive, it would be my tough luck. On the sixth day of our Puerto stay, I headed to the airport. I had a bad feeling my precious part wouldn't be there. I should've had more faith in the Mexican postal service.

"*Hola, algo para* Brito?" I asked.

The man behind the counter spun around and sifted through some brown-paper packages on a shelf. He turned around with a flat, rectangular package in his hand and passed it to me. The inch-thick box felt as heavy as a bar of lead. My jaw hit the counter, and my eyes bugged out cartoon-like. The chain!

"*Muchas, muchas gracias!*" I headed back to the others, gripping the package like a life raft.

With Omar pointing and instructing, I got my hands greasy and wrapped the beautiful new chain neatly around the bike's sprockets. We were ready to blaze.

* * *

A year or so earlier, a buddy of mine, Mike Digger, had bussed his way through Central America. Digger had returned to California rattling off a ton of Spanish. He spoke highly of a Spanish school in Quetzaltenango, Guatemala, where he reckoned his vocabulary had quadrupled. Digger had paid a hundred dollars a week to stay seven nights with a family—meals included—and had received five days of one-on-one tutoring. I talked with Omar and Zachary about checking out this school. They liked the idea, too; my Spanish lagged, but theirs was worse.

From the beaches of Puerto Escondido our trio motored inland toward the city of Oaxaca. The new chain worked perfectly, and my bike rode as smooth as ever.

We cruised single-file along a road that spiraled up the forested Sierra Madre del Sur Mountains. The fresh mountain scent kept me alert. The air grew cooler the higher we climbed, and at each rest stop I added a little more clothing to compensate for the dropping temps. We were traveling in the middle of winter, and it felt like it. I thought I'd left the icy mornings behind, but mountain ranges lay scattered intermittently along my path, and with them came lofty elevations and brisk, biting air.

After freezing my bones in frayed tee-shirts and worn out Levis in South Africa, I'd vowed never to leave home again without a good set of thermal underwear. So far on this trip, my longjohns had been called to duty far more often than I would've anticipated. I was always grateful to have them.

Our last full day in Mexico came to a dramatic close. After a brief stay in Oaxaca to check out the ancient Monte Alban ruins, we'd descended the mountains and returned to near sea level. By dusk we'd made rights, lefts, and more rights in a search for a place to stay. We rode past miles of grassy fields as night showed its dark face.

My dead headlight had passed its job to Omar, and my busted taillight was being trailed by the ever reliable Zachary. With most of my weak spots covered, my only dilemma was how to keep Omar in sight. I had to lift my tinted visor to see anything at all, and the thick dust kicked up by his tires battered the gravelly road and assaulted my eyes. I wanted to fall back as much as possible, but losing sight of Omar's taillight in the blackness would be worse than suffering through his blinding cloud. I would just have to bite the dust to avoid biting the dust.

I don't know why, but my bike sounded much louder in the dark. Her scream buzzed through my entire body.

We began hunting for a place to camp. The wide open area we were riding through lacked hidden nooks and crannies, and the side of the road would not do. Then, through the black, we saw dull lights in the distance. We had lucked into a place to stay. Under low-wattage floodlights, the isolated hotel had a ghostly glow. Pulling up, we were disappointed to see that it was a quality place. I headed into a clean office. These people were not into bartering. At sixteen bucks each, the room put a dent in our wallets. The upside was that, just like in Acapulco, our room had hot showers and soft couches, so we would all sleep comfortably. Once we got over the shock of the price tag, it plain old felt great to be done for the day.

We had hit the southern tip of Mexico. Before taking off for Guatemala the next morning, we stopped for breakfast to use up the last of our remaining *pesos*.

9

GUATEMALA

Don't Stroll the Late Night City Streets

I liked knowing I wasn't alone, that the three of us would tackle the border together. I knew that juggling my gear through lines as I pretended to understand the officials' Spanish would be a tiring trick. Instead, after we'd checked out of Mexico and arrived at Guatemala's faded, poorly maintained immigration offices, Omar and Zachary guarded the motorcycles while I disappeared inside to get my passport stamped. Then we rotated, two of us always staying with our gear.

An officer came out and took down our license plate numbers. The whole time, I was busy bartering. He wanted so much for this and so much for that. Our insistence that we carried only a certain amount of dollars was a lie he wouldn't buy. Nevertheless, we eventually reached a monetary compromise, and because I carried small notes stuffed in different pockets he had no way to tell how much I actually had on me.

Within three hours we had our permits and were ready to ride. Getting our belongings over the border intact had been a task tough enough with three men; alone, it would've been grueling.

My only trouble waited in a little plywood booth where a thick-mustached guard did one last check of my passport before lifting the gate to let the vehicles pass into the country. The Israelis were first. They flashed their passports at the smiling official and he graciously motioned them through. But when I handed the man my passport, his smile took a dive.

"That'll be nine *quetzals*," he said.

"Nine *quetzals*? What for?" I asked, confused.

"The fee for the gate," he added with a hint of hostility.

"Fee? Why? I didn't see anyone else pay anything," I protested softly, referring to the Israelis, who were now long gone.

"Israel is our friend," he said, obviously getting annoyed.

"I'm your friend," I claimed sweetly.

"No, you are not. Israel is our friend. America is not!"

Something must have slipped past me concerning my country's current relationship with Guatemala. I thought our countries stood fairly cool with each other. Apparently, this gentleman thought otherwise. Not that it would've made a difference, but I couldn't remember what in the hell we had done to them.

Looking straight into his eyes, I searched for a neutral thing to say.

"Look . . . there are over two hundred and fifty million people living in America. You couldn't possibly expect each and every one of them to think, act, and feel the same . . . right?"

It didn't work. The dude just sat there eyeing me with a blank stare, unwilling to collaborate. Resigned, I reached into my pocket and paid the meager tariff, which was more about principle than fee. With a smirk of satisfaction, the man tossed me a little check-marked piece of paper we both knew no one would ever look at.

* * *

The two-lane mountain road ascended into cooler terrain toward Quetzaltenango, alias Xela (Shay-la). The fresh air boosted my energy as it filtered through my lungs. I felt very comfortable riding with the Israelis.

At our next rest stop, we pulled out our cameras and snapped a few shots. In the distance, we spotted a small farm nested in a picturesque valley. I walked to the edge of a steep drop-off and couldn't help but admire the mysterious misty mountain summits. I was officially in Central America.

We reached the cobblestone streets of Xela by mid-afternoon to find men, women, and children of Mayan blood parading around in their traditional brightly colored clothing.

Among the many Spanish schools in Xela, we managed to find the one we were searching for. The address Digger had given me led us to an open door along a dingy blue concrete wall that faced a quiet narrow street. These schools were popular with travelers looking to build their knowledge of the local language. Families offered rooms in return for a percentage of the school's profits. We needed places that could accommodate our bikes, so the boys and I split up amongst those who had the space.

The congenial Ernesto and Maria, my new foster parents, were very hospitable. Their home had an interesting design, with the doors to several rooms opening onto a large central den with a cement floor. All of their possessions were well used, but well kept. In one corner sat an intricate weaving machine the size of a grand piano. The grandfather, who rarely spoke, worked this machine by himself in silence. The kitchen stuff—the stove, pots and pans, utensils, and the long kitchen table—looked as if they'd been passed down a generation or two. My room had only a simple single bed draped with layers of colored blankets and a small, plain wooden desk with a sturdy kid-size chair. Everything worked dandy.

The living was the easy part. Communication was another story. Even though I answered "*Sí*" to every comment Ernesto and Maria made, most of the time I understood hardly a word they said. Their dialect sounded noticeably different, or it may have been their accent. I don't know. My Spanish wasn't refined enough to grasp the difference. It would have been easier rapping with a three-year-old, if I could've found one. That was fine by me. I did comprehend lots of their shorter phrases, and I got all the practice I could absorb in the one-on-one sessions at the school.

Sometimes Ernesto and Maria would share the kitchen table with another student, a German in his early fifties. His white flipped-out hair and circular bifocals made me think of a cross between a hippie and a mad scientist. For what it was worth, I worked on the fundamentals of Spanish with him. Our mealtime conversations didn't always have to make sense to be fun.

"*Buenos dias,* dude," he'd say.

"*¿Como está, Einstein?*" I'd reply.

The Israelis and I had shared this idea that we were going to isolate ourselves from one another, other Westerners, and the English language in an earnest attempt to sharpen our Español.

Once we hit Xela, this isolation lasted about two hours. As soon as we had settled in with our families, we regrouped to explore. The town square, flanked by old colonial buildings, bustled with activity. It didn't take long to run into . . . well, others like us.

A group of Canadians around our age had driven an old school bus from British Columbia to Guatemala to make a donation of the bus itself. It sounded like a great trip for the young and the restless. They had some interesting stories to tell. Among the group floated a flaxen blonde named Sara; fun and flirtatious, she added spirited pizzazz to the afternoon.

The Canadians told us about a local hot spot to check out. That night we arrived at the hip cantina, where a small stage and an open mike allowed transients a moment in the spotlight. The Israelis and I listened as a traveling musician strummed cover tunes on his guitar: "Heeeeey baby, baby, it's a wild world." He sounded good, too.

Young people from all over the world sat at big round tables drinking pitchers of beer. As usual when a bunch of intoxicated philosophers get together, they came up with some interesting and comical jargon. Take the lively Norwegian backpacker, for example: he was the most fun to listen to. As he got drunker, the passion in his Viking blood boiled as he expressed his love for his country to a table of five different nationalities. "I tell you," he beamed with pride. "There is no place better on this earth!"

For kicks, the others disputed his claims. His enthusiasm had every person at the table—the Canadian, the Austrian, the Englishman and the Frenchman—feeling patriotic.

This particular night, my attention turned to the Canadian

Sara, who arrived out of the blue as Omar and Zachary were leaving for the night. She and I sipped a beer and chatted about how great it was not to be at home working. The guitar player had long since stopped strumming, and background music played in the dimly lit bar. A light fuzz filled not only my head, but everyone else's, too.

After talking for a couple of hours, Sara and I left the soft glow of the pub at around two in the morning. To make sure she got home in one piece, I accompanied her to her home-stay.

The streets were cold and empty. I would've sprung for a taxi, but they didn't seem to exist. Instead, we walked down one dark street after another, making a right, and then a left, and then another right. Twenty minutes later, we stood at the step of Sara's windowless front door. She leaned in for a goodnight kiss and gave me a warm, nuzzling hug. That heated me up, but only temporarily, as she then disappeared behind the heavy wooden door of her host's house.

With Sara safe, I faced the daunting return trip alone. I stepped into the darkness and embarked on a long, spooky stroll. Tightly bolted doors and tall cement walls bordered the narrow streets, and all the dwellings looked the same.

Walking the back streets of a heavily populated Central American city late at night was sketchy and foolish, and the fact that there was not another soul in sight made it a lot more worrisome. Recognizing my complete vulnerability to the evils of the night, I moved briskly in what I hoped was the right direction—left, then right, then left again. Despite my efforts to glide weightlessly over the crude cobblestones, my steps echoed noisily. A nervous streak seared my spine. After turning down one street after another, I knew I was horribly lost.

In my growing paranoia, I sensed someone lurking close behind me. I kept glancing over my shoulder, but saw no one. The strange sensation started to get to me. I started to jog. Clop, clop, clop, clop. That didn't help. The jogging intensified the echoes, and the uncomfortable loudness forced me into a run. A rare dim streetlight cast my moving shadow, which I caught out of the corner of my eye. That freaked me out, and I ran faster. The echoes increased. I'm running from myself, I thought. This is absolutely ridiculous, right? It may have been silly to run from my silhouette, but I wasn't taking any chances. My legs wouldn't slow.

Running from the sound of my own footsteps, I could swear I heard voices. The people with those voices must certainly hear me running. I looked over my shoulder again, and saw nothing. They must have hidden.

I felt like a frightened child in a haunted house on Halloween, waiting for the boogie man to jump out of a dark corner. The countless gaps and crevices in the city walls made perfect hiding places for the wicked. No matter how freakishly similar the neighborhoods looked, I kept searching along until, somehow, I miraculously stumbled upon the blissful familiarity of my family's street. I flew straight up to the front step of my homestay, and with a tight fist I hammered on the door. *WHAM, WHAM, WHAM!* I didn't bother acting polite. Disturbing the household was exactly what I wanted to do.

Seconds later came the muffled sound of sliding deadbolts.

Ernesto, in his bedroom attire, opened the door with a smile. *"Buenas noches,* J.J."

I stood there flushed and sweating in the chilly air, trying not to breathe heavily. But the mist coming from my mouth gave me away. *"Buenas noches, Señor Ernesto,"* I said.

Relieved to be off the streets, I headed for the safety of my room.

Not surprisingly, I wasn't too popular at breakfast. After a grace period during which I ate a couple of tamales, Maria broke into a story. She stared straight into my eyes and delivered her lecture.

"Mira, J.J., tienes mucha suerte, porque es muy peligrosa la noche. Dos calles lejos, a las tres de la manana, un hombre fue apuñalado con un cuchillo, y murió." Her eyes widened as she slowly repeated the word. *"Murió. ¿Me entiendes?"* She closed her speech with, *"Tienes cuidado en la noche, porque es muy, muy peligrosa."*

Here's what I got out of it: "Last night, at around three o'clock in the morning, not two streets over from our own, a guy was attacked with a knife and murdered. Here in Xela, that's not uncommon. You're a moron for running around in the wee hours of the morning. You need to be careful, especially when it's dark. It's very, very dangerous."

Maria gave sound advice. I wondered whether the voices I'd heard the night before had been just my imagination, or whether they had actually belonged to the victim and his killer.

* * *

Our personal tutoring continued all week. When the weekend hit, Omar, Zachary, a few others students and I went on a field trip to the nearby Fuentes Georginas natural springs. A town bus carried us to this peaceful setting, where hot sulfur pools nestled in the looming mountains.

The students from the Spanish school soaked in the thermal pools alongside local families. Depending on where you were in the pool, the water temp ranged from lukewarm to scalding. I hopped into the water and swam slowly around, stretching my muscles. It felt so nice. Had it not been a weekend with so many frolicking people, I'd have easily fallen asleep.

Three well-mannered surfer-looking guys appeared and smiled a hello to our group. We all got to talking. Jack, Jeff, and Jessie hailed from North Carolina, and, to my surprise, they did in fact surf. The Carolina boys were traveling in a van to Panama. But our conversation was cut short when we realized something was wrong.

Amongst our group of students was Sharon, a sweet, like-able twenty-three-year-old Australian. Sharon had passed on dipping into the springs to take a short walk up a mountain trail. She had gone alone, and she'd been gone over an hour.

We grew concerned. She didn't seem the type to wander far. By the end of the second hour, six of us prepared to track her down.

Her friend Beth was fighting back tears. "I hope she's okay. I have a terrible feeling she's in trouble."

"Let's get moving," Omar said. "Those clouds are dropping fast."

We climbed high to a tree-studded ridge. "SHAAAARON!"

we called into the dense forest again and again. No response. I hiked along the ridge until I came to a grand vista, and scanned the vast, deceptively peaceful valley below. The sun that had shone earlier now hid behind a disheartening mist that blanketed the silent mountain peaks. A knot twisted in my stomach.

By the end of the third hour, we'd made our way back down and declared her missing. One of our Spanish instructors telephoned the police from the small restaurant at the springs.

The bummer was that a girl had vanished. The cool thing, which shocked all of us, was that one hour after we phoned the authorities a large canopied military truck filled with a contingent of machine gun-toting soldiers roared onto the scene.

The officer in charge waved them out, "*¡Valla, valla, valla!*"

In their black boots and dark uniforms, the men were dressed like soldiers but looked more like angels. They filed out of the truck and charged up the mountain, double-fisting their intimidating automatic rifles. Omar recognized their firearms at once.

"Hey, J.J., see their guns?" he said. "Those are Israeli weapons the Guatemalans are holding."

Though I knew less about guns than about my motorcycle's engine, I experienced a sudden gain in perspective as to the relationship between the two countries.

All of us down below waited impatiently as the men combed the mountainsides. The forest absorbed all sounds, and we couldn't hear anything. No calling out, or footsteps snapping twigs. The quiet could've driven a person mad.

The hours dragged, with no sign of Sharon. The grey afternoon light grew darker, and the fog thickened. A heavy scent of desperation hung in the wet air.

A soldier appeared from the trail, alone. Then another, who had found nothing. We bit our nails as, one by one, the soldiers emerged from the forest empty-handed, twenty men in all. They'd started out so confident and strong, but now, as night crept in, the soldiers were forced to abandon the search.

In the twilight hour, our field trip bus reluctantly departed the springs for town, leaving the lost girl behind in the rapidly falling temperature. She'd been wearing no more than sandals, a light rayon skirt, and a thin, long-sleeve shirt. No sweater, no jacket, no nothing. Since she was an occasional smoker, we had questioned whether she might have a lighter to start a fire. But we found she'd left all such belongings behind, so that possibility got ruled out. I bet even Rambo would've had trouble creating a spark with his bare hands in those damp, misty mountains.

* * *

My spirit remained low that night. At dinner, I explained what had happened to Maria and Ernesto in my broken Spanish.

"Una estudante está perdida in las montañas, y la noche está muy fria."

Maria gasped, "*Ahhh! Qué triste.*" She kept saying, "*Qué triste.*"

I didn't eat much before I excused myself and headed for bed. Crawling under the cold sheets, I wiggled and burrowed into a warm spot. Even beneath five blankets, battling the chill was a chore. Poor Sharon had to be out there in the freezing night air, alone. I wished I knew where the hell she'd disappeared to. Here I lay, safe and warm, while her life had suddenly turned perilous and fragile. Restless, I dozed in a whirl of guilt.

* * *

Late the next afternoon at school we got the news. They had found Sharon . . . alive!

She returned to school the day after that, bruised face and all. While not quite her normal cheery self, she sat at a table with some of us and recounted her horrible ordeal in vivid detail.

"I only planned on a short hike, and walked along the ridge through the trees for awhile," she said. "When I turned around to head back, something seemed different. The pattern of the trees had changed. I couldn't believe how quickly I'd become disorientated."

Sharon had strayed too far. On her way back, she'd passed the trail that led back to the springs and had headed deeper and deeper into the thick forest. Before she knew it, she was desperately lost.

"I knew I'd slipped up when I couldn't tell if I was coming or going," she said. Sharon's voice mixed of relief and fatigue, and her eyes had lost their sparkle. "I wandered for ages. My legs got so bloody tired. And I was so scared, because I couldn't find my way back."

Weary and riddled with anxiety, Sharon had staggered across a rocky stream and slipped on a slick stone. She'd fallen hard into the shallow, freezing water. More dazed than ever, she'd risen to her feet and continued on, trudging in all directions for the sake of moving. Before she knew it, darkness had surrounded her.

"I had a lighter in me little bag, and thought how it would've been nice to make a fire. But I'd left the bloody bag behind," she said. "The night was so cold. I didn't sleep a wink. I just curled into a ball and shivered."

For hours she had toughed it out, chilled to the bone. When dawn had crept up she'd continued on, still frightfully lost. But luck had been on her side, and she'd stumbled upon a small farm around midday. The gracious farmers had brought her back into the care of her host family, where the traumatized girl had cleaned up, eaten a hot meal, and slept twelve hours straight.

After hearing the story, I tried to put myself in the same scenario. But the memory of my lost and lonely day riding across the Baja desert dimmed in comparison, and I could only grasp a tiny speck of how she must have felt. There was no denying that Sharon's experience had been more intense than my own.

* * *

Following the week of *hablo, hablas, and hablamos*, the Spanish instructors held a little graduation ceremony, complete with printed cloth diplomas bearing our names. We sat on chairs in a circle on a concrete slab in the yard behind the school.

They expected an acceptance speech from each graduate. I had always had problems with public speaking, even in English, and when my turn came around I struggled to spit something out. "*Hola,*" I said. "*Muchas gracias para total. Está muy bien, yo creo yo apprendar muches* . . . is that right?"

Everyone clapped anyway.

Omar and Zachary's speeches were even shorter, with Omar's "*Muchos gracias!*" receiving the loudest applause.

Then it was time for the Israelis and me to be on our way.

We stuffed our cloth diplomas into our pockets, and when we fired up our already packed and ready-to-go motorcycles a thunderous roar filled the yard. The instructors and the other students gathered to wave and watch us exit single-file onto the street.

Passing Xela's main plaza, we spotted the Canadian crew and stopped to say a quick goodbye. Among them was Sara, the girl I'd walked home from the bar earlier that week. After donating their bus, she and her friends had searched for ways to get back home. Funny enough, some guy had offered Sara a ride north on his motorcycle.

"Yeah, I'm not sure whether I'm going to take his offer," she said. "I want to check out all my options. We'll see." Then the little flirt leaned over and whispered in my ear, "I wish I could get on the back of your motorcycle!"

Heck, I was ready to give her a ride right then and there. But, um, we were heading in two different directions.

* * *

Our next stop was Lake Atitlan, one of the most majestic spots in Guatemala. High above sea level, and cradled by volcanoes, the lake had been a haven for hippies and draft dodgers back in the Sixties. It still held a psychedelic atmosphere, with colorful shop advertisements and relaxing cafés. The boys and I found a room at a small family-run home-stay. We unloaded our gear and took off on a joy ride through town.

As we passed a flashy hotel, we stumbled upon an army of traveling bikes. I counted twenty leaning on their kickstands next to each other. The bikes belonged to a club that organized an annual run to Guatemala. Unlike our enduros, these bikes were large Gold-wing-style cruisers.

What set my Honda apart from the other bikes was the surfboard racked on its left side and the fact that she was quite a bit older. But I wouldn't have traded her for any other. So far, my baby had been true to me, and I loved her dearly.

* * *

Another off-road style rider crossed our path, a German who had dismantled his machine, boxed it, flown it to Argentina, and reassembled it. He was heading toward Alaska to do the "American 10,000" as I decided to call it, from the south to the north. Man, could this guy ride!

We first saw him—or rather, he saw us—while we were on an excursion along the dirt road that circled the lake. Zipping by from out of nowhere, he rode up next to us for a few seconds and then sped away, as if egging us on to follow. He did this twice.

The boys were handicapped in the form of two Israeli chicks they had met in town. The girls were riding on the backs of their bikes. I, however, having no board on my racks, felt light on my feet. So I battled for all it was worth to keep up with the unknown antagonist. I opened throttle and took a racing stance, keeping my body still while using my arms and legs as shock absorbers. I did my best to copy the guy, who rode like a jockey on a racehorse.

It was no contest. The guy smoked me, gliding effortlessly over the bumpy terrain and leaving me to eat his dust.

Watching all this ate poor Omar up inside. He was our group's logical answer to the mystery rider, and he was dying to cut loose.

"I wanted to take that guy on so bad. Watching him was killing me!" he told us later in an impassioned voice.

If I'd been thinking at the time, I could've taken the girl off Omar's hands and he could have done his thing. Maybe it was better it hadn't happened that way; we would have had a blazing drag race on our hands, and risked injuring our front man. But who am I trying to kid? It was his life, and I would've loved seeing those guys battle it out!

Apparently the whole macho race thing was infectious, which would explain why I had felt pulled to keep up with the crazy German. I must have done alright, because later, during a break by the lake, Zachary commented on my effort.

"Hey, J.J., I saw you out there. Your riding has really improved."

"Really? Cool. Thanks." The compliment boosted my ego. I understood that if anyone would have been likely to notice a difference in my riding skills, it would've been Zachary, the guy directly behind me for the last two thousand or so miles.

* * *

Back at our small family-run homestay, I befriended Victor, the son of the caretakers. At roughly twelve years of age, he was the eldest of the three children and the greatest help to his parents. From the moment our trio arrived, Victor assisted us in any way he could. He dragged an extra mattress down a flight of stairs and across several tile porches so that our two-bedded room could comfortably accommodate all three of us. He did all this with such cheerful enthusiasm, I thought, What a nice kid.

The next day, thinking he might get a kick out of it, I offered to take young Victor for a spin on my bike. "Yo, Vic, *¿quieres una ride on mi moto?*" I asked. He gave me a huge grin and a nod.

We got the go-ahead from his parents and we were off. The young lad's only problem was trying to figure out how to hold on. He finally slipped his fingers loosely through my belt loops.

Riding in a mountainous region, we soon approached a steep climb. I remembered Doc—the man who had sold me my bike—and how he'd flown up a hill with me on the back. I couldn't resist. As Doc had with me, though not to quite the degree, I opened throttle and charged up the mountain. Victor grabbed on tight to stay aboard.

"*¿Como está?*" I shouted through the wind.

"*¡Bien!*" he cried out.

We twisted our way up the steep, winding incline. Except for his death grip, the kid felt so light I could hardly tell he was there.

The lake glistened to our left. The evergreens were every-where. I imagined how differently I'd grown up compared to Victor, mentally matching my Orange County home against his rural small-town life. Chances are, he didn't recognize the natu-ral beauty in his own back yard the way I did, and I hadn't ap-preciated my home's conveniences the way he would.

My thoughts fizzled when we found a cool spot to stop at an outside marketplace high above the lake. We pulled over for a bite to eat. We strolled up to a vendor's pastry cart and loaded up on drinks and sugar-puff snacks. Victor reached into his pocket for some *quetzals*.

"*No, no, yo pago,*" I insisted. He looked at me and shook his head.

"Come on, *por favor,*" I pleaded. "I invited you on this ride," I said in English. I don't know whether he understood that. I had a hell of a time convincing the humble boy to put his money away. But he finally did—a testament to his character.

Heading back home, we had a spectacular view of the volcanoes framing Lake Atitlan. The whole way back, I kept our pace nice and mellow so Vic could enjoy the ride.

When Victor and I motored up, his parents were outside their house to greet us. They were all smiles, appreciative that I'd taken their son cruising. Young Victor was stoked. And seeing the delighted looks on all their faces . . . well, more than anything, I was just glad I hadn't crashed with these nice people's kid on the back of my motorcycle.

* * *

The next day, the Israelis and I left Lake Atitlan and traveled to Antigua, a touristy colonial city.

The place oozed charm and old-time Spanish architecture. Every stone street was home to some kind of magnificent cathedral or a ruin reduced to rubble by some past earthquake. We roamed the town in awe of its three-hundred-plus-year history.

* * *

We had reached the inevitable: things were about to change. Geographically, my Israeli friends were leaning east and I was leaning west. Their agenda pointed them to the Caribbean side of Central America, toward long, punishing roads I didn't care to bike across. I aimed at cruising toward the Pacific to loot its wave-filled treasures on the far more accessible side of the Central American isthmus.

Omar had once said, "Riding together creates a strong bond. On the highway, you're vulnerable and exposed. Anything can happen. If you go down, your partner can save your life."

He was right. We'd developed a strong camaraderie traveling across desolate open highways, snaking across treacherous mountain trails, surviving city traffic mayhem, and outrunning village dogs. I felt comfortable with my new bros, like we could depend on each other no matter what. I didn't want to see them blow a tire and eat the street any more than I wanted that for myself. We had experienced new sights and sounds together, stumbling through language barriers and wrong turns and learning about different cultures. Most of all, we had shared the excitement of exploring by motorcycle.

If I hadn't been traveling with a surfboard, I probably would have continued on with Omar and Zachary. But the irony of it all was that without the board I doubt I'd have met them at all.

Either way, the time had come to say goodbye. I was going to head out the following morning in the opposite direction and continue on the path my heart was paving. I wasn't carrying that surfboard around for decoration.

10

EL SALVADOR

Long Rights Beckon

February 13th, 1996, is a day I'll have trouble forgetting. Dawn was cool and quiet. Dark clouds loomed high above, yet it didn't feel as if it would rain. In front of our rented room in Antigua I loaded my bike slowly, unenthusiastic about leaving the safety of our little group.

Omar awoke and came outside. I'd already said farewell to Zachary.

"You can still come with us if you want," he said, noticing my reluctance to leave.

I stopped to study my rig. "I am a bit torn. But the waves are calling."

"I understand," he said.

"Be careful out there," I said, finally psyching myself up enough to put on my helmet, get on the seat, and give my bike a few good kicks. Vvvvrrrooommm! I revved her up to a respectable temp, and slapped Omar a high five. "Good luck!" I said, and eased away.

"*Vaya con Dios,*" he said, arm raised.

I watched him disappear in my rearview mirror.

* * *

Leaving Antigua, in the heart of Guatemala, I stayed alert on the lonely morning ride. The greenery of the highlands gave out a fresh crisp scent. For a while, the ride was easy. My first major obstacle was the metropolis of Guatemala City, not too far away. I managed to roll right into rush hour, and that was when my relaxing ride turned ugly.

If I had ever sweated at seven in the morning, it had never been quite like this. Cars honked, taxis swayed, and buses closed in on me as I tried to maintain a straight line. At one point I got boxed in by a bus at my nose, one on my tail, another three feet to my right, and I could easily have stuck a foot out and kicked the last sucker just to my left. The smelly fumes were trapped in my helmet—a lousy way to get smoked out. Toting the surfboard, I wasn't ultra-maneuverable, and I had the feeling all the other drivers were out to nail me. You'd think I would have been used to that, coming from Southern Cal, but this place made California gridlock feel like a mellow day at Disneyland. I didn't understand the road signs, and couldn't afford to look at them for fear of tangling with the crazy motorists.

When at last I managed to negotiate the pandemonium and skirt the city to find the bliss of open highway, my heart rate slowed to a mild roar. The road dropped down into the hot coastal lowlands, where I was surrounded by tall, thirsty grass. The engine's constant hum calmed my nerves.

The wind blew and the sun blazed, both piercing the weave of my denim jacket. Feeling vulnerable without my fellow riders, I experienced a strange type of exhilaration. The thrill of riding alone made me think of how it must have felt to gallop a sturdy steed across the wild, open Texas range in the 1860s. The only man who could come to my rescue sat there gripping the handlebars, and his Spanish sucked.

But I was optimistic, my bike reliable, and together we made time.

I had no intentions of surfing the Guatemalan coastline, though I'm not sure why. My gut guided my every move. At this point, I was aiming toward the waters off El Salvador. Maybe my onward push stemmed from the rumors of its long right pointbreaks.

The Rio Paz separates Guatemala from El Salvador, but a bridge over the river linked the two countries. Vendors and potential pickpockets littered the area, waiting to make a sale—or in anticipation of the slightest chance to lighten your luggage.

Getting out of Guatemala was simple. Fast lines, a couple of departing stamps on my passport, and they were happy to be rid of me. From there, I took a deep breath and began the stressful ride across the bridge toward El Salvador, preparing to deal with sticky-fingered officials and black market money changing rip-offs.

Right away, a Latino teenager saw me passing by and took chase. "Hey, wait! Wait," he hollered in perfect English. I ignored him and continued to ride, keeping my mind on the immediate future.

* * *

There were times when the U.S. dollar proved invaluable. That was why I made it a habit to load my money belt with a few hundred in tens and twenties. Earlier, preparing to exchange a couple of Jacksons for some colones, I had pulled out two twenties and stuffed them into my front pocket. I found it unbelievable that these plain-clothes money changer guys hung around the crowded area with two-inch-thick stacks of bills in their grip. It seemed to me that having so much cash exposed in public would be flirting with danger, but not even the seediest characters were giving them a second look. Maybe there was some sort of "Don't rob the money changer" code that everyone followed. I stopped to talk to one of these currency-bearing cowboys. We traded.

I motored over to the poorly maintained immigration offices at the El Salvador border, where I endured heavy stares from every direction as I got off my bike and removed my helmet. I avoided prolonged eye contact with anyone and put on a face of stone. Although a nervous streak the size of the Amazon River rushed down my spine, I pretended to be thoroughly self-assured. I wanted the locals to think that if this *gringo* was daring enough to arrive at their border alone on a motorcycle, he might be some ominous kick-ass martial arts expert, or maybe concealing a lethal weapon. I hoped they wouldn't call my bluff.

By this time, the boy who'd followed me across the bridge approached from behind. The kid's messy black hair was a perfect match for his ratty blue jeans and stained yellow tee-shirt. He must've been around fifteen years old.

Breathing heavy from his run, he asked, "Hey, do you need any help?

I knew from experience that a street kid in a foreign country who spoke perfect English often spelled trouble. They were usually bold, cunning, and more persistent than a used car salesman. One way or another, they'd pocket at least some of your money.

"No thanks," I replied, hardly acknowledging him as I shouldered my pack. He didn't budge, only stood and watched me pull my board off its racks.

I headed to the door of the small, weathered building and stepped inside. My heart sank and my shoulders slumped. I couldn't believe it. Directly in front of me was the most chaotic mess of humanity I'd seen since waiting in line to buy a ferry ticket on a hot, busy day in Southeast Asia. On one side of a long, low counter, two officials clicked away on antique typewriters, while at least a hundred Latino dudes on the other side clawed their way to the front. Many held papers and stretched their arms out to be recognized as they tried to out-shout one another at full volume.

What a mess! I thought. How in the world am I supposed to get through that? Standing frozen in the doorway with my board bag heavy in my hand, I muttered, "Oh, Crap . . ."

Needless to say, I didn't join the crowd. Instead, I went over to lean quietly against the wall.

Seconds later, I heard a familiar voice. "Give me your passport."

Normally, the last thing I would do would have been to give my passport to a strange kid who could almost pass for me. But the situation looked bleak. I was desperate . . . I complied.

Holding my important blue book in his hot little hand, the boy blended into the masses.

It was nothing short of a miracle. Half an hour later, he

scrambled to the front and handed my passport to an official. Relieved, I left to check on my bike.

Good thing, too. Once outside, I saw with horror that my bike lay on its side! I ran over to pick it up. Two men sat on the hood of a rusty pickup truck only a few feet away. All of my nervousness had vanished. My baby was on the ground, and it ticked me off to think that someone would have maliciously knocked her down.

"WHAT THE F**K HAPPENED HERE?!"

The two dudes laughed at my rant. "Shit happens," one of them said coolly, in decent English.

"YEAH, SHIT HAPPENS!" I grumbled, lifting my bike from the ground.

Nothing had broken. If the fall had busted the clutch or something, I'd have been screwed. I should have been more careful. These guys looked dodgy, but I kept mad-dogging them anyway.

The one who'd spoken before noticed my scowl. "It's a windy day," he said in a casual tone.

That was true. I took a second to peer at the swaying branches of a tree. But I knew they were just mocking me, and I wasn't about to trust anyone who spoke English—which reminded me to go check on my boy.

"What's your name?" I asked him.

"Miguel," he answered.

"What's next, Miguel?"

"We wait."

Within a couple of hours an official was standing behind

my bike, writing down my license plate number. Ah, the joy of progress, however painfully slow. Time and again Miguel came to me and said, "Okay, wait." And with every "wait," I'd reluctantly shell out a few extra colones to "complete the process." They wanted money for the stamp, money for the sticker, money for the paper they wrote my information on, money for their mamas.

Some bogus charges were to be expected, so I'd already divvied my *dinero* up among the pockets of my jeans. I never pulled out all my dough in one chunk. Their fees always started at around a hundred colones, but I'd haggle them down to twenty or thirty. I could be a fierce barterer and sensed that young Miguel was one of the conspirators. But that didn't bother me at all. No matter where you are, there's always a price for freedom.

I am happy to say that in only five hours I had a vehicle permit in my hand and my passport stamped. With permission to ride freely into the country, I gave Miguel sixty *colones* and bought him a bottle of Coke for his trouble. He was stoked, and I ecstatic. If not for the young hustler, my back would still be leaning against that wall.

* * *

El Salvador opened up before me. Happy to leave the border behind and never look back, I stuck to the road closest to the coast. I wasn't sure of my destination, but figured I'd know it when I saw it.

The landscape became mountainous, and the asphalt road turned to dirt. Before long, I spotted a team of men laboring on the road in the mid-afternoon sun. They swung heavy picks into the hard ground. The sun's rays shimmered off their shirt-less, sweating backs. The instant the workers spotted me, they signaled with their hands toward their mouths. At first I couldn't tell what they were trying to tell me. Then I saw that they were thirsty and didn't have water. No water! This whole scene was disturbing, and I bet that the non-laboring gents who ran the show had their water. Without stopping, I unzipped my bag and reached for the small, half-full bottle of water. I tossed it to the dehydrated mob and they scrambled for it. I hope they shared.

The mistreated, sweaty men reminded me how fortunate I was to be from a wealthy country. To think that back at home I'd had a restaurant job bussing tables—not the highest posi-tion on the American totem pole, but that job had allowed me to save enough money to buy a new surfboard and travel to practi-cally anywhere in the world I wanted to go. Yeah okay, maybe I had to be penny-wise and rent a closet instead of a bedroom. And eat rice and oats from bulk bins instead of pricy packaged foods. And so what if I bought clothes from thrift stores and all that business. What I'm getting at here is that I did all that in the spirit of adventure, whereas the average El Salvadorian had to use their own money-saving techniques just to survive, with minimal extras. And I didn't have to pound the ground in the heat of the day without water for a pittance.

Riding past the laborers on a motorcycle made me realize that even though my last job had been as a busboy, I had more than these folks would most likely ever have.

Someday, I thought, maybe I can do something good for others.

* * *

Catching up to a public bus bouncing down the unpaved highway, I noticed children with perplexed looks on their faces peering at me through the back window. Then in the dusty glass I saw something else: a rider wearing a black helmet and tinted visor. He had some strange thing at his side, and didn't look like he was from around here. To see my own reflection was a trip. It reminded me of a Bon Jovi song, the one with the cowboy on the steel horse. When I refocused on the children, I saw the whole back of the crowded bus checking me out. I sped around the big vehicle and into the distance.

I came to a tunnel, a crude hole carved out of the mountain. It was long, narrow, and pitch-black except for the light of the opening at the other end. Feeling uncomfortable, I made a cautious entry, unsure as to what awaited me on the other side. It was the perfect setup for an ambush. Riding through the darkened passageway, I wondered how much a *gringo* ransomed for. In an effort to stop tormenting myself, I turned my thoughts to the ocean. Soon I burst out into daylight.

Having made it through without a scratch, I felt confident entering the next tunnel. Man, it was dark in there. Then I saw something odd up ahead. That's funny—it's got two openings at the end. *OH, CRAP, IT'S A BUS!*

My heart raced. The bus took up most of the room in the tunnel, and I hurried to inch my bike as far over to one side as I could. Pressing bike and body against the wall, I leaned hard and dug my shoulder into raw, jagged earth. With my headlight broken, I hoped the driver would see me in the darkness. I tensed up as the thing neared. The bus lights blinded me, and the sound of the engine grew louder. *Hooooooonnnnnnnk!*

The bus roared past an arm's length away, showering me in tunnel dust and prolonging its horn blast for added drama. I figured that meant he must have seen me. Either way, I didn't waste any time yanking the throttle and racing the hell out of the black hole. When I emerged into the sunlight, it took me a moment to collect my wits. I would've been cool with dying while surfing wild waves at some hazardous location, or even being gunned down fighting brutal banditos. But being splattered to bits by a bus inside a mountain didn't strike me as glorious at all.

* * *

After a while, I noticed the afternoon sun dropping. I'd been in El Sal for only a couple of hours, but had seen enough tunnels and buses to want to call it a day. The smell of saltwater indicated that the sea was nearby, although I couldn't see it . . . until . . . .

I'd just motored through a small village when the road—now solid pavement—made a sudden curve, bringing the ocean into view directly to my right. Small waves peeled along, and I saw three people bobbing in the water. They were surfing!

I turned around and headed back, spotting a dull homemade sign for lodging on the tree-shaded beach side of the village. On the other side of an open chain-link gate, a little off the road in a peaceful setting, sat a small unpainted cement building. I rode through the gate, parked, and pulled off my helmet.

As I stretched my arms and back, a round-faced woman appeared from nowhere. "*Hola. ¿Tienes cuartos?*" I asked.

"*Sí.*" She nodded and left to get her keys.

Waiting, I took a look around. Four doors lined each side of a huge open hallway, and I spotted hammocks swinging lazily across the middle. The woman returned and opened one of the rooms so I could have a look. Grey concrete floor and walls, a small table and chair, a 40-watt light bulb dangling three feet from the center of the room, a bed, and a raw bathroom equally decorated. Oh, wait. This must have been the presidential suite. It had a fan! I'd found heaven.

The room cost thirty *colones* a night (roughly $3.20 U.S.), and the lady wouldn't budge on the price. I was more than fine with that, just happy to be somewhere. I rolled my bike into the room. It felt so good to change out of my hot jeans and into my cool boardshorts. I slid my board out of its cover, waxed it up, attached a leash, and strolled down a dirt trail to the beach.

Small three-foot rights rolled down the point. The other surfers had gone, and I was alone. I jumped into the water, submerging my whole body, and felt the stress of the day wash away. The surf wasn't going off, but I didn't care. I stayed out until the sun melted into the sea.

If only Omar and Zachary could see me now.

Tired from a hectic day, I hit the sack soon after dark.

* * *

The next morning I woke to a faint, distant rumble that pulled me abruptly out of bed. Feeling refreshed and ready to surf, I stretched to get the blood flowing, grabbed my board, and made tracks toward the beach.

At first I couldn't believe it. Not another human to be seen on the sands or the sea, and the surf had picked up . . . way up! A magnificent empty wave peeled down the point. And behind it, another. Two more followed—a scene worthy of a surf movie.

I bolted to the water.

Euphoria filled me as I paddled over one impressive wave after another. I reached the lineup between sets and sat on my board. The anticipation had me burning. I took a few deep breaths and kept a sharp eye out to sea.

Seconds later, the horizon warped. The swells marched in, and I paddled over the first two. Another deep blue wall of water loomed up in front of me, with a long beautiful shoulder. With the takeoff zone all mine, I swung around and stroked into my first ride. Hopping to my feet, I pumped high on the face, driving hard. I was flying!

The wave kept building, and a sweet section formed up. I dropped down and eyeballed a spot on the steep and inviting open face. Aiming for the top of the wave with a ton of speed, I leaned into the turn of the century. Burying the rail, I pushed hard on the deck, my board cutting through the water and whipping under me to a quick but complete stop. A nice fan of spray complemented the move. Momentum carried me to the next section, and a solid bottom turn boosted me toward a smackable lip . . . *WHACK!* It was so easy.

The wave allowed me five more good turns before it lost steam. Paddling back out was an absolute pleasure, and watching the good, empty waves, I almost pinched myself. If this wasn't paradise, it didn't exist.

A dozen long waves and almost an hour later, I felt at total peace with the universe. During those watery rides it seemed like I was the only person on the planet.

But I wasn't. From my placid trance I was awakened by another surfer who paddled up from out of the blue while I waited for a set. Naturally, we struck up a conversation.

"The waves are firing, huh?"

"Yeah, it's super fun."

"Hey, I'm Stan."

"What's up, Stan? Good to meet ya. I'm J.J."

We swapped waves all morning as a trickle of other surfers joined us in the water.

After surfing, Stan gave me a short tour of the village eateries. There were three small *comedores* nearby, where you could fill your stomach with beans, rice, and oily eggs for nine *colones* (a U.S. buck). *Pupusas* were made of maize and had fillings such as cheese and cabbage. They were a cheap yet hearty snack, available everywhere.

Food and shelter ran me about seven dollars a day, thirty-five a week. The waves were free. This may have been considered chump change in the States, but it was probably a fair amount to the average Salvadorian. And frankly, it was plenty enough for me, too.

* * *

That evening I heard a knock, knock, knock on my door, and opened it to find Stan in the entranceway. "What's up?" he asked cheerfully.

"Not much. Come in," I replied, stepping aside.

Stan made himself at home at the table and chair in the corner of the room. I closed the door and plopped onto the bed with my back against the wall. I enjoyed having a visitor.

"Do you smoke?" he asked, grinning.

"Smoke what?"

Stan busted out a clear plastic sandwich bag that wasn't filled with a sandwich. Grabbing the shriveled, pungent, fluorescent green plant from the bag, he began to pluck it apart. Then, after a pile had developed on the table, he pulled out a little white piece of paper and rolled up a big, fat joint.

Leaning back in his chair, he struck a match and fired the thing up, puffing clouds of transparent smoke into the air. A sudden cough rattled his larynx. He flicked an ash on the concrete floor and crushed it away with his bare foot, then took another hit and passed the doob to me.

Standing at well over six feet, Stan hailed from Northern California. He had just finished a stint in the Peace Corps at a small, out-of-the-way village in Honduras. His mission: to bring awareness to the villagers about the importance of preserving the environment. Evidently, he'd met with trouble on that count.

"Those villagers don't care about things like pollution," he said. "They're barely feeding their families. And if you think about it, it's really us." He paused and scratched his messy blonde hair. "Western cultures have all the money. And that means we have all the stuff, which in one way or another usually equates to more damage to the planet. I'd bet the average first-world household creates more landfill in a week than a whole third-world village can produce in a month. I'm down here when I should be at home helping to make a change."

Stan looked at me through red eyes. Not zoned-out eyes, but the eyes of a man in thought. He wanted to leave future generations with a clean, beautiful, bountiful planet.

Looking back, I see that I hadn't fully appreciated the earth until after high school, when I'd started traveling. Keeping the earth clean is important to our future, and to our kids' future. I'm thankful that there are planet preserving organizations like Surfrider Foundation, and that more and more people—powerful influential people—care and are making a difference.

On the flip side, customs and cultures had sometimes confused me. I was once in an isolated village on the Indonesian island of Sumba, where they purposely left litter on the ground as an ostentatious sign of wealth. The garbage showed that they had the means to purchase packaged goods—or so I was told when I tried to pick up a cookie wrapper off the ground. Bogus tale or not, I didn't want to chance being ostracized by the village chief, so I left it alone.

Anyway, after a year and a half in Honduras, Stan had finally gotten frustrated enough to abort his green mission. While he fretted because protecting the environment had never quite registered with his subjects, he had managed to flee with something of value—the Spanish language. His Spanish rocked!

Although he claimed to have spoken very little before his otherwise fruitless expedition, his extended vocabulary and uninterrupted flow of speech absolutely inspired me. I liked my new friend. Stan had a passion for the environment, but also, within, he seemed to harbor a rebel. He sorta reminded me of a cross between a tree hugger and a rock star.

Neither of us said anything for a couple of minutes. Just before I went comatose, Stan spoke again.

"Fun waves today, huh?"

"Oh, yeah, it was so nice out there." I had surfed twice that day, and felt tranquil from all the action. One of the great things about surfing is feeling worn out after a good day of surf. That after-surf mellow mood can be almost as gratifying as riding the waves.

Although I must have resembled Jello melting into my bed, inside I felt collected and happy. Thrilled to have arrived at this place, I was beginning to see the fine line here between peace and pain. And to be relaxing in my room without a care was . . . well, I couldn't have asked for more, except that everyone else in the world feel as content as I at that very moment.

* * *

El Sal had a different feel to it, for sure. During the 1960s and '70s, revolutionary activity had torn the place apart, resulting in a war that had lasted twelve long years and ended over 75,000 lives. The government and the guerrillas had ratified a peace treaty in 1992, only four years before I showed up.

In the coastal town of La Libertad, I saw the war's lingering effects on the many despondent men curled up on sidewalk benches or lying on the ground under the cool shade of the trees. Some men clasped one of those cheap bottles of rum sold in many of the town's small shops. For two bucks, you could get a fifth of rocket fuel. No, the booze wasn't quite that bad, but it was cheap enough for the mentally destitute and monetarily busted.

Although I dared not pass judgment, I yearned to lift them from their despair, to brush them clean and inspire new life. Seeing grown men lying in the streets brought me down. I could never pretend to understand them.

* * *

One sunny day in town, as I was stepping out of a run-down convenience store, a man in his early forties approached from the crowded streets. From the outset, the man gave off a negative vibe that I wasn't sure how to take.

"Hey man, how's it going?" he asked. His tone wasn't friendly; it freaked me out. He reached his hand out for me to shake. Although uncertain of his motives, I reciprocated respectfully. Our hands locked.

The guy's English was clean, but his clothes and face were filthy. His hair shot off in every direction and his eyes were bloodshot. Is this guy drunk? I wondered. He gripped my hand for an uncomfortably long time. I lightened my grip, but that only made him squeeze tighter. He wasn't trying to be my mate. In fact, it was obvious he hated me.

I tried to free my hand and be done with the everlasting shake, but his grip intensified as his face contorted. He refused to let go. After too many seconds of his malice, I wanted my hand back.

Without saying a word, I ripped my hand free. The time bomb exploded. With all his vocal might he screamed, "FUUUUCK YOUUUU! FUCK YOU AMERICAN PEOPLE! YOU THINK YOU CAN DO WHAT YOU WANT?! WE HAVE GUNS HERE! WE WILL KILL YOU!"

He backed into the street, swinging his arms in the air and making his outrage a public affair. People on the street watched us in silence. The onlookers didn't seem to share this man's harsh attitude—about killing me, at least.

To evade the confrontation, I stopped looking at him and turned calmly back into the store. He stood there a moment mumbling obscenities in Spanish, and then walked away.

I'd done nothing to provoke this guy, beyond being American. With him, I guess that was all it took. The U.S. had backed the Salvadorian government during their civil war. I supposed he must be a rebel, and that he was going to hate me no matter what. Good thing he didn't have a gun, because he probably would have pointed it at me and pulled the trigger.

When the episode was over, I felt sad. The simple fact that I enjoyed peace and opportunities while this man had been in a physical fight against his own people was difficult for me to digest. Sometimes I wondered whether I was too sentimental to deal with a dose of the real world. Why did some people cruise while so many others struggled?

Maybe I could've made a donation somewhere instead of using the few grand I'd saved to travel and ride waves. But I didn't have enough money to make a real life-changing difference for anyone. Or did I? Maybe my guilt stemmed from the selfishness I wanted so much not to attribute to myself. At least I've been spending my busboy-earned dollars in their countries, I rationalized. That way I'm spreading the wealth, even if just a little.

I didn't dwell too long on negative thoughts, figuring if I

were lucky enough to be satisfied with my life, it'd be a shame not to enjoy it.

* * *

A phone call home was past due. Given the nature of my trip, I had promised my folks I'd make an extra effort to stay in communication with them, but I often lagged. Today, though, from a rusty public telephone booth in town, I dialed "O" for operator. As the operator connected the call, I noticed a grim fellow appear from behind a wall. He was taking too much of an interest in me.

"Hello, Mom? Sorry it's been a while, but don't worry, everything's fine. I'm in El Salvador," I said, keeping an eye out for the dangerous looking man near the wall. He finally strolled away, thank God.

"Oh, Mom, the surf here goes off! And my bike's still rolling along fine."

"That's great, sweetheart," she said, relieved to hear me alive and jovial.

I told her the Salvadorians (with the exception of the man who had cursed me out) were very hospitable. And that the country's coastline was a surfer's smorgasbord. Warm water, fun waves, and affordable food and lodging, El Salvador had it all, I said. I explained that the country was scary enough to keep the number of international surfers down to a minimum, which was good for me, though it was unfortunate that the people remained so poor that the local surfing community stayed at a minimum as well.

"Well, Mom, gotta go. Say hi to everyone."

"Alright. Be careful. I love you."

* * *

Over the next few weeks, I joined forces with my new surfing buddy, Stan, to surf and explore. Often, we'd hook up with the diverse crew that came and went at our accommodations. We surfed with a dreadlocked Swede named Ivan. An experienced windsurfer from Sweden's Baltic shores, he was new at riding boards without sails, but he could do it. He drove a brown Chevy van with Louisiana plates and was heading to God knows where.

Another surfer we met was a shy Canadian, originally from Quebec. The Canadian hung out with Cory, who also surfed and hailed from Kansas. Yup, Kansas. A notch past the beginner stage, Cory made great use of the long point waves in El Salvador. He said he had started surfing in the Dominican Republic, where he'd lived for a while. That fascinated me. I couldn't have known that two years later I would go to the D.R. myself as part of an eight-month stint in the Caribbean.

Thinking of the D.R. reminds me of the story of Lupe. Fast-forward with me to late 1998, the year I discovered the perks of crewing on sailboats. Having taken a flight to South America, I hopped aboard an American couple's private yacht in a Venezuela marina and sailed with them across the Caribbean Sea to the Dominican Republic.

There, I jumped ship and spent a month in the beach town of Cabarete. After renting a cheap room, I made some friends and enjoyed an islandy Jimmy Buffet-song existence—surfing days, bartending nights, and afternoons spent lazing in a hammock with a beautiful woman I remember dearly.

Eventually, the urge to move on had me hunting for a ride to explore the West Indies. I said goodbye to my friends and headed for the mellow port town of Luperon. Walking the docks there, I was recruited by Lupe, a rail-thin Columbian lady whose voice sounded not unlike that of a dying chimpanzee.

"Hi. I'm Lupe," she said.

"Hey there, do you know anyone heading to Puerto Rico?" I asked.

"Yes, yes. I'm going there. You come with me," she insisted.

We had hardly said hello before she grabbed my arm and hauled me off to the marketplace to buy provisions for the passage. She seemed a little off. Realizing that she was my new captain, I felt uneasy.

At the market, I picked up some bread, some mangoes, a few bananas, and a gallon of water. Lupe must have been broke; she didn't buy jack. I paid for the food and was ready to leave when she took one last look around the market.

"I don't eat much, but I love to eat ftttthrrruit!" she said.

You are a fruit, I thought.

I grabbed a few extra mangoes for Lupe, and we walked and talked our way to the harbor. In between her stories of estranged husbands and her unending search for paradise, I asked, "So Lupe, how long have you been sailing?"

"Oh, I've sailed a lot. A lot."

Her beat-around-the-bucket response made me feel even less at ease than before.

Things got even worse when we arrived at the anchorage and I saw Lupe's boat—a tiny, toy-like craft with thin, chaffed rigging. My next bit of reasoning made me feel somewhat comfortable about the situation: I still have my surfboard. If Lupe's toy boat started to sink, I could paddle for shore. It was wishful thinking, but this false sense of security gave me the courage and/or the stupidity to take the risk. I boarded the boat and helped weigh anchor.

Daylight was dying as we sailed out of the sheltered bay. Out on the open ocean, the cool trade winds amplified and rocked the boat. When the craft heeled, I could easily reach down and drag my hand in the water. We'd rise and fall with the breathing seas, and I'd sometimes get sprayed from the bow ramming into a wave.

Normally, all this sea action wouldn't have bothered me, but I'd already doubted my captain's competence. At first I thought, Well, she got this far. But from where? I didn't know. A rocky shore lay to starboard—a hazard for a sailboat, but to me it meant land and the chance of survival if our vessel were to flounder.

Not long after midnight a tired Lupe went below, leaving me in command of the ship.

We continued to pitch and roll in the dark, unwavering swells. My right hand gripped the tiller, and my other hand held tight to the gunwales. The night wind swept across my face and whistled through the rigging. Chills ran down my spine. Every nerve-racking gust felt capable of capsizing us into the black water. That feeling of danger gave me a rush. The ocean is massive, and we're so small.

At around three in the morning, while at the helm negotiating stubborn weather, I noticed Lupe through the companion-way. She sparked up the galley stove and filled a large ceramic bowl with broth, placing it right over the burner. I found it curious she didn't use a pot. The gimbaled stove teetered precariously with the listing boat.

She'd almost completed the task when the boat bucked violently over a steep wave. The bowl went airborne. The ceramic shattered on the cabin floor, and the soup drained into the bilge.

Lupe began to weep.

"Come up here and take the tiller!" I demanded.

She did.

Hoping to relieve Lupe of her frustration, I headed below and cleaned up the mess.

Although I considered mutiny, I learned something from her. Sailing her small boat gave me a new perspective on seamanship. And seeing her as a single sailor, a female from Colombia no less, I admired Lupe's courageous spirit. As long as we weren't blown to Haiti, the Dominican Republic's ruthlessly corrupt neighbor, I was good.

I'd passed off my hope of reaching Puerto Rico as a fairy tale. In fact, after two blustery days at sea, we sailed from the Atlantic side of the D.R. around to its Caribbean side. There, I said adios to Lupe and ran yellow-tailed back to Cabarete, where my friends were shocked to see me.

The next vessel I boarded had an "old salt" for a captain, and together we sailed across the Mona Passage to Puerto Rico and islands beyond.

I cannot think of Cory, the Kansas guy in El Salvador, without remembering Lupe and that sailing trip in the Caribbean.

* * *

Now, back to Central America.

One afternoon our odd bunch of surfers—Stan and I, the Canadian, the Midwesterner, and Ivan the Swede—piled into Ivan's van to search for surf. We drove off the beaten path and arrived at a spot where the waves were inconsistent and only so-so. We waited and watched. A couple of decent ones rolled through, so our group paddled out for the heck of it. Having logged in a little more sea time than the others, except for Stan, I positioned myself down the point near a couple of waist-high rights with some potential. I caught a fun little wave with a steep takeoff and three lumpy, but fun, walled-up sections. After my first ride I paddled back out and immediately nabbed another. The tide must have started lending a hand, because the ocean suddenly awoke from its nap. Like magic, the consistency increased and suddenly we were all getting our fill of waves that peeled farther and farther down the point. We ended up having a great session. The ocean will do this type of turnaround when least expected.

Up the coast, I could see another possible right-hander peeling just in front of some big rocks. The image captured my imagination. With a bit more swell, those waves would really come alive.

But so would the break where I was. Surfers dream of these kinds of possibilities.

* * *

One sultry Saturday evening Ivan, Stan, and I headed to

San Salvador for a night on the town. We were accompanied by Pierre, a forty-five-year-old Frenchman, and Bob, his Oregon buddy. Those two were a riot, smoking and joking and drinking as Ivan's heavy Chevy wound its way along the two-lane highway toward the capital.

Pierre and Bob made no secret of their plans. They were heading to the puta houses for a little paid action.

"I love the putas," Pierre said. "There's no confusion . . . no problems."

"Well, they may not steal your heart, but I'd watch out for your wallet," Stan joked.

Stan and I were surprised when Ivan, who was our age and not a bad-looking cat, agreed to join them. I'm not sure whether Ivan understood what he was doing; his English wasn't that great. To us, it sounded like an itchy option. We wanted to meet some real people on the swinging side of town.

We parked the van at a cheap motel in a seedy part of San Salvador. "Alright," we said, "whoever's not at the van tomorrow when Ivan's ready to go finds his own way back."

We split up and taxied to our destinations.

Stan worked his Spanish with our cab driver while I peered into the dreary streets, where darkness ruled the hood. The cabbie knew where to go—the Zona Rosa—and our beat-up taxi motored closer to the city. Soon, the streets here looked brighter, cleaner, and felt surprisingly safe, with casual patrols of armed police strolling along the well-lit storefronts.

Right away, I noticed hip, well-dressed Latino teenagers, both guys and gals, having a tailgate party in the back of a clean, late-model pick-up conveniently parked in the lot of a liquor store. I had a high school flashback. With the stereo cranked up, the teens laughed and sipped on freshly bought *cervezas*.

The carefree atmosphere stood in sharp contrast to the dismal area we had departed less than fifteen minutes earlier, making the gruesome gap between the rich and the poor even more evident.

Stan and I grabbed a small bottle of rum and some O.J. and sat on a nearby park bench to enjoy a relaxing evening cocktail. The thriving scene had yet to kick in. Like the tailgaters, we were just getting primed. I couldn't get over how incredibly safe I felt in San Salvador. It was all about location. The presence of gun-toting cops didn't hurt, either.

By ten o'clock, the Saturday night pulse vibrated in the streets. I wondered if the area had recently undergone a metamorphosis. With their country being ripped apart at the seams, many wealthy El Salvadorians had fled during the revolt, and a good number of them had headed to North America.

We met Jose and his brother. They'd lived in New England for years before returning to post-war El Salvador, their return motivated by the low cost of living. I suspected that many of the revelers around us had lived through a similar experience and were familiar with North American culture. Stan may have had the upper hand in Spanish, but I was often able to resort to English for more involved intermingling.

As the night wore on, Jose offered us a couch to crash on at his place. That sounded good to us; we couldn't be bothered trying to find our way back to our seedy motel. We finally dragged our partied-out bodies to Jose's. The place was large but scant on furniture, as if only recently occupied. A long, lone couch sat in the center of a large white-tiled area big enough to be a dance floor—but no one did any dancing. Instead, Stan and I split the couch, one sleeping at each end, curled up like cats. We didn't wake until noon. Jose drove us the one hour from San Salvador to the coast in his shiny S.U.V. Our night out had come full circle.

* * *

That evening, I relaxed in a hammock in the large free-for-all patio outside my room. After a night in the city, the sheer peacefulness of the sprawling tree-studded property dissolved the last of my hangover. A soft breeze messed with my hair.

Marta, the middle-aged mother of three who ran the place, sat at a table at the far end of the patio. She knew I'd spent the previous night in the capital. "*¿Como era la fiesta?*" she asked.

"Oh, *muy bien,*" I said.

"*No regresaron anoche.*"

"*No,* Stan *y yo dormimos con un amigo,* " I said, hoping I made sense.

"*Ahhhh, bueno. Es muy peligrosa la ciudad.*" She talked as if the city were a billion miles away. "No me gusta la ciudad. Hay muchas problemas. Estoy feliz aquí, cerca de la playa."

Although my grasp of Spanish was poor, Marta's words made sense. I knew exactly what she'd said: that she loved her nice, quiet village life away from the crime and grime of San Salvador, where so many people struggled to survive. El Salvador was beautiful; you just had to be in the right places. Waving a hand skyward and speaking softly, Marta motioned to the mango trees that towered above as she described the untroubled air around us. "*Qué tranqilo . . .*" she said.

Tranqilo was one of my favorite Spanish words, but I sometimes got it confused with tequila.

I didn't ask Marta how she had carved out her wonderful little haven. She was a fortunate woman, and she knew it. I was happy for her.

All her talk of peace and quiet had made me tired. "*Buenas noches,*" I said, and made my way back to my room.

Lying in bed, I had a lot to think about. My thirty-day motorcycle permit was due to expire, and I would either have to renew it or ride out of the country. Drifting off to sleep, I decided to bail soon for Nicaragua, via Honduras.

* * *

The next morning, Stan and I grabbed our boards and hitched a ride up the coast to another seaside pueblo. We weren't surprised to find foreign surfers camped near its peeling waves. We strolled past the village and onto the beach, where a large thatched canopy shaded a few relaxed visitors. I noticed three familiar dudes sitting on the sun-beaten sand, drip-drying next to their boards: Jack, Jeff, and Jessie, the North Carolina surfers I'd met briefly back at the hot springs in Guatemala. Their van was tactically parked next to a large tent, a setup that suggested they'd been there awhile.

I cruised up to them. "Hey, guys!"

"Hey, how's it going? It's J.J., right?" said Jack.

"Yeah, it's going great, man. Whatcha been up to?"

"Surfing," said Jack, his thick brown hair still damp from his morning session. "Lots and lots of surfing."

I peered down the point at the small but perfect waves. "This place is pretty sweet, huh. I'm gonna miss it when I go."

"So are we. Ya heading out soon?" he asked.

"I think so, probably in two or three days," I said.

Jack looked at Jessie. "Oh, really? Us, too. We're on the move."

This coincidence hit me fast. "Hey, do you wanna team up to cross the border?"

"Sure, sounds cool, let's do it," Jack said. In one swift stroke of luck, I had found friends to travel with through my least favorite hurdles of Central America: the borders.

Stan and I paddled out and caught some nice rights, and were soon joined by the others in the warm, inviting water.

* * *

Two days later, the Carolina boys' van rumbled onto Marta's compound. I'd been in my room making sure I hadn't left anything behind when I heard Jack's muffled holler come from outside.

"Whoooooo! C'mon, J.J., ya ready? It's time to roll!"

"Whoooooo!" Jessie and Jeff hooted too, obviously pumped to hit the highway.

Just as raring to go, I came charging out of my room with high fives for everyone. "Heck yeah, guys! I'm ready!"

Bright sun splashed through the mango trees, making my bike glow. She waited on her kickstand, already packed, warmed up, and ready to ride. I always loved the excitement that whipped through me as I readied for a day on the road. And these guys absolutely intensified the feeling.

Stan and Ivan were on hand and immersed in our enthusiasm.

Jack looked over at Ivan. "So, ya gonna stick around awhile?"

Jack's upbeat talk must've made Ivan realize he didn't want to miss out on anything.

"Hell no, I'm going, too!" Ivan answered. He fired up his van.

Equally on a whim, Stan ran to his room, grabbed his board, chucked his dirty laundry in his backpack, and jumped in with Ivan.

"Let's blaze this joint!" Stan yelled, and we roared outta there.

Two vans and a motorcycle made tracks down the battered highway toward new horizons. I'd pulled my gear off the bike and thrown it into Ivan's van. This was great. I could swiftly maneuver around the larger vehicles and easily dodge road ruts. Zipping around into the freedom of the wind, I had an absolute blast . . . until we reached Honduras.

11
HONDURAS
Border Blues

Honduras had been a dreaded obstacle in everyone's mind. Because of the way the borders slice up Central America, we had to cross a small chunk of Honduras to reach Nicaragua. Since Honduras lacked decent surf, we intended to blow quickly through the country.

As it had when I crossed into Guatemala from Mexico, having amigos when we reached the Salvadorian immigration offices gave me a "no problema" feeling.

We breezed out of El Salvador, but were stopped fast in our tracks at the entrance to Honduras. Compared to the other countries, the Hondurans demanded a substantial tariff—a whopping thirty-five bucks per vehicle—and they wouldn't haggle over the fee.

This created some friction.

We were fortunate in that we had Stan to translate. His Spanish was unrivaled by even that of the Carolina boys, who spoke far more fluently than Yours Truly.

Stan traded words with one of the officials. Never losing eye contact, he stood square in front of the man and maintained an attentiveness that changed his usual surfer-boy looks into those of a true diplomat. Even so, I'm sorry to say that we were getting nowhere. As Stan struggled to sway the rigid Honduran officer, a frustrated Ivan threw his arms skyward in a heated refusal to pay the inflated fee.

"I don't care. I'm not paying."

Big mistake. That only pissed off the head officer, who made a "the hell with you guys" face and told us to get lost. The rest of us clammed up to avoid aggravating the situation further. We hoped to reconcile the old-fashioned way.

There in front of the small immigration building, articles from the vans filtered into the hands of uniformed Hondurans. The large vehicles carried plenty of spare stuff for expropriation—snorkel gear, tee-shirts, shorts, flip-flops, girlie mags, a half-bottle of rum. One cheerful official lifted a flimsy red Bill-a-Bong tee-shirt by its shoulders and held it flat against his buttoned uniform. He looked down at his chest, picked up his head, smiled, and gave us a satisfied thumbs-up. We all said "Looks great!" and thumb-upped back, but really, we wanted him to get on with it.

At first, they seemed satisfied. But then they wanted a couple more items, and a couple more. At last, the pilfering topped off with a few bucks, and we finally got the go-ahead to cross the border.

We got permission alright, but there was a catch. The officers refused to properly permit our vehicles, rendering our transportation illegitimate. Our passports remained unstamped. We had unknowingly bartered for an escort soldier holding a machine gun to ride shotgun in one of our vans and vouch for us at the checkpoints along the way. He could then help us out of the country on the other side. It was a take-it or leave-it proposition.

Having no desire to go back to El Salvador, we grabbed the soldier. He hopped into Ivan's van and lit a cigarette. "Vámanos," he said.

We were happy to finally be on our way, but from there on, things went downhill for me.

What should have only been a short trip to the Nicaragua border turned into an exhausting nightmare. Our rented Honduran did his job at the checkpoints just fine. He did get us through. But he also insisted on stopping in a small town along the way so he could do something. Whatever that something was, it took him forever. We had already burned far too much daylight at the border. I relied on the sun as my guiding light, and it was fading fast. The headlight on my bike was shot, and even with large vehicles to follow I'd risk striking one of the potholes scattered along the lousiest-kept road to grace my tires.

With every idle second, my stress mounted. I paced the curbside, staring at my bike and dying to get back on the road. The late afternoon sun dropped out of the sky, cooling the quiet streets of this little town. Finally our inconsiderate soldier casually returned, got into Ivan's passenger seat, and sparked up another cigarette. I wanted him to choke on it!

Dusk deepened, making us all anxious to reach the other border. I followed as both vans roared out of town and sped faster and faster down the highway. I lost ground. The needle on my speedometer was pinned past the red as I rallied to keep up.

Thud! my bike jarred on a pothole. This is risky, I thought.

I maintained a Herculean grip on the handlebars as I battled to remain upright on two wheels. The sky darkened, prompting me to lift my tinted visor. Our road, however, fluctuated between battered pavement and raw dirt, and lifting the visor let in the dust kicked up from the vans. The stuff obliterated my vision. Visor up or down, I couldn't see. I peered through a tear-shedding squint as the distance between me and the others grew. Now I'd become both sluggish and blind. Whether or not my friends realized I was having trouble following no longer mattered; obviously, falling behind was my problem.

When the gap between us increased, my eyeballs regained vision. But then the road started winding. Every now and then, my friends' taillights would vanish around a protruding landmass. I was thinking how great it wouldn't be to get lost out here with my legal documentation in violation; I simply didn't have any. Worse, I'd been foolish enough to leave all my gear—with the exception of my passport and travelers checks, which were inside my money belt (I'm not that foolish)—in one of the vans.

I concentrated on the last hint of daylight as my engine screamed its solitary howl into the evening air. A genuine uneasiness crept over me. Taking a good jolt here and there, I rode peeping at the ground whenever I could to avoid the ultra-dark spots, the dangerous potholes. Running off the road and into the jungle was a serious possibility, as no other traffic lit the way

Two sets of taillights appeared in the distance, and then disappeared around a bend. The occasional flash of red lights ahead gave me hope. I did my best to follow the curving, dilapidated road.

Then I lucked into a straightaway, and with it, a chance to catch up. This was when not having my gear weighing me down came in handy. I changed tactics. Squatting half-crouched—as I had chasing the German biker in Guatemala—and loosening up my elbows and knees, I punched it and let my bike feel her own way across the bumpy terrain.

The bike bucked and bounced under me. All I had to do was go straight.

To my great joy, the vans' glowing taillights grew larger. I kept gaining ground, and realized that now I wouldn't be lost. Once I caught up, we hit better road, and following the others became less of a challenge.

At last we reached the Hondura/Nicaragua border. In the darkness, our soldier guided us to a grass field near what looked to be military housing—his destination, no doubt. The moment we parked, he fled without completing the job he'd promised: helping us get out of the country.

Not that it mattered. By this time, the immigration offices were closed. We wondered whether the soldier had deliberately wasted time in that darn town to make it impossible for us to cross when we got to the border. We felt used.

Blocking the view from the outside world by facing the open slider doors of the vans toward each other to create a wagon circle effect, we camped like a band of urban cowboys. My bike leaned against Ivan's Chevy. Finally able to relax, I felt like a dusty mess. I never admitted to the others how I'd worried that I wouldn't be able to keep up.

Jack and Jessie pitched a large tent between the vehicles,

and Jeff offered me the extra place to crash in their van. It sounded a lot better than being confined behind the narrow walls of my mini-bivy. Ivan and Stan, of course, bunked in Ivan's van. There being six of us and soldiers with guns nearby, we felt safe, and we slept uninterrupted in the field fronting the barracks.

* * *

In the morning, before the border opened, Stan got a head start on mustering up a way for us out of Honduras. We'd bribed our way into the mess without proper documentation, and now we had to fix it.

The auction began. Stan had met a local guy who said that with enough help from our ever-changing currency, he could get us stamped into Honduras and simultaneously out of the country to boot.

We all coughed up our passports and stayed close to our mediator. Watching him tactfully negotiate the transactions gave us confidence. One by one, he handed our passports over to an official behind the desk. And one by one, the official stamped each of them . . . twice.

No one knew how in the heck our hired man had pulled it off. We were so eager to straighten out our situation that we didn't care that both borders had ended up costing more than if we'd just paid the full amount in the first place. Take note: sometimes, you just gotta pay.

12
NICARAGUA
As Easy As It Gets

Once we'd made it out of Honduras, we didn't screw around with Nicaragua. We quickly recruited another guy to arbitrate our legalities. The middleman made life easy. Thanks to him, I experienced my smoothest border transit up to that point. Vehicle permits and all, we slid into Nicaragua without a hassle.

The day heated up as I followed the vans across the dry, grassy plains of Nicaragua's western lowlands. For the first time since leaving California, I rode without the protection of my denim jacket. I wanted the cool breeze to brush my arms. It did, but at a price.

After twenty or so minutes into the country, a swift-moving, blackish but translucent cloud dove out of the sky. It flew right into my path—or was it the other way around? With little warning, a thick swarm of bees blasted into me, machine gun style. *Plat! Plat! Plat! Plat! OOOOOOOUCH!* The little suckers were ricocheting off my helmet and torso. Some bees stuck to my body, frantically buzzing to detach themselves from the stingers that penetrated my thin shirt and sunk into my shoulders and chest.

I swept them off with one hand and steered with the other.

If I'd been allergic to bee stings, I'd have been a sick man. I couldn't believe the timing. Well . . . yeah, I could, but just said "whatever" and continued to ride in a tee-shirt. The moving air soothed the welted flesh. Luckily, I'd had my helmet on during the unlucky encounter.

* * *

From the main highway, we took a dirt road that branched off toward the ocean. The path was full of dips and whoop-de-dos, perfect for my enduro. Man, it was fun. With all my stuff off the bike and in Ivan's van, I felt light on my wheels. My bike and I easily outran the larger vehicles for a change, and we playfully kept ahead of the gang.

The road paralleled the Pacific, passing under palm trees and along secluded beaches. Before long, we spotted a nice beachbreak, and our crew screeched to a halt.

We jumped out of, and off of, our respective vehicles. The midday sun projected a lime color through the waves, and an offshore wind groomed the surf into perfect peaks of light.

"Let's hit it!" Stan hollered, yanking off his tee-shirt.

Everyone scrambled for their boards.

The burning sand fried our feet, forcing all six of us to sprint across the beach. Our scattering group jumped into the empty surf, paddling and hooting.

Soon we were stroking into clean green waves. Thirty yards away, I saw Jeff catch a beauty. Right after that, Jessie picked one off. A little farther away, Stan dropped in deep. It was on!

Alone, I'd paddled over to a peak that offered a nice, punchy right. On my third ride, I scored a real gem. The drop was steep and the lip threw far out over my head. I slid down into the trough and stood in a hollow, emerald-colored pit. Oh, the sweet view, looking out as the wave curled over me! I flew out of that and carved a fast, sweeping roundhouse back into the bowl. From there, I pumped down the line and pulled a long floater, gliding across the roof of the wave, launching out ahead of the pitching lip and freefalling five feet to the bottom. After scooting back onto the wave's shoulder, I kicked out to go catch another one.

Paddling back out, I wasn't thinking about the college degree I didn't have, my income that wasn't coming in, or how I might pass up making something of myself, as my parents feared. Nope. That stuff never crossed my mind. All I could think about—what mattered more than anything—was riding my next wave.

* * *

That night, we camped on the beach and boiled a pot of beans over an open fire. But after we ate, we stayed clear of the fire. The next morning we hit the road.

* * *

Traveling became rhythmic, like music—camping, surfing, camping, surfing, surfing, surfing, camping—as we made our way down the coast toward Costa Rica. We spent very little money. Everything seemed so incredibly easy, setting up camp at one empty beach after another, a wavelength from the ocean's blues and greens. The air always had that fresh, salty smell.

Late one afternoon, Stan and I sat quietly on the beach, our toes buried in the sand. We'd been camping under the stars for almost two weeks and by now had fully adapted to the peace and isolation. Turbulent waves crashed under a storybook sunset. Orange-red clouds roasted near the sun just above the Pacific horizon, losing color as they moved over us and eastward toward Nicaragua's towering volcanoes.

"Man," said Stan. "It oughta be illegal not to watch the sunset."

"Yeah . . . ." Equally inspired by Mother Nature's raw beauty, I knew exactly what he meant.

* * *

From the beaches, we picked up and headed to Granada, one of the oldest European settlements in the Western hemisphere. Located on the edge of Lake Nicaragua, the largest lake in Central America, Granada is full of impressive colonial architecture.

We parked our vehicles on a side street and strolled around, enjoying the history. Beautiful old homes lined the street. As we passed one particularly grandiose residence, I saw that its stately white front doors were wide open. I couldn't resist the invitation to peek inside.

This place had all the frills. Victorian-style couches and tables, a home library, doorways bordered in crown molding, and a huge staircase that circled half the room and led up to the second floor.

The most interesting frill of all rested on an antique chair. Wearing dress pants and a buttoned-up shirt, a feeble old man sat observing the outside world. The elderly gentleman had fair skin, slick silver hair, wise eyes, and a narrow nose—the look of a European. He could've been the great grandson of an affluent colonial-era politician. That's what I pretended, anyway.

Our eyes connected.

I wondered how much that man had seen in his lifetime. He must have been almost a century old. I imagined him in his prime, trotting down the cobbled streets of Granada on a studly stallion, en route to join fellow aristocrats to have a drink and discuss wealth, war, and women.

Was his first language Spanish? Did he have heirs to his prestigious home? Had he gone through a wife or three? Had he lived a fulfilling life? Something intrigued me about the well-to-do old guy.

Although I only spent five seconds lost in his eyes, I'd have been thrilled to talk to him for a few hours and hear his story about the old days. But I kept walking. I didn't have the nerve to bother him.

* * *

We left Granada for a small beach town at the southern end of the country, where the Carolina boys and I said goodbye to Stan and Ivan.

"*Adios*. Careful heading back," I said.

"See ya. Watch yourself heading down," said Stan. He gripped the bike's throttle. "Me and Ivan are gonna ride motor-cycles through here some day. Man, from where we sat in the van, riding the bike looked like a blast!"

When they finally drove off, a warm, fuzzy feeling grew in my stomach. They wanted to ride. My bike and I had actually been an inspiration.

The Carolina boys and I stuck together and headed for Nicaragua's southern border, less than a hundred kilometers away. Looking around at the foliage, I realized this was the last I'd see of this country. Jack drove the van nice and slow. They were probably soaking up the scenery, too.

We said "See you later" to Nicaragua.

13
COSTA RICA
The Final Session

The hassle-free Costa Rica border was the first I'd seen that had the vehicle permit fees posted on its wall. What a concept. I felt the air grow lighter. Waiting in line at the immigration offices here didn't cause me to sweat as it had elsewhere. Plus, I didn't have to lug my board around, since it was locked in the van. That was nice. The officers issued our permits without questions.

"That was flippin' easy," I said, shocked.

"Yeah. If only all the borders were this organized," said Jack, sharing my disbelief.

I hopped onto my bike, the boys climbed into their van, and we rolled into Costa Rica.

A celebration rocked through my veins. Awesome, I made it!

Although back home I had claimed I didn't give a rat whether or not my bike carried me all the way to Costa, that if it broke down I could just hop on a bus, I saw now that in all that hoop-la I had only been fooling myself. I was so elated. The smells here were fresher. The trees appeared healthier. Even the road seemed smoother. Obviously, it had mattered. I had done what I'd set out to do, and rejoiced in the accomplishment.

The Carolina boys and I headed for Playa Hermosa, a long stretch of beach halfway down the Pacific side of Costa Rica. We arrived on Hermosa's sand at dusk and parked for the night. This ended up being my final commute with the others.

Come morning, the sun reflected brilliantly off the breaking seas. We all paddled out, eager to taste a few. As usual, I had left my gear locked safely in the Carolina boys' van. When the session ended, I lazed under the cool shade of a huge tree while the others prepared to continue south. Once they were ready, I pulled my bag from their van and strapped it to my lone bike.

"Guys . . . it's been a pleasure," I said.

"Yeah," they said, "great traveling with you."

Their van roared to life, and the boys clunked the heavy doors shut. They drove off and disappeared in the distance.

Seconds later, a mini-van taxi pulled up carrying three surfers. Fired-up to get into the water, these guys unloaded their boards in a hurry. One thin, dark-haired dude jogged up to me and asked, "Do you have any wax?" His accent sounded Israeli.

"Sure," I said.

Digging into my bag, I reached for the plastic baggie where I kept my wax. "The waves have been fun all morning,' I said. "Oh, by the way, are you staying in Jaco?" I handed him the baggie.

He could see my rig and the fact that I was free-floating.

"Thanks . . . Yeah, in fact, where we stay, a guy left just this morning. So there's an extra bed. And it's cheap."

"Really?"

He hurried to wax his board. "We'll show you where. But first, we surf!" He shot across the beach and into the water.

I pulled my board off its racks.

* * *

While swapping waves, I learned that these guys, Tom, Eli, and Seth, were indeed Israeli. I told them the story of Omar and Zachary—how we'd met in Mex and ridden together to Guatemala. Having by now bumped into a number of Israeli surfers throughout the world, I was surprised at how many keen wave riders originated from that little Mediterranean nook.

After we surfed, I followed the Israeli-filled taxi into the touristy beach town of Jaco. We stopped at a basic white stucco one-story, four-bedroom house that had beds for rent. The owners used the house like a hostel, community style. They'd crammed four beds into every room, and each bed cost five bucks a night. Roommates changed almost daily, and the whole casa was shared by all the guests. The use of a kitchen meant I could make inexpensive hot meals. I didn't cook with a silver spoon, and a dollar-fifty bought a day's worth of easy-to-make pasta and sauce—the only thing I made for lunch and dinner. The bananas I ate for breakfast required no cooking.

The place had an ever-changing roster of tenants, and I met some colorful characters. For example, one afternoon a lone Frenchman came through the door shedding tears. He was the same age as most of us in the house—early to mid-twenties—but the guy suffered from a chronic illness: he had a broken heart.

"I fell in love with a beautiful woman in Mexico City, and then found out she's got six months to live," he sobbed.

"Ouch, tough break," said Eli.

With his swollen-eyed sobbing and sniffling, Romeo (or so I'll call him) was a mess. I wondered whether his lost love's allegations (hers to him, not his to us) were a crock or not. It was obvious he was telling us his truth. Either way, he was drowning in that sometimes deceptive emotion that often transforms a sane brain temporarily into a lame brain.

Romeo had a desperate need to express his grief. The minute he staggered into the house, he sank onto the couch and spilled his guts. His story of passion kept five of us dudes glued. He clutched a tear-stained photo he'd eventually pass around the room. The girl in the picture was an absolute knockout, however I had a sneaking suspicion this chick had told a bogus tale to get the lad juiced up and had never intended on kissing the poor frog into a prince. But I kept my notions to myself.

Romeo moped around the house for a full day, dragging his sorrow behind him like a rusty anchor. Then he split—back to Mexico, I think.

* * *

Ironically, although I felt relaxed riding my bike around Costa Rica, it was the only place in Central America where I was stopped by police.

Eli, one of the Israelis, wanted to join me on my bike for a surf session at Playa Hermosa, eight kilometers down the coast. Costa Rica had a helmet law, and he needed something to put on his head. We rummaged through the kitchen cabinets and found an aluminum strainer. He placed it on his head. It was too big. I took a mini bungee cord, hooked it into the mesh, and strapped it under his chin.

"How do I look?"

He looked ridiculous.

I rode slowly with Eli sitting behind me, one arm around his board and the other gripping the bike. We made it to the surf without a problem, and caught some waves. However, on our way back to town, we passed a police car. I cringed when I saw him dart out of his hiding spot and flash his lights. We pulled over.

When the cop walked up we were chuckling, because . . . well . . . we knew how stupid we looked. Inspecting Eli's make-shift helmet, the copper struggled to control his laughter. As he turned the strainer in his hand, the corners of his lips fought not to rise.

"*¿Qué es esto?*" he asked.

"Uh, umm ...." I puppy-eyed him.

In this case, my lack of Spanish might have been useful, but I dredged up my best apology nonetheless. Since we had no money, no passports, and no permits on us (other than the shiny sticker on my bike's frame that proved a permit had been issued), there wasn't much he could do.

I understood the officer's brief speech to mean that it wasn't kosher to ride with a strainer on your head, and please don't be such dumb tourists. A real helmet must be worn in Costa Rica. "*¿Entienden?*"

Finally, the cop returned the strainer to Eli, who placed it back on his head. The sympathetic officer let us ride home in this fashion. We appreciated his leniency.

My next run-in with the law wasn't quite so comical.

Eli and I had returned to our place from the beach one afternoon to find the whole house involved in a full-on fiesta. A few new people had arrived, and salsa music bounced off the white walls. Hands held quickly emptied plastic cups of rum and coke. I had two choices: join them, or run.

"Do you guys want to play Quarters?" I asked. Quarters was a drinking game we used to play in high school . . . ah, I mean, college.

Everyone gathered around me. I set a glass on the center of the kitchen table, aimed for it, and bounced a silver Costa Rican coin on the wooden surface. The coin pinged near the rim of the glass half-filled with rum and coke (when a slam dunk is made, the person who made the shot picks someone to drink the beverage down) and danced off the side of the table. Then they all wanted to try.

As with any drinking game, and drinking in general, moderation is the key. Everyone knows you shouldn't soak up so much booze that you wobble. But the rum was cheap, and easily bought down the street. By nine that night, most of us were hammered. I was among those who had blown off the whole moderation thing.

Motivated by alcohol, a few of us walked to the disco. Going out may have been my great suggestion. Bed would've been the smarter choice, but spending the evening dancing with Costa Rican women seemed a divinely inspired idea.

I don't quite remember who I was with, but I do recall acting rambunctious as we waited in line at the disco. We laughed and provoked each other. A few feet away, the club's open doors enticed us with the echoing beat of a wild time.

In line in front of us were a couple of Ticas. Silly me, I didn't see their boyfriends, right in front of them. I hit one up. "Hey there, cutie!" I'm sure I said it sloppily.

An extremely ticked-off Tico, who had probably found us annoying ever since we'd arrived, got in my face. "Hey, buddy, that's my girlfriend!" he snarled, like a lion protecting his lioness.

"Easy, tiger, I was just saying hello." I would have been mad at me, too.

Hidden in the dark, a police car I'd been oblivious to was parked nearby. Two officers had been watching, and the guy whistled to the cops and hollered something with the word borracho in it. I knew borracho meant drunk. I guess it was obvious. In a flash, an officer seized my arm.

"Oh, man, I just said hello," I protested. But I could see that it was useless, and the policemen weren't being forceful, so I didn't put up a fight. They casually escorted me to the back seat of the cop car.

I was too tired to dance anyway.

* * *

I woke in the fetal position on a smooth concrete floor, my head feeling funky. The ground felt cool against my skin. As my eyes focused, it took only seconds to recall my last memory— the cops, the cops' car, and the ride in the car. Shit, I'm in jail!

The afternoon fiesta and getting borracho hadn't been a dream.

Concrete walls and thick metal bars separated me from the free world. Scanning the room, I saw another prisoner, a local, sleeping over yonder in a ball of his own. I rose to my feet and stepped toward the morning light shining through the jail door. The air outside smelled crisp and coconutty.

I grabbed the metal bars and shook the cell door, "Hey, let me out of here!" I cried out, like I'd seen in the movies. No one came. I was already bored.

I'd never been jailed before, and it occurred to me that it might be an interesting place. Tiptoeing around my sleeping cellmate, I gave myself a tour of the block.

Partitioned off by a narrow barred door, another room housed easy-to-steal stuff like bicycles and radios, giving the impression that the cell doubled as the local lost (or caught) and found. Other than that, the place was bare, with not even a cot to sleep on. The black-bar front door remained the most exciting feature in the joint.

Although the entrance/exit opened directly onto a quiet street close to the beach, I stood confined, and could only reach an arm through the door and swipe at free air. That made me want out even more.

With nothing to do and no guards around to antagonize, I lay on the ground, curled up, and drifted back to sleep.

A loud clanking jolted me out of my slumber. A chubby man in a police uniform appeared through the black bars. At last! I jumped to my feet and over to the door, pressing my back flat against the wall. The officer grinned, and I grinned back. Big joke. Funny to him, no doubt, to have a foolish tourist caged.

The guard twisted the key and pulled the door barely ajar. Then, ever so slowly, he widened the gap. He paused, a cat toying with a rat.

Open, open, open.

Neither of us said a word. When I saw just enough clearance, I slid calmly along the wall toward the opening in small, sideways steps. Now the guard and I were face to face—on the preferred side of the bars. I gave him a gracious smile, and he let me walk away.

I felt lucky. I'd had no idea how long they were gonna hold me or what they might do to me. No interrogation, no paperwork, nothing.

I took a casual stroll on the beach in the direction of my place. A particularly carefree feeling followed, a feeling of joy. Even the fuzziness of my hangover felt good.

Back at the farm, the boys were hysterical because I'd spent the night behind bars. Eli, who'd passed out before we left for the disco, laughed. "Tell me, is the hole in your butt sore?"

"Yeah, yeah. It wasn't like that, strainer head!"

After the jokes about my incarceration got old, I saddled up the Honda and departed Jaco to head inland.

Next stop, San Jose.

* * *

The tree-studded countryside grew more and more picturesque as my bike and I motored into the rolling hills, up the winding road and past the occasional vista. I barreled toward the city, aiming for a hostel address I'd written down from one of Eli's guidebooks.

Riding in Central American cities—even in tourist-friendly Costa Rica—confused the snot out of me. Traffic signs were mystifying, that is, when I actually saw one. Other motorists devoured me.

Finding the hidden hostel, just another door cut into the large walls of the metropolis, took great effort. But I found it, and its convenient location in the bustle meant I could easily take care of business on foot. I was fortunate that the caretaker lady didn't reject me and my greasy machine.

The hostel was plugged deep into the city walls. From the sidewalk, I had to push my bike through the narrow front door, wheel her down a maze of long hallways and past the couches and bookcases of the lounge, roll her through the communal kitchen, and dodge umpteen curious backpackers before reaching an open-air patio. Now I could relax. My motorcycle would have a safe nest in which to rest while I dwelt in the city.

* * *

I had come to San Jose specifically to buy a plane ticket. Once the travel bug had sunken it's teeth into my bloodstream, I'd become fascinated by the history of worldwide colonization by European explorers. The Dutch and Portuguese had crossed oceans, and their relatively few sailors had dominated scores of civilizations. The British, too, and they had fed the entire globe their language. The French had claimed nooks like Tahiti, Reunion Island, and New Caledonia. The sea floor sparkles with gold-laden Spanish galleons. Before planes and trains, cultures had mixed and people had migrated by horseback or wind-powered sailing vessels. And within the space of a few hundred years, in the age of exploration, the Europeans had spread to far-off territories at a faster rate than any other people ever before. By comparison, I imagined it had been a slow go for the Native Americans who crossed the Bering Strait and walked to the corners of the Americas in an earlier time. Anyway, I dug thinking about how the world had come to be the way it is today. My new-found curiosity would've shocked my high school history teacher.

All along, I'd planned to sell my bike in Costa and fly to Europe. I wanted to do stuff like stand at the edge of the earth in Portugal and eat a potato in Ireland.

I'd heard about a travel agency in San Jose that issued a student discount travel card. I wasn't a student, but no one cared. As long as you were under twenty-five and gave them twenty-five bucks, you were good to go. The money you dropped on the Go Card would save you a couple hundred on airfare. I walked into the building and waited my turn in line. They snapped my pic, and presto, in minutes I held the card.

A flight to Madrid, Spain, cost around three-hundred-fifty bucks. For four hundred, I could fly, via Madrid, to Amsterdam, the Netherlands. These were the cheapest choices from San Jose, and I chose the latter. My flight was scheduled to leave in three weeks. I purposely left some time to enjoy Costa Rica's surf, and to sell my bike.

* * *

I'm not sure whether the university had anything to do with it, but while relaxing on the steps outside my hostel I noticed that San Jose had an unusually high concentration of stunning girls (this does not include the transvestites). I must have been coming down with Latin fever. As the girls passed, I swear they seemed eager to throw a quick tease. Many sashayed by with either a lusty stare, or an exaggerated shake of her booty. One even blew a kiss.

Joel, a tall, friendly Aussie I'd met at the hostel, joined me outside to chat. We tried not to gawk at the mocha beauties.

"Yeah, mate, I took an interesting taxi ride earlier today," he said. "The cabbie was an absolute riot. Talked heaps. Said he'd come back at five to take me to some dinner party shindig. You wanna come?"

"Um, sure."

True to his word, the cabbie, Mario, returned to play tour guide to the big Aussie. Joel and I were kicking-back on the curbside when the small white sedan rolled up sporting a "TAXI" sign on top. Inside the car, a man with a mustache boiled with enthusiasm.

I guessed him to be forty-five.

"Joel, you are here!"

Joel leaned into the window. "Hey, Mario, mind if me mate J.J. comes along?"

"Sure, sure, not a problem." Mario looked at me with a big grin.

We climbed in, me in the back.

"This is not a paid ride," he said. "I am done for the day." He flipped a switch, turning off the meter.

As soon as we took off, Mario reached into the car's ashtray and pulled out a skinny marijuana cigarette. He lit it and sucked.

I'm telling ya, the dude's dented taxi, his Spanish accent, the joint sticking out of his mustached mouth—I thought I'd magically stumbled into a Cheech and Chong spoof.

"I know this *cantina*," Mario said, holding his breath. "It's not very nice inside, but it's real cheap, okay?" He defended the dive as if we cared. He already knew we were into it. Follow the locals, I always thought. I preferred spending money in hole-in-the-wall places, where it looked like the people needed it most. Not to mention the fact that they were all I could afford.

We drove on, and the buildings got shabbier. Our cab stopped in front of an open door on a small side street. As soon as we went inside and sat at the bar, Mario ordered three beers.

"Okay, I pay mine, you pay yours, and you pay yours," he instructed. "That's how I like to do things, so it's not confusing."

Joel and I were cool with that. He was the host. Each beer cost ninety cents.

Mario was uninterruptible. Plants, politics, his wife's love-making techniques—he volunteered all sorts of random information, one word after another rolling off his tongue.

I enjoyed the bar's dankness, the paint-chipped walls and the stench of stale cigars. We stayed for three rounds, and then got back into the cab. Mario must have been plenty high.

On the city's outskirts, in the quiet alley of the neighborhood he called his own, Mario pulled up to a white steel gate. Behind the gate lay the driveway of his humble home. He got out and rolled it open. Potted palms and flowers were strewn about prettily, and once the gate to the street had been re-closed, the cozy floral-filled patio felt especially peaceful.

A young boy charged out of the house and flew straight to Mario. "*Papá, Papá!*"

The father flung his son into the air. "*Hola, mijo!*"

Holding his boy in his arms, Mario went right up to one of his potted plants and gently lifted a delicate pink flower with two fingers. "See this flower? This flower is a most típica of Costa Rica."

I got a kick out of the way he said that.

Then his wife, a good fifteen years younger than he, appeared in the doorway, smiling shyly. We were invited inside, where their spotless kitchen boasted 1960s style cabinetry.

"My wife doesn't speak a word of English, and I like it that way," Mario said. We got the picture. He rattled off our evening plans to her. Apparently she wasn't invited, but she didn't seem to mind. She had a submissive air about her; it was clear she didn't question her husband.

Mario's son had his father's energy. He ran around everywhere like a little locomotive, talking up a storm. Then, while his mom and dad blabbed to each other, the kid seized the moment. In the matter of one minute, he built a ladder stacking books on a chair and climbed up to a cookie jar intentionally shelved high in the kitchen. He sneaked himself a cookie, smiled at me, and then disappeared for a couple of minutes. I didn't blow his cover.

* * *

We drove to the outskirts of the city, to a large, very nice house. Though the place had been converted to a restaurant, it still had the cozy feel of a personal residence. We'd left the dive bars behind. Most of the guests sat outside on long wooden benches under the shady branches of a big tree. The friendly atmosphere felt like a family backyard B.B.Q. A live band played upbeat background music. Now I understood why Mario had wanted to show us this side of Costa Rica.

It didn't surprise me to see Mario mingling with many he knew in the crowd. Joel and I grabbed ourselves a cerveza and relaxed on a bench. A plump gentleman of about sixty sitting next to me struck up a conversation. Like everyone else, he was neatly dressed and good-natured. The man listened closely to what I had to say. The beer had loosened me up, and I spoke my best Spanish yet. Without twisting up terminology, as I often did, I told him how I'd ridden to his country on my motorcycle. He asked if I had faced any dangers. I said that nothing too terrible had happened.

"*Yo vengo de Los Estados Unidos, con mi surfboard.*"

"*¿Es peligroso, no? ¿Has tenido problemas en otros países?*"

"*No mucho, porque tengo suerte.*"

He acted surprised that a young lone gringo would ride so far just to ride a few waves.

The nice man bought a round, and then started talking a little too fast for my comprehension. I think he thought I could understand Spanish. I reverted to nodding and blankly responding "*Sí,*" just to be polite.

* * *

Eventually, Mario fetched Joel and me and drove us back to the hostel, ending his tour. We thanked him for his hospitality.

Joel and I stood at the front door of the hostel.

"So what-da-ya-say mate, feel like headin' out for a beeya?"

"Absolutely."

After voting to party on, we walked to another cheapo bar that reminded us of Mario's favorite haunt. After a few ninety-cent beers, we ended up at a happening nightclub. Ha, I had finally made it to the disco.

We lapped through the crowd to check out the scene, and then Joel headed for the dance floor. I got to talking with a brown-eyed girl, but my Spanish plain-old wasn't good enough to converse over the club's blaring music. It was a miracle that I ended up with her phone number.

The nightclub had a big dance floor upstairs, and I joined Joel and bopped around amid the hot and sweaty crowd. It had been a long day, and we were both growing tired.

Joel tapped my shoulder, "Hey, J.J., let's get going, eh?"

"Yeah, sure," I said. "Which way are the stairs again, any-way?"

"We can leave from up here. There's a slide right over there."

"A slide?" At first I thought he'd said slide.

"Yeah, mate, a slide. Like at a playground."

Now I thought he might be too drunk.

We maneuvered through scores of people toward the . . . No way! An actual slide spiraled down from the second story to the sidewalk.

I'd never seen such a thing at a nightclub. Or anywhere else.

Joel looked at me with a huge smile. A giddy feeling washed over me. We both chuckled at the thought of taking the plunge. Then we burst into uncontrollable laughter. I dared him to go first.

"Wait, go upside down and backwards." We laughed harder.

Positioning himself on his back and sliding head first, Joel launched down the chute.

I followed, on my back with my feet toward the sky. Wooohooo! A perfect crash-landing into Joel, who'd slammed onto the sidewalk seconds before. We were laughing so hard we couldn't get up.

Two police officers stood over us, staring down but not smiling. When I saw their silhouettes through watery eyes, oh man, their presence made everything even funnier! The officers didn't seem to think we were such great entertainment, but they didn't cuff us, either. We finally stopped laughing long enough to stand up.

"Thanks, that was the greatest!" we told the cops. And we left.

The next morning, almost sober, I rode out of San Jose and toward the Pacific. My bike buzzed down the mountainous two-lane highway. The whole country lay before me, and I had one small dilemma: choosing where to surf next. Waves were every-where. Maybe head south toward the Panama border? Continu-ing south felt natural; after all, I'd been traveling that direction for months.

Several miles outside the city, I braked for breakfast at a bright yellow fruit stand. The old mustached vendor sold me some ripe bananas and mangos, and motioned for me to rest on a smooth sliced-log bench. He asked where I was headed. I said south, maybe. He noticed the surfboard on its racks and flung his head northward.

"Hay buenas olas al norte," he said.

"Al norte, huh?" How in the heck would he know?

"Sí, al norte."

The fruit seller seemed so sure of himself. I wondered why. Hmmm, this guy doesn't look like he'd know a good wave if it crashed on this fruit stand. How come he's telling me to go north? Maybe he's all-wise. This could be a sign.

My mind fumbled with what to do as I mounted my bike and waved to the vendor. *Al Norte.*

Soon, a fork in the road provided a north or south option. The fruit man's suggestion held fast, and I chose north, rip-roaring up toward the Nicoya Peninsula, a hefty chunk of rural land that jutted out into the Pacific.

It took half the day to reach Costa Rica's northwest. Once there, it was only minutes before I wandered off the main road and got lost on one of the many dirt tracks that crisscrossed the region. I hoped to find one of those beaches mentioned by the fruit man, but instead rode aimlessly under canopies of large trees crawling with white-faced monkeys. At one point my front tire almost squashed a two-foot-long iguana that darted across the dusty trail.

Scrambling to find my way out of the wilderness, I came to a place where the dirt track stopped at the banks of a dried-up rocky riverbed roughly eight feet deep and fifteen feet across. A single foot-wide plank over this natural drainage ditch bridged the gap to the track on the other side. It was clear that the bridge was meant to be crossed on foot. I, however, attempted to motor across.

It would've been easy for Evel Knievel.

A fall from this narrow wooden "bridge" probably would not kill me, I figured. But it could easily shatter the unity between the Honda and me—and after all we'd been through together. I'd have to be careful.

My real worry was that if I tweaked myself tumbling off the side, yelling for help out there in the sticks would be a waste of breath. But I'd been on that darn dirt track forever, and for some ego-driven reason my confidence pushed me to go for it.

As a pre-test, I walked out over the dry rocks directly to the center of the plank and bounced to gauge its strength. The wood hardly bent. Good.

Okay, I'll do it. Just don't fall.

My hand twisted the throttle, revving the engine with the front wheel on the bridge and the back wheel still in the dirt. I took a deep breath, focused on a tree directly across the riverbed, and released the clutch. A strong start onto the plank stabilized my balance.

Afraid I might be distracted and thrown off course, I dared not look down. My smooth and constant acceleration kept me advancing across the narrow beam. The wood creaked and bowed under the weight of my bike. The ride felt floaty, like being suspended in mid-air. The front wheel led bravely, guiding me forward. I glided perfectly over the plank to the safety of the other side.

I let go of my breath. In hindsight, I saw that I shouldn't have taken the risk. Backtracking bites, but plummeting into a boulder-filled ditch? No, thanks.

It took me a while to find my way back to the main drag so I could continue down the dry, dusty peninsula.

A variety of lodges (some American-owned), from budget to over-priced, nestled near a right-hand reef break. Directly facing the surf, a new resort (an Italian project) was nearing completion. Several cabanas were under construction, some finished. The café and pool were open for business. Riding past the resort, I motored through the dirt parking lot and onto the sand to take a look at the sea. A stubborn afternoon breeze raked the ocean surface, reducing small, belly-high waves to junk.

Although a bit saddened to see the beachfront become marred by the presence of a new resort, I assumed that the surf was the reason for all the development. I'd stick around to find out.

Before reaching the beach resort, I motored past an inexpensive looking accommodation. I cruised back to it and parked near a large hangout area in front, where a lone, beer-gutted expat lazed in a hammock, his meaty flesh blobbing out through the nylon weaves. Behind him, I saw a large mural of a wave.

Nice Picasso, I thought.

"Hi. Do you have any camping areas or dorms?" I asked politely.

Picasso browed me and shot me a rude reply. "Naw, I don't do the dorm thing anymore. If you want a room, its twenty-five bucks a night."

I said, "Thanks anyway, I'm after a five-dollar bed," and turned to go.

My disinterest must have sparked his, for Picasso suddenly

changed his mind. "Well, I guess I've got a dorm bed you can have. But its eight bucks."

I almost declined because of the dude's lousy attitude. But, not being in the mood to hassle sleeping on the beach, I took his offer.

"Yeah . . . where?"

"The room's around the corner," he said. "I'll have Irma get you the key."

Without moving, he gave an obnoxious shout. "IRMA! Bring a key to the dorm! And bring me a bag of potato chips, too, will ya?"

A middle-aged Costa Rican soon shuffled out of the kitchen, apparently annoyed by his call. She didn't even try to fake a smile when she handed me the key, and walked away without a word.

Picasso's slave, I thought.

I unloaded my bike and walked around the decent-sized wooden building and opened the door. The dingy room had eight dust-covered beds, and I set my board and bag on one. The place was absolutely dead, which could've been why the guy had caved and rented me a bed. Maybe he figured eight bucks beat nothing.

Boardshorts replaced my dirty jeans. The day still held enough light for me to catch a few windy waves and wash off the travel grime. I stripped the cover off my board and waxed up.

Although the main surf break was a ten-minute walk away, I rode my bike to the beach to keep her with me. The thought of selling her soon made me that much more attached.

The sun hung low in the sky when I parked on the sand and paddled out. The waves may have been crappy, but they were empty, and after the long day's ride, stroking through the warm ocean felt therapeutic.

Soon, a surfer appeared running down the beach, a board tucked under his arm. He joined me in the waves. Waiting between sets, he struck up some small talk.

"So where are you from?" he asked. His heavy Southern accent caught me by surprise.

"California. And you?"

"North Carolina," he said. "So when did you fly in?"

"Well, I didn't exactly fly here." My bike stood in plain view, and I let her tell the story. "See that motorcycle on the beach?"

"Whoa, you mean you rode that thing down here?" he said. "That's got to be one of the most hardcore things I've ever heard of."

His accent added tons of color to his words, and it'd be a lie to deny that his statement made me feel pretty cool. Chatting, I found out we had similar names. B.J. had been in Costa for many months. A surf-stoked goofyfoot, he was a darn good surfer. Even in the choppy crap, he skimmed fast backside floaters and squeezed into surprise hollow sections. The eighteen-year-old had shipped his truck from North Carolina and worked as a cook for a nearby resort. It seemed like a full-on thing to do for a kid his age. It appeared he was as serious about his fun as I was.

"I cook at the big lodge down the road," he said. "That's all I do, cook and surf."

I could relate.

* * *

After the session I rode back to my rental, dripping wet. Through the kitchen window, I saw the local lady I presumed to be Picasso's slave . . . I mean, wife. She'd been mopping the kitchen. He hadn't budged from the hammock. Using his belly as a table, he munched on a fat hamburger.

"If you want some food, tell Irma and she'll fix it up."

Stuffing his face in public was smart advertisement—the hearty burger was aromatic—but I made for a lousy customer.

"I'm alright, thanks. I'm turning in."

Picasso couldn't have known that it was against my principles to spend more than two dollars on a single meal. I had a bundle of bananas stashed in my bag for dinner.

* * *

In the morning, I hopped on the Honda for a surf check. On these cop-free country dirt roads, I had quit wearing my helmet and rode under the warm sun in my shorts and flip-flops. After parking in the gravel area at the beach, I sat on my bike and studied the waves awhile. They were as small as they had been the day before.

A large Ford pickup pulled up a few feet away, and out popped a cheerful gringo who immediately chatted me up.

"Hi there, my name's Joe," he said, stretching his hand out to shake.

"How's it going? I'm J.J." I shook his hand. "Small waves this morning, eh?"

He smiled, "Just wait. Boy, this place gets good."

"Hope I get a chance to see it." I still wasn't sure of my plan of action.

Joe said he had a bungalow for rent and to come check it out.

"It's just up the road on the left," he said. "My house is under construction. You can't miss it."

Unlike Picasso's, Joe's attitude was personable and cool. He knew how to round up customers. I agreed to stop by later, and we left it at that.

After hanging at the beach, I went to pack my things.

* * *

Picasso appeared in the outside lounge area. My things were ready to go, and I handed him the money for the bed.

"Here ya go, man. *Hasta la vista,*" I said, glad to be leaving.

I'd come to the sudden decision that my bike was officially for sale. I wanted enough time to ask around before my flight to Europe. What the heck, I thought, and hit up Picasso.

"Hey, my bike's for sale." I said.

"Does it run good?" he asked.

"Run good?" I said, and kicked her over to show him.

On the damp dirt fronting his property, I cranked the throttle hard and the engine screamed. Waaaaaamm! I gripped the handle bars tight and popped the clutch. Together, my bike and I spun two huge doughnuts, the rear tire spitting up a muddy blizzard. She made me proud.

"What do you want for it?" he asked.

"Five hundred."

Picasso paused. "Well I don't know about five. I'd give three."

"Three? I ain't that ready to sell." Nice try, buddy, I thought, but I'm not about to give her away! "I'll letcha know when I'm desperate." I dropped the subject, loaded my gear, and bailed.

* * *

This part of Costa Rica was arid, with dry grass, yet there were plenty of trees. I cruised along the dirt road. Wire fences defined the rectangular perimeters of land parcels. Then I saw Joe's lot, exactly as he had described it—a block house under construction, two finished bungalows, and a dilapidated trailer where he, his wife, and two young daughters were living while they waited for the construction to be finished. Tenderly cared-for saplings had been sown everywhere on the piece of property, and there stood Joe, hose in hand, watering his future. When I motored up and parked on his lot, he was glad to see me.

"Hi there, J.J.!"

"Hey, Joe, cool place you got here."

We talked while he watered. I told him my situation—a few weeks left before I took off for Europe. I told him my bike was for sale, and that ideally I'd like to sell my wheels just before I left so that I could ride her in the meantime. Oh, and of course, that she was priced at five bills.

Not only was Joe interested, he didn't hesitate. In fact, he upped the ante.

"Look, I'll give you the five hundred for the bike. You can stay, free of charge, in one of those bungalows until you leave. My wife is a great cook, and you're welcome to join us for meals anytime . . . AND I know the area, so I can drive you around in my truck whenever you don't feel like riding the bike."

Apparently, he badly wanted the bike. I liked his offer. The bungalow. The food. The cash. Deal! We shook, without the Boy Scout palm-spit deal seal.

Selling the motorcycle at five, and flying across the Atlantic for four hundred and twenty dollars—man, that meant the three-fifty I'd spent on the bike had covered transportation from California to Central America, and all the way to Amsterdam. A true bargain.

* * *

I carried my gear to my new pad and lay on the bed. The freshly built single-room wooden bungalow stood on poles ten feet off the ground. Being up there gave me an Indonesian feeling. High above, monkeys bickered with each other in tree branches, adding an exotic flavor to the air.

Selling the bike had been easier than I'd figured. Now I was back in vacation mode, with nothing left to do but relax and enjoy the surf.

* * *

On the land adjacent to Joe's, in plain view across a low property-dividing hedge fence, sat a small—well, I don't know what you'd call it—home? Wood pillars supported a thatched roof over a yurt-shaped concrete foundation around thirty feet in diameter. A shoulder-high cinder block wall circled halfway around the hut; the other side had no wall at all. Hammocks hung between the un-walled pillars.

The interesting open-air hut could hardly be called a complete house, but it was absolutely habitable. In fact, someone lived there . . . a Northern California man named River. He was house-sitting for a friend.

Although he held deeds to land of his own, River had yet to build. "My property is on the other side of the road," he said. "The former owner desperately needed money, and sold me four lots for twenty grand. I'm selling three of them for twenty-five grand each, and then building my house."

When my new neighbor invited me over for tea, I sat at the table in the center of the hut and took a good healthy look around. The hut's rough-around-the-edges alternative style pleased me. Its lack of walls generated an airy ambiance, and the fact that half the place was walled created a sense of privacy. And the hut had its luxuries. Electricity powered up a ghetto blaster, a fan, and a full-sized refrigerator. A wide plywood counter, sink, and two-burner propane camping stove made up a kitchen. And next to a queen-size bed, on block-and-plank shelving, a thrift-store library held interesting readables. I particularly enjoyed one thick book of random ocean facts and stories that included a Titanic's survivor's view of her maiden voyage.

Newly planted palms dotted a flat field of thirsty golden ankle-high grass. A deep well had been dug to allow fetching a bath and scooping out water for cooking. You just threw in the rope-tied bucket, let it sink, and reeled it in—and presto. Hidden way over in an obscure corner of the lot stood a small three-sided plywood shelter. The un-plied open side faced the bush, blocking the view of anyone who straddled the seemingly bottomless black pit. Ahhhh, paradise.

Little did I know when I first visited River's place that I'd have a chance to sample his unprocessed lifestyle. He needed to take his girlfriend to the airport and spend a few days in San

Jose. And when River asked me if I would mind house-sitting while he was gone, what do you think I said?

Four days later, I carried my bag and surfboard from my cabana on Joe's property across a gap the size of a football field to River's place and plopped my stuff in the shade of his hut. I sat at the table and scanned the vast lot.

"Thanks," he said. "I didn't really wanna leave the place empty. There's a case of beer in the fridge, just help yourself. I'll be back in about three days, five max."

"Um, sure. Do whatcha need ta do. Don't rush," I said, getting comfortable. Ha, and I was doing him a favor.

River jumped into his truck and zoomed off.

I could hear the afternoon breeze skim across the tops of nearby trees. My feet pushed off the ground, leaning my chair back. Stroking the bristle on my chin, I studied my new pad with its Tarzan's-studio-apartment flavor. My mind fantasized about the things I would do to the place if it were mine. Maybe over there a fire pit, or a rope swing. Over there, a fish-cleaning station.

In my eyes, this existence characterized the quintessential surfing lifestyle. Then it hit me. A sudden tingly sensation gushed in my stomach. This was how I wanted to live! This defined me. Right then, I promised myself that someday I'd go somewhere warm, buy some land, and construct my own surf cabin.

Costa Rica had opened my mind with its twenty-thousand-dollar plots of land and easy-to-build bungalows. Sure, some money would be necessary. If I had to, I could earn enough cash to do it bussing tables. But from what I saw, the best tools were creativity, resourcefulness, and desire.

* * *

The morning after River left, I hiked toward the beach with my surfboard tucked under my arm. The path to the ocean skirted a big grassy meadow and trailed through a mini-forest cut by a stream easily crossed via a felled tree. Birds ka-kooed. Lizards lurked. And oh, yeah, a long, thick snake slithered within a foot of my foot. Spotting the thing, I froze in my steps, and it cruised by as casually as if I were invisible.

I arrived at the beach and walked past a handful of Italian girls socializing on their towels. Among them was Natia, a lively girl I'd met a few days before. When I strolled by, she smiled and waved. I waved back, happy to be recognized.

Paddling out to join a few other surfers, I enjoyed the clean and powerful five-foot surf. The rays of the late morning sun sparkled off the ocean's surface, darkening my bare back. Floating on my board, I stuck my face in the water to blow some bubbles and taste the sea salt on my tongue.

Good beach days never got old.

After a couple of hours of fun surf, my last wave deposited me on the sand. Natia sprang up from the group and bounced in my direction. She came right up and threw her arms around my neck. Her sun-warmed body pressed onto my water-cooled skin. She kissed my cheeks.

"Hello, J.J., tonight is the full moon." She had my attention. "I'm hosting a rave at our house. We live not far up the road. Can you come?"

She couldn't have asked me an easier question.

* * *

That night I rode, dead headlight notwithstanding, on the dirt path brightened by a lively moon. I could've walked to the Italians' from my place, but couldn't pass up my last opportunity to be a cool guy rocking up on his motorcycle. Ha, and I wish that were a joke.

I motored up to a house on several acres of jungle property. The front porch was strewn with guests. From out of nowhere, Natia appeared and greeted me with more cheek kisses. In her cute Italian accent, she said, "I'm glad you come." Being the hostess, she told me to get social and introduce myself to whomever.

Inside the house, I entered a bareley-lit room filled with strange, rhythmic music that sounded like African drums mixed with Techno. There wasn't much verbal mingling going on. The room was designated for dancing. A group of mixed-gendered dancers swayed, some hugging, in a seductive back-and-forth motion. I could tell that this wasn't an occasion of alcohol, but of ecstasy.

Through a large open window, a sweet scent of smoke wafted in. I left the room and headed outside to investigate. Low and behold, under a cluster of moonlit banana trees stood three Italian guys, smoking cloves. I wandered over to see whether they were friendly. The tallest one noticed me.

"Hello," he said. "You are Natia's surfing friend, no?"

"Um, yeah. I'm just cruising around." I didn't want to give the impression of lurking around.

"Come over and join us; we were just talking," he said.

"Thanks. I don't really know anyone. Well, besides Natia."
And I didn't even know her.

"No problem," said the Italian. "I saw your motorcycle.
Where did you get that?"

"California. I came from California."

He looked puzzled. "What? You rode here from America?

"Yeah. You know, to surf."

"You rode here . . . through Mexico? To go surfing?"

"Well, yeah."

He rattled something to his friends in Italian, and they all
chuckled. "How long did that take?"

"How long?" I had to think for a second. We were in mid-
April, and I had left right after New Years. "I guess about three
and a half months."

"Wow, you must really like surfing."

"I do."

I didn't bother trying to explain to him that the journey to
the waves was a special experience in itself. I relied on my motorcycle to tell that story.

After the party, I thanked Natia for the invite and enjoyed a
leisurely putt home.

* * *

A few days later, River returned from San Jose and I moved
back into one of Joe's bungalows.

The morning after that, Joe did a wave check at dawn. I
heard his truck return from the two-minute drive to the beach,
and he hollered up some good news from below. "Hey up there.
Rise and freaking shine. Let's go. The surf's cranking!"

I hopped out of bed, charged down the bungalow stairs, and threw my board into the back of his idling truck. Joe gassed it to the beach.

My jaw dropped when we pulled up to overhead spitting barrels. They were epic waves, the best I had seen so far.

"Wow, Joe. You weren't joking!"

"I told you this place got good," he said

What a day—no wind, all glass, and nobody out!

Moving faster than Joe, I gave my bones a good stretch, grabbed my board, and stroked out through the channel toward the breaking waves. Thick, clean cylinders funneled across the impact zone, and I had a spectacular view into the wave's stomach.

Once outside, I impatiently waited for a set. The water stayed flat for only a moment before the ocean's surface rose from out of the deep blue sea. Oh, yeah! I paddled with conviction, strategically passing over the first wave of the set and positioning for the second.

Down the steep, smooth face I dropped. The wave pitched and barreled over me as I angled into the crystal cavern. Being inside the wave felt like another world. My vision sharpened. A low-pitched rumble filled my ears. And each second felt like a minute as my board and body followed the sweet spot of the wave's curve and glided all the way through the glass-like tunnel. The wave stayed perfectly hollow, allowing me to shoot out of the tube with ease. I followed the tube-ride with a huge carve on the open face. Man, it felt good.

Joe was watching from the channel. "Beautiful!" he yelled.

We traded perfect waves while the morning sun sparkled above the trees on the beach. The barrels I scored that morning were worth every mile I'd ridden to catch to them.

* * *

That week I rode my bike less frequently. And then, finally, it all came to a halt. On my last day in Costa Rica I completely changed gears and prepared to move by foot. Leaving was hard. I remembered young Solina in La Paz, and how she went her way when the time came.

My motorcycle leaned against a post at one of Joe's bungalows and waited for me to go. Our ride had ended. Though I was the one leaving, I stared at my bike like she was a serious girlfriend who had recently broken up with me, painfully ending the relationship. Emotions for my baby welled up from my core. Up and selling her plagued me with guilt. But I knew she understood. She'd represented both security and freedom.

On the gas tank and fenders, much of her original red bled through where the black paint had been chipped or scratched away. The tread on the rear tire had burned down to almost nil. A fine coat of dust belied her true beauty.

I was so proud that she hadn't quit. Not once. Not during times of ignorant neglect, nor while crossing the center of Mexico's scorching Baja Desert. She had never stopped nipping at the heels of Omar's newer, stronger set of wheels, and had given me her all climbing up the misty mountains of Guatemala. She'd powered through the long chiseled-out tunnels in El Salvador and carried me across Honduras in the haunting darkness. Together, we had excelled on Nicaragua's isolated dirt trails and cruised through its captivating colonial cities. And after many fond memories, she had escorted me safely to my destination, the country of Costa Rica.

According to the odometer, we had clocked over six thousand miles. In our dying moments together, I looked at her the same way Doc had the day I'd taken her off his hands. Only now did I truly understand how he must have felt. This wasn't just a soulless body of fuel lines and steel. This baby had heart.

She was my friend.

I finally broke the last tie and tore my reminiscing stare from my beloved bike. With my bag on my back and my board in its cover tucked under my arm, I turned and walked away.

THE END